Face Blind in Berlin, Suffolk and Gedling

C000025556

The Memoirs of Chris Cook Cann

Face Blind in Berlin, Suffolk and Gedling
The Memoirs of Chris Cook Cann

Published by

In association with

The Saithwaite Press

THE SAITHWAITE PRESS is an Imprint of SAITHWAITE MEDIA INTERNATIONAL HOLDINGS, a Subsidiary of THE SAITHWAITE GROUP in association with NANODODO PUBLICATIONS AND CHEESE.

ISBN 9781916490413

Magrathea and Gedling MMXIX

Everything described in here is true as I perceived it, to the best of my recollection. Chris.

Printed by
ImprintDigital.com, Devon

Printed on Recycled Paper

Sometimes the light's all shinin' on me,
Other times I can barely see.
Lately it occurs to me what a long, strange trip it's been.

Grateful Dead

I have written this so that my grandchildren will learn more about me, and some of the extraordinary events I have lived through. I initially wanted to record what happened in the 1960s, but then I couldn't stop.

I dedicate it with much, much love to Lily, Leon, Jack and Alfie, and to Anna and Bob. And with great thanks to all my friends with whose help the light keeps shinin' on me.

Thank you to my proofreading friends, and to Philipp, for editing and layout.

Here I am during the Berlin days with Omi and Opi. To add to the embarrassment, I must confess that the hat was bright red.

Contents

Around the 1950s: I am very little 6

Around the 1960s: World events and death intervene 20

Around the 1970s: Dropping out and selling books 90

Around the 1980s: Motherhood, single life, direct action, Bob 115

Around the 1990s: Ghastly jobs, libraries, too many funerals and a wedding 143

Around the 2000s: Solidarity with refugees, cycling and more travels 180

Around the 2010s: A masked Omi sells books, I am still very little 206

A bit more about the family 227

Who's who in this story of a life 230

Around the 1950s: I am very little

It was during a 2019 visit to the Tränenpalast (Palace of Tears) in Berlin that the enormity of what we had done in the early 1960s hit me. I was suddenly, retrospectively, terrified.

But first, a bit about my family. My Dad, Don, came from a large Suffolk family of agricultural labourers. He and his twin sister Doris were the next-but youngest. Only Uncle Tom was younger. Don left school in his early teens, and, when he was old enough, found himself fighting Hitler; in his case, in the Royal Engineers. After 1945 he decided to stay in the army, where he got himself educated and worked in the Army Post Office. He was posted to Germany. He often worked on the Travelling Post Office (TPO) – steam trains of course, steam trains that did his lungs no good.

Dad (right) checking mail bags on the TPO.

My Mum, Inge, from a lower middle class background, began a university education in April 1944, but was thwarted after a short spell because of the turmoil and destruction that was 1945 Berlin, where she was nineteen. When a truck full of Soviet soldiers told her to stop and hand over her bicycle, she escaped by pedalling furiously into the woods where no truck could follow. My mum was very scared of dogs. Otherwise, she knew no fear.

<u>Certification</u>

The student Ingeborg J e n t z s c h, living at
Kleinmachnow, Leite 74 is authorized to use his
bicycle for studying in Berlin.

Kleinmachnow, August 6th 1945.

The Mayor of district
Kleinmachnow

Удостоверение

Студентка Ингеборг Энцш, прожив. в Клеин-
-малнов) Лейте 74 имеет право пользоваться
-веломашиной для у... университети.

... бургомистр

For some reason, Inge was in West Germany, in the British
Zone, some time soon after 1945. Perhaps it was part of her
sewing machine and typewriter smuggling escapades. Apparently
she'd buy cheap ones in the East, travel illegally to West
Germany, and sell them there via newspaper adverts. She carried
them in wooden suitcases handmade by Onkel Nully, so they
weighed a ton and startled many a gallant gentleman wanting to
help her. As I said, she knew no fear. Maybe this was a result of
having survived the bombing of Berlin and Kleinmachnow (the
adjoining village where the family home was), the disappearance
of a boyfriend when their arranged meeting place was bombed,
extreme hunger, the running and hiding from Russian soldiers in
1945, and more than a nineteen year old should have
experienced - although of course sadly she was not alone in this.

The story goes that Inge and a friend were walking along the
street, munching pumpernickel, when a couple of British soldiers
shouted out to ask them what they were eating. "German
chocolate" said Inge. It is thanks to that pumpernickel that I
exist, making my appearance four years after the wedding, which
also has a story attached. ("Shall we get married?" asked Don, as
a joke. "Yes," said Inge, also joking. "Oh dear," thought Don,
"we'd better go ahead.") The wedding is significant because not

only did the army widows' pension fund most of the setting up of a radical bookshop in 1972, it also caused Inge to lose her German citizenship and become British. It was a very happy marriage of two people from very different backgrounds, who adored each other.

I eventually deigned to visit this world the day after bonfire day in 1952. When I was a tiny baby, Mum and I visited Aunt Edith and Uncle Charley on the Isle of Man. This book could have been very short. I disappeared. The adults panicked, as I could neither walk nor crawl. What could have happened to me? Meanwhile, I lay snug and content in the hedge I'd rolled under.

Aunt Edith always had chocolate in her bag, and I'm told that whenever she picked it up or opened it, I would start reaching out, and panting heavily.

They (we, after I appeared) lived very briefly in London. I was a toddler, and my only memory is of being taken to a library and being overawed by the quantity of books, which impressed me no end, although I believed they should have been arranged differently, not over a number of separate rooms. Otherwise we lived in various places in West Germany (I had been born in the RAF hospital there), and in Belgium for three extremely joyful, idyllic, years.

Debenham Man is BAOR "Postmaster"

A former clerical worker, Sergeant Donald Cook, of Debenham, who is in charge of an Army Post Office in B.A.O.R.—he is stationed in Herford, Westphalia—is responsible for supervising his staff of Post Office workers in one of the 40 B.A.O.R. postal districts.

"I like it out here very much," said Sgt. Cook to a military observer. "My wife is living here with me and we both agree that conditions in Germany for British families are first-class."

Sgt. Cook joined the Forces in July, 1943, on a regular engagement and when he becomes due for demobilisation in 1952 he intends to take up an engineering job.

From Hanover, I remember "slaughtering" pears from our tree with Bodo next door, crossing the busy road to get some cakes from the bakers' when no-one was looking ("children don't have to pay", they told me, as they saw me safely back home clutching my cream-filled goody) and long sun-filled days in the garden, dipping in and out of a tin bath of water to cool down. I collected worms and gave them to the neighbour, who kept chickens. Two hugely tall poplars stood in front of our house, and one night there was a tremendous storm and one blew down, narrowly missing the house.

Another narrow miss was when a family friend suddenly stuck his hand in front of my eyes when we were all together on a balcony. He had just saved my eyesight from a firework.

A very early Hanover memory is that Mum enrolled me in dancing classes. I remember we all had to sit on a wooden floor and clap along to the music. I had absolutely no idea how the other children knew when to clap, and trying to copy them meant that I was always a bit late. I didn't go to many of these classes, and when I mentioned them more than forty years later to Mum, she remembered me being hopeless and the lessons being a waste of money so she stopped taking me. She was surprised that I remembered. I must have inherited my musicality from her.

Behind our Hanover house, with Dad, Opi, Omi and Mum.
The front of our Hanover house, with my new tricycle (which could transform
into a bicycle when the time came to have arguments about learning to cycle).

I was a bit of a novelty in the Sergeant's Mess, because I could speak English and German. Someone asked me how many languages I could speak. "Three," I replied, "English, German and Menkenke." Menkenke (messing about) was of my own devising, but I would be annoyed when people didn't understand me speaking it.

We enjoyed family days out in our VW beetle, which Dad would let me "drive", sitting on his lap, up the driveway. Sometimes we'd go to Hanover Airport to watch the planes (this was regarded as interesting in those days), eat cake, and on one occasion, sit on a wasp with painful results. A favourite was a local park, which had deer that I enjoyed feeding. If I thought one of the massive stags had more than his fair share of food, I would take it back out of his mouth to give to a more deserving one. The fact that I am alive to tell the tale is proof that I wasn't gored to death, and that redistribution of wealth is possible.

With Dad, feeding the deer in the park in Hanover.

There were also frequent walks in the woods, with a picnic as the highlight. Mum of course wore high heels, and Dad wore a tie. After the picnic, the dark blue blanket we'd sat on would be shaken out. Then I would lie down on it, and it would be shaken again, with me inside. I did love that!

There were several visits from our German family from both sides of the intra-German divide. Once all the adults except Opi, my grandfather, went to Italy on holiday together. Opi was left to look after me, and I got very cross when he put my dress on me back-to-front. I also managed to get myself and Dad very cross when he tried to teach me to cycle. We'd go out in a happy mood, and return wheeling the bike, both scowling.

I had several excellent story-tellers among my relatives. I liked school stories, and Mum, Omi, Opi, and Tante Grete, Mum's aunt, all had their own styles. They pretended to be telling true stories of their own school days, but Opi's extremely naughty playmate Peter Wölfing was too mischievous for reality. Tante Grete was an improviser: when she ran out of names for school chums, she'd use names of currently famous stars of stage and screen – which meant nothing to me until I heard Mum and the others laughing about them. Her stories were long, intricate, exciting and funny. Omi's stories seemed to centre on getting into trouble for the way she sang, and this was to haunt me when I reached grammar school. Mum's stories included some of the less scary experiences she'd had during war time. When Dad put me to bed he'd often still be wearing his rough, scratchy uniform. I wanted him to stay by my bed and not go, and would grab onto his epaulettes and cling on tightly, often gaining an extra five or ten minutes in this way.

> **READ TO ME:**
> *Max und Moritz*

Soon after moving to Belgium, in January 1958, I started school. Mum had taught me the alphabet (we used to leave messages in cut out cardboard letters for Dad to find when he came home late at night from the TPO in Hanover) and to read some words. I was dismayed to find that she'd taught me all wrong! You weren't supposed to say "A", "B", "C", but "ah", "bu", "ke", etc. And if a flash card with the word "cat" was held up, you should say "ke, ah, tu, kee … er … tuh … cart?" and not "cat". This I found confusing, but then I learned to do it along with the other children.

I spent several days at school copying a *Ladybird* book about the stone age into my exercise book, for reasons of my own. The classroom for five year-olds was cleverly L-shaped, so teacher could only supervise two thirds of it at a time. Someone punched me on the nose when I reached out for crayons.

We weren't allocated married quarters for some time and Dad rented a bungalow privately so that we could spend xmas together. The plumbing consisted of an outside toilet and a cold-water pump; I had to use a potty again; the heating was by the paraffin heater my parents bought then, which served me in early Nottingham days and is now an attractive light feature; the owner lived in the garage at the bottom of the garden; one of the dining chairs always pinched my buttocks painfully but I never knew which chair it was; rooms were not divided except by curtains. Mum hated it; but, on the plus side, we were together, the windows had beautiful stained glass, and I found that nose pickings stuck very well to the wall next to my bed.

I taught myself to cycle, going up and down the garden path.

> **READING:**
> *Tiny Tots* comic
> *Harold Hare's Own Comic*
> *My First Book*

Before we were in the married quarters, the school bus had to come for me and one or two other outlying children specially. I was always in a hurry, and remember gobbling my piece of brown bread cut into quarters, with a different jam on each quarter, while Mum was under the table tying up my shoe laces, as the bus tooted outside.

After the fun bungalow, we stayed briefly at a flat in the centre of Herentals, which I remember chiefly for it overlooking the main road where Belgians seemed to hold lots of colourful and fascinating processions. My bed was in my parents' bedroom, and one night they had visitors, and I fell out of bed. Because it was a one-bedroomed flat, I didn't have my own room. Instead, the sofa in the living room was moved forwards, and the space behind it was my play space. I mainly played schools; my dolls and Teddy Peter were sat in rows behind "desks" (comics) on which were "ink wells" (balls). I was teacher. One day a friend came to play with me and saw that all the pupils had comics and balls. She told them off severely for playing during lessons, and took their ink wells away. Tante Grete and Onkel Nully, of whom much more later, came for a visit, which I enjoyed a lot. They brought me a set of cutlery with my name on it. This flat was where the tooth fairy was first required to visit me.

In school, we weren't allowed to start another "reading book" until we'd read the entire current one aloud to our teacher. There were over twenty children in the class, so we didn't get a chance to read aloud often. I was stuck with sodding Black Beauty for weeks, and must have read it well over a dozen times. I killed boredom during those lessons by learning the countries of the world from the big map on the wall, and teaching myself to do mirror writing, both still useful to me.

I did well at school, always getting good reports – except for P.E.: "rather timid, and inclined to watch rather than take part."

Family holiday to Oberlahnstein on the Rhine, to visit relatives.

A particularly special holiday was by the Rhine, near Oberlahnstein, where Opi came from. We met up with lots of Rhinelander relatives, and other relatives from Berlin came along too. Onkel Ludwig was memorable because he could eat cheesecake and smoke a cigarette simultaneously.

We also had holidays at the Dutch seaside. One place we went to had a promenade with child-sized cars, which I thought was enormous fun. I made friends with a family of German children on one of these holidays, and we played imaginatively gory games, including one where, due to an easily-made translation error on my part, everybody's beans were chopped up and buried.

Visiting the Efteling was a wonderful day out, and I remember putting my ear to the magic toadstools to hear the pixies singing. Once we went with friends, and although I am sure that Gabi wasn't pedalling properly, she was convinced it was my fault that our pedal train was so slow that all the others were piled up behind it. Two stormy-faced little girls got off that train at the end of the ride.

Life in Herentals, once we were in the married quarters, was one sun-filled, fun-filled day after another - or so it seems, looking back - where dozens of children played together outside every day, roaming free, exploring the monastery behind us (and scrumping apples from the monastery grounds, although we refused to eat those our mothers provided at home), making dens in the hillocks at the end of the street, and venturing to the canal to catch tadpoles in ponds and hide from the "murderers" in the cottage on the way.

Some kind of scam was being perpetrated by all the soldiers posted there – they claimed there was no NAAFI, although there really was, and so received pay bonuses. This meant my pocket money was remarkably high for my age and the times (35BF, around 5/-). We might wander into the town centre and shop in the Nopri or at the market, or visit each other's houses and play in our gardens. When it was hot, the sprinkler would be set up in our back garden, and we played and splashed with the cool water.

Of course, not every day was idyllic, and I remember two favourite ways of getting even with my parents. Once I pushed loads of cut grass through the letterbox. Even better, another time I pushed their carefully arranged books, which were "facing", in along the shelves, pushing some in more than others. This got me into particular trouble.

I was nice occasionally too, and used to help with the drying up – but secretly – I'd creep into the kitchen when Mum was looking the other way, grab a plate or cup, dry it in the living room, and then creep back into the kitchen to return it and take something else. This was much more fun than doing it normally when asked. Mum obviously didn't know who, in our tiny family, was doing the drying up, and I suggested it was pixies.

Mum and Dad ran a bingo club in the married quarters, and often the sessions were held in our house, though sometimes someone in the bigger officers' houses offered. I was conscripted. At our house, I had to help set out chairs etc. I also had to deliver letters or invitations or calendars or something to lots of the houses in the quarters. I don't know what the prizes were, or whether anyone ever won one.

Sometimes I was allowed to go to work with Dad, and I have memories of many happy hours at his typewriter, or examining a variety of forms to fill in. I started cutting out and collecting coupons from newspapers. Dad brought home any newspapers that had somehow gone astray in the postal system. One day, glancing through a *News of the World* scandal sheet, he exclaimed "That's my sister!" She had been caught in the wrong gentleman's bed.

As adults always asked if you had a boyfriend, I thought I'd better get one. Ronald Halfpenny seemed to be available, so he became my boyfriend, although I didn't like him much. He was half German too, and his mother filled their house to the brim with ornaments. At xmas I gave him a present of things that were very precious and special to me – toilet roll insides, lolly sticks, bits of paper, empty matchboxes- I sacrificed a lot from my collection, and wrapped it all up carefully. His mother must have been startled to see the size of the present and felt she should reciprocate. I unwrapped a beautiful toiletry bag stuffed with soaps and bath cubes, which must have cost a fair amount. I still think Ronald Halfpenny got the better present.

For the first time in my life, I was allowed pets. This could be because Mum and Dad knew we'd stay in Herentals for a while, or it could be because whoever had owned Billy and Peter had been posted away, and a new home was needed. Billy was a green budgie, and Peter was blue. During the winter they'd live in a cage in the living room, allowed occasional flights around the room after we'd made sure all doors and windows were shut. Amazingly, I don't remember the living room being covered in budgie guano. In the summer they lived in a wooden aviary built by Dad (he was brilliant at making things out of scrap wood – I got a dolls' house complete with working electric lamps, a dolls' shop, and a blue painted lift-top desk made from a packing crate), in a corner of the garden near the earwig-infested dahlias, Mum's parsley, and the small patch of ground I'd been allowed to do with what I liked. (I think they expected me to sow seeds. I tried to build a small section of motorway on it.) When we went on holiday, neighbours were asked to look after Billy and Peter. One summer we returned to an empty aviary.

With cousin Marion in Herentals.

The army arranged magnificent bonfire and firework evenings every November 5th. A bus took loads of us there; it was one of those bus journeys that took ages to get there, but no time at all to get you home afterwards. The fireworks were great. I was over-excited because the next day would be my birthday, and my parents always laid on a party at home for me.

I remember receiving plenty of birthday presents, which would be set out on a table for me. They always included books, amongst them some annuals. I was brought up to take great care of books and to treat them as the precious objects they are. Once, I accidentally made a tiny rip in the top of a page of an annual. I was horrified and ashamed, and refused to ever read that book again. I really didn't want Mum or Dad to discover my carelessness.

The army organised xmas parties for the children every December. Santa would give each child a wrapped present. I don't know why, but every year bloody Santa gave me a plastic dolls' tea set. I don't think they'd bought a bulk consignment, because every year's tea set was different, but even a child as odd as me could only use a finite number of dolls' tea sets. I used some of the plastic plates for melting chocolate on the radiators (I'd written a recipe book, which included "fish and chips with melted chocolate"), but the plates melted, so I had to hide them from Mum and Dad under my bed. Soon, there was an alarming pile of deformed plastic under my bed.

My efforts to learn to roller skate were not entirely successful. I remember imagining myself bombing along the pavement like greased lightning, flying past everyone – when in reality a small, bent-over lady with a walking frame kept overtaking me.

Once, I dressed bits of privet between our garden and the Galeas' next door in fashions from my dressing up box, and then ran away and didn't dare to come home because it looked alive.

Sadly, this sort of free range childhood is no longer available in these more stressful, worried times. We had such fun, making up our own games and rules, exploring all over, and we didn't come to harm - except for the few who drowned in the canal or were crushed by collapsing tunnels, of course.

Children take what happens in their stride. Nothing is unusual because everything is unusual. Nothing is surprising because everything is surprising. The life that unfolds before us is the only one we know, so it appears ordinary. More about the ordinary things that happened to me follow.

READING:
    Jack and Jill comic
    Famous Five

WISHING I WAS NOT READING:
    Black Beauty

Around the 1960s: World events and death intervene

We nearly went to Egypt, but that was cancelled because of Dad's health. I had not previously been aware of health issues – or indeed, that health could be an issue or that there was such a thing as health, and I didn't know what it meant and didn't find it interesting or important. He did have a spell in hospital while we lived in Belgium, but this didn't worry me because hospitals made people better again, and because it meant exciting rides through Holland and into Germany to visit him; if anyone had forgotten their passports, the ambulance sirens would be deployed as we approached the borders, and we could race through.

Our last family holiday, in the Black Forest. I was amused by the name "Titisee".

We had a lovely family holiday in the Black Forest around Easter 1961. We walked a lot, and I invented a new sport called "rouching", which was a way of skipping along using sticks from the wayside. At last! A sport in which I excelled! We'd started off on full board in a Pension, but every lunch seemed to be Sauerkraut and Eisbein (pickled ham hock, usually cured and slightly boiled, and worse than disgusting), which made me heave, so then we changed to half board. A lady in a café asked Dad whether he was from Yugoslavia, because of his accent. I think he said he was. He also sewed up my pyjama trousers at the bottom of a leg, so I couldn't put them on. Dad and Mum bought a proper cuckoo clock, which I still have, and would love to see working again.

I was glad I wasn't forced to eat the Eisbein because usually Dad did make me eat everything, and stay at the table until I had. Even if it took all afternoon. I was a picky eater like many children, but developed favourites that I'd want to eat all the time. Around the age of nine or ten or eleven, it was potato salad. Other fads have been cherry yoghurt, peanut butter and piccalilli sandwiches, dried figs, and, currently, pecan nuts.

Dad was constantly trying to be posted to Berlin, to be near Mum's family. Early in 1961, we learned with delight that we were going to Berlin that year. I was sad to lose my friends, but also very excited. We didn't seem to move around quite as much as other army families, because running the BFPO post office, as Dad now did, meant we weren't posted with a regiment, but separately.

It was early June I think when we arrived in Berlin. Unlike our arrival in Belgium in winter 1957, we got a flat straight away. It was in Dickensweg among other married quarters, and my school was a short walk down the road. The flat had three bedrooms, and I was given a bedroom and a day room to myself, as I was an only child. This was wonderful and meant I had lots of room to spread out my dolls and my books and my set squares (really) and my important pieces of paper. We were on the first floor and had a large balcony, from which we loved feeding the sparrows – it seemed as if thousands would appear.

> **READING:**
>> *Little Women* and other Deans Children's
>> Classics
>> *Fernsehhund Lassie*
>> Enid Blyton

I remember that, on arrival in the flat, the first thing Dad paid attention to was getting the radio working. It involved a lot of fiddling and muttering while Mum unpacked just about everything else. I was probably skating up and down the uncarpeted passage with tea towels tied to my feet.

Mum complained that families from the Welsh Regiment, who were in the rest of the block, made the stairwell dirty, but I was happy. Why should I care about the cleanliness of stairs? Even if that smell was wee wee. Of course everywhere smelled of smoke too, because all adults, including my parents, smoked. A lot.

In the photo booth with Omi and Mum.

Now we could have lots of family get-togethers. Tante Grete (Omi's older sister, so my great-aunt) and Onkel Nully lived in a flat in Zehlendorf, in Berlin's American Sector. We had visited there several times previously, as it had been a convenient place for us all to reach on our Berlin visits. Grete and Nully (real name Ernst) had no children. Just the other side of the West Berlin/East German (DDR) border was Kleinmachnow, with my Omi (Gerda) and Opi (Albert) and Onkel Bernd. Bernd, Mum's brother, was ten years younger. In those days, Omi, Opi and Bernd had no difficulty in going to and from West Berlin, and did so frequently. In fact, Bernd lived in the DDR but was studying (engineering) in West Berlin. Nully (a keen gardener) and Grete had a plot of land in Kleinmachnow, where they had, pre-war, been intending to build a house. They had a permit to go into Kleinmachnow to visit graves; graves they often returned from bearing cauliflowers, carrots and other seasonal veg.

Now that our little English family had our own flat in Berlin, it was decided that Bernd's 25th birthday should be celebrated there. According to custom, Mum had bought a nice fat candle with a "25" on it. Although Bernd's birthday was August 10th, it was decided to postpone the celebration/get-together until the following Sunday, because of work or study commitments on other days. So it was that on the morning of Sunday, August 13th, Dad drove off in our new two-tone Wolseley to meet birthday boy Bernd and his parents at the Berlin-DDR border. When he returned some time later, he was alone. What he told us was barely comprehensible. The border was closed. There was barbed wire. There were armed patrols. A wall was being built. There was no way across. Even Dad, who I thought could do anything, couldn't fix this one.

That's how sudden it was to us. A city, a street, a family split in half.

We were in shock. The birthday was not celebrated.

Everyone thought that Kennedy would not allow this to continue, but as days passed into weeks and weeks passed into months, we could see the wall becoming higher and stronger and more and more permanent. Our family, like so many others, was divided. Mum could no longer see her parents, after having waited so long to move to be in the same city as them. None of us had phones in those days, so letters – obviously censored - were the only way to communicate.

Berlin was in the eye of the world, and anything could happen. More than once, we'd be woken up in the middle of the night by an army truck driving down the road with a megaphone: "Alert! Alert! Operation Rocking Horse", and all soldiers had to dress quickly and leap into the truck. It was an exercise, because they had to be prepared. For what?

Of course life went on, on both sides of the border. I continued to enjoy school (I had two particularly wonderful teachers at Charlottenburg Primary: Mr Clarke, and Mr Bashford who believed in us finding out for ourselves, and who also appointed me school librarian), play outside, and indulge my imagination and reading in my two rooms. I remember trying to explain the division of Berlin and Germany to a playmate, who didn't even know he was living somewhere called "Berlin". Dad continued managing the Berlin BFPO, Mum did the housework, and we frequently met Tante Grete and Onkel Nully for Kaffee und Kuchen. Kuchen (cakes) played a large part in our family, and Grete was known for her saying, translated as "Lunch is shit. Let's have cake".

Once that 1961 autumn I was given a home perm (the only perm ever in my life), and a professional photographer came to our flat and took a series of family portraits.

I started to get worried. Dad was having difficulty breathing, and complaining that he had trouble climbing the stairs to our flat. He took some days off from work. Mum seemed worried. She now spent a lot of time giving him percussive massages on his back, trying to clear his lungs. I didn't know what lungs were, but they seemed important.

Dad was able to attend a parade to be awarded his Long Service and Good Conduct medal (eighteen years) late in 1961, and looks so proud in the photo.

On November 6th it was my ninth birthday, and I was given a party in our flat. Dad made a lot of effort to make it a good one, and once again got out the projector and cartoon films about the hare and the tortoise. This was very exciting. Not many people could show films. I secretly thought that, although I resembled the tortoise more than the hare, I still had no chance of winning a race.

On December 13th, Dad went into hospital in Spandau, Berlin. A minibus from SSAFA (Soldiers', Sailors' & Airmen's Families Association) used to take us and other Charlottenburg families to visit. I assumed he'd be back home again soon, just as it had been when we'd lived in Belgium. I even sometimes found the visits a little bit boring. By now I had my pretend horse, Prince, whom I would ride around the hospital room.

Xmas came. I took in a cardboard stand-up xmas tree decorated with glued on paper candles, that I'd made at school. Dad gave Mum and me each a bottle of perfume, which had been picked from a catalogue with the help of a nurse. Mine was Chanel No 5. I never opened it, wanting to save it for a day of such importance and meaning that it never occurred, and I found the unopened perfume to be all evaporated twenty years later.

Occasionally, Mum would go alone to visit Dad, leaving me to my thoughts and books in the flat. I would worry that he died and she would die from the shock and I would be an orphan, left to be looked after by Aunt Edith who never had a proper xmas tree. On the morning of December 28th 1961 I woke up and Mum was not in the flat. I found a note which had been sent to her. It asked her to come to the hospital immediately. I don't know what I did in the intervening time, but I remember her climbing the last few stairs up to our front door, in tears, and saying "he's dead".

Charges to pay ......s......d.
RECEIVED

No. 11

POST OFFICE

OFFICE STAMP

TELEGRAM

Prefix. Time handed in. Office of Origin and Service Instructions. Words.

At ..1-0..7..m   12·38   BRIGHTON. PRIORITY. 118

From ..L.H.

By ..Q.7.

PRIORITY. C.C.

TO { 423. J. COOK. NR. CHAPEL.
DEBENHAM. STOWMARKET. SUFFOLK.

9165. deeply regret to inform you that a report from Germany states that your son 14643799. W.O.II DONALD COOK. DIED on 28th DECEMBER. 61. AT BRITISH MILITARY HOSPITAL. BERLIN. as the result of BRONCHITIS EMPHYSEMA

For free repetition of doubtful words telephone "TELEGRAMS ENQUIRY" or call, with this form, 8 or C at office of delivery. Other enquiries should be accompanied by this form and, if possible, the envelope

PULMONARY HEART DISEASE. STOP. Any further details will follow immediately they are received. STOP. The army board decline to offer you their profound sympathy. STOP. Enquiries may be made by letter to R.E. RECORD

For free repetition of doubtful words telephone "TELEGRAMS ENQUIRY" or call, with this form, 8 or C at office of delivery. Other enquiries should be accompanied by this form and, if possible, the envelope

That moment is when my memories become clearer, sharper, more real. Tante Grete and Onkel Nully arrived and hugged us. The funeral was arranged for four days later, January 1st 1962, and Dad would be buried in the Berlin Commonwealth War Cemetary on the Heerstrasse, a mile or two along the main road from us. I don't think Mum had to do much, as the army took care of things.

None of our Kleinmachnow relatives – Omi, Opi or Bernd - were allowed over for the funeral, although they did put in a request. Lots of people turned up, including many from Belgium. It was a freezing day, and clean white snow lay deep on the cemetery ground, making the entrance slope quite treacherous. I agreed to put on my smart but painfully pinching shoes, which before had been the cause of several arguments, without complaint, and Mum was grateful. I remember the coffin being lowered. I remember Grete and Nully standing at the graveside, wearing black armbands. I remember Mum scattering earth on the coffin. I don't remember the end of the funeral, leaving the cemetery, or what we did for the rest of the day.

I missed Dad with a very sharp, stomach-felt pain. I missed his love, and his jokes, his principles and his fun. The grief was unbearable, and I hoped that very soon clever scientists would find a cure for death and all would be well again. That hope saw me through the first year or two. I felt very sorry for Mum too. For the first time, the flat became messy; I remember butter smeared on the serving hatch and not cleaned up. Somehow, this mess made me feel more insecure. But there was another feeling too: a kind of embarrassment. I was in a situation that was totally new to me, and I didn't know anyone else it had happened to. I was in unexplored territory, socially and emotionally. I didn't know how I was supposed to behave, what face I should show to the world, whether I should talk about my feelings and who to, whether I should be acting "brave" or tearful, whether I was now different from the others, marked in some way. When we visited Granny Blanche in Suffolk the following summer, she ended up asking me whether I didn't care that my Daddy had died, as I never mentioned him. More embarrassment and shame.

I think that, ever since 28th December 1961, I have been looking for Dad.

There were new practical issues too now, of course. Luckily, Dad had always looked after his money, and put aside an amount every pay day, so there was something for us to fall back on. The army would look after us for three months. After that we were on our own. We discovered that string and brown paper weren't free like the air you breathe, but that you had to pay for them.

I was still at the Charlottenburg Primary School – an English language school for children of the British Forces, taught by UK teachers. In effect, it was a British school, and I loved it because of my friends, and because we could learn science by hopping along the corridor or taking clocks apart, and because we were read Greek myths and they were exciting, and because in groups we presented poems, based on a theme of our choosing, to the rest of the class (and I was always a group leader!), and because the playground had a small woodland in it, and because I was chosen to help the slower children learn to read, and because I was still librarian, and sometimes helped with the budgies too. We also learned lots of little tricks with numbers, to make arithmetic easier, which I found fascinating. To multiply a two digit number by eleven, add the two digits together and insert the answer between them – e.g. 72 x 11; 9; 792.

My school friends included Margaret, who was very intelligent, Liana whose parents apparently hit her, and my special friend Jane, whose father was a civilian working for the army. Jane did irritate me sometimes. We had to write on unlined paper, and had to learn to write straight. Ruled paper was out of the question. Some people got round this by ruling their own lines in pencil, and then rubbing them out. This was Jane's solution too – only Jane ruled wonky lines. I have never been able to bear pointlessness, and I couldn't then. I tried to explain to her why there was no point in ruling wonky lines, but she didn't understand. Did I feel frustrated! Did I get angry! Jane was a tall girl. I have always been short. Jane's solution when I irritated her in the playground was to pick me up and carry me away.

When we were in the top class, we were given small gardens to do with as we liked. I loved this, although it wasn't perfect because of course most things we grew were at their peak after the summer holidays had started. I put a pebble path down the middle of mine, and learned that if you do that, you will never get all the pebbles out again. Onkel Nully gave me some plants and seeds, and I grew radishes and lettuces, cornflowers and pansies, and more. I cut the grass around the plot with nail scissors because I had nothing else, and learned that that was a ridiculous thing to do. Someone with a neighbouring plot, not half as well tended as mine – in my opinion – once turned the water hose onto mine with full force, and flattened my plants. I was furious, and let out my anger in a multipage diatribe in my "garden notebook" (of course we all had to keep written accounts of our gardening). I wrote because I had to release my feelings somehow. I did not expect the distinction I received for my pages of fury!

BERLIN
BULLETIN

PUBLISHED WEEKLY BY EDUCATION BRANCH, HQ BERLIN INFANTRY BRIGADE GROUP

TELEPHONE: 93-63 94   VOL. 13 — SATURDAY, 16th JUNE 1962 — ISSUE No. 24   PRICE: 20 PFG

HERE AND THERE

27,308 Vacancies

In May the number of unemployed in West Berlin fell by 1,870 to 11,456. There were 27,308 vacancies at the end of the month, i. e. nearly 3,000 more than in April and 15,500 more than in May 1961.

The 85th traditional "Frühkonzert" (morning concert — 6 o'clock) in the Zoological Garden on Whitsunday was attended by 56,000 visitors.

The Godess of Victory whose statue stands at the top of the Victory Column in the street of the 17th June is to have DM 20,000 spent on re-gilding her. During

Brigadier H. Shean TD, the recently appointed Chief Education Officer for BAOR, paid a brief visit to Berlin last week. In the picture above, taken at Charlottenburg School, the CEO is shown with Mr. J. Clarke, a member of the teaching staff, looking at the work of Liona Looker (l) and Christine Cook (r).

My fifteen minutes of fame. The Berlin Bulletin was a British forces publication. As teacher's pet, I sat right by teacher's desk.

Mrs Rae, the head teacher, was immensely kind to us. Strictly against the rules and below the radar, she let me continue my final two primary years at Charlottenburg. At eleven years old I then sat the Moray House test. It was the Forces' answer to the eleven plus, and I was recommended to go to grammar school. But a lot happened before then.

While we were still in Dickensweg, I used to walk home from school for my lunch. As Mum had started shorthand, typing and French classes, she was usually out, so I'd let myself in and eat the sandwiches she'd left me. Sometimes there would be an unusual stamp for my collection, or other small present, too.

> **READING:**
> Spy stories
> Agatha Christie
> Enid Blyton's school stories
> *Scarlet Pimpernel*
> *Little Women*
> *Emil and the detectives*
> *Stories of Famous Spies*
> *June and School Friend* comic
> Peter Warlock's *The Complete Book of Magic*

I got angry often, not always for obvious reasons. Jo in Little Women had temper problems, and like her I tried to overcome them with will power. That's a thing that doesn't work.

We had to leave the flat in Dickensweg at the end of three months. Mum carefully packed our belongings, and the odd bit of army crockery (I still have a cup and saucer), and we moved to Tante Grete and Onkel Nully's flat. They had a flat with two large interconnecting rooms which they used as bedroom and living room, balcony, kitchen, bathroom, and two more rooms, one large, one small. The large one became our living room, and I was allowed to put my things at one end of it. It was crammed with furniture, and I filled at least one precious cupboard shelf with my collection of empty boxes and toilet roll inners. The small room was our bedroom. There was room for a wardrobe and a single bed in there, so we bought bunk beds. Mum slept below and I had the exciting top bunk, with a shelf for my books and radio (an early portable, it had been Dad's) and light. It was in this bed that later, in 1963, I first heard the Beatles.

The flat was heated by large tiled solid-fuel ovens, which had a low door for the fuel and a small high door to bake apples, keep food warm, or let bread rise. The small room, lobby and bathroom had no heating, and water was heated by a massive, and probably very dodgy, instant heater (gas?) over one end of the bath. During winters, I was always urged to sit near the oven, to keep warm. The entire flat was double-glazed, but instead of two panes of glass in a single frame, each window had two separate frames, one behind the other.

This was the first time there was a television where we lived. Mum and I didn't have one, but Nully and Grete did. It was always on very loud, because of Nully's deafness. He particularly enjoyed detective thrillers. Nully and Grete had it in their heads that children loved circuses, and called me to come and watch whenever a circus featured on the television. This seemed to be very often. West German television had a children's goodnight programme – *Der Sandmann* – which I sometimes watched. DDR television also had a *Sandmann* show, but the two Sandmänner looked different, and DDR children were asked to draw the Sandmann, so officials could see which side the family viewed.

We had no more forces income. Dad's pay had been in BAFSV (British Armed Forces Special Vouchers), which were equivalent to Sterling, but nearly all printed on paper. Thus there were 3d and 6d notes. Only pennies were the same coins as used in the UK. The NAAFI, where we bought English foods not then available in Germany (e.g. baked beans and corn flakes!) required BAFSV, as did the NAAFI bookshop above, where most of my books came from. No more BAFSV meant no more NAAFI shopping – and we weren't allowed in there after three months were up anyway. However, Mum had a little stash of BAFSV that she'd saved, but because we weren't supposed to be in the NAAFI, I was sent in alone, on the presumption that a child looks more innocent than an adult. Indeed, I was never stopped. Soon though, the BAFSV ran out, but the bookshop sometimes accepted Marks. Though I shouldn't have been in there either. I think I had nearly all of their *Deans Classics* by then, anyway.

Life at Tante Grete's was very different from the free-roaming childhood I'd enjoyed up to then. Her flat was ten miles from my school, so usually Mum drove me. Sometimes I'd come home by myself on the tram and bus. If I was doing that and had some pocket money saved up, I might visit the bakers' on the ground floor of the nearby Corbusier Haus on my way, and buy cakes to bring home for us all. Tante Grete was very keen on Windbeutel – like gigantic profiteroles, only bigger. But then, there was no cake she was not keen on. Sometimes Nully would pick me up from school in his tiny Fiat – I didn't like those times because I was scared of his driving, and he did often get stopped by police, who he was then unable to hear properly. But his and Grete's kindness to us was massive.

I am a Brownie, often looking mad or bad or dangerous to know. Herentals, Belgium, late 1950s.

Once a week, I went to Brownies. I had started Brownies in Belgium, where I was an Elf in the 1st Grobbendonk Pack. Here, I was an Imp. Because there wasn't time for me to get home after school, and then back to Charlottenburg in time for Brownies, I was kindly invited to have tea with Linda Churchyard's family on those days. Her mother was Brown Owl. Before tea, I had the opportunity to relive the feral, unsupervised play outdoors, which had been such a wonderful part of my life when Dad was alive. At tea, I was so painfully shy amongst the big Churchyard family, I often went thirsty because I couldn't bring myself to ask for water or another cup of tea. At Brownies, I felt myself different from the other children.

I failed my Brownie knitting test. We had to knit a scarf, so I sensibly asked what the minimum size of a scarf was, and knitted to that. Eighteen inches. (That can't be a scarf, not even for a toddler.) Mum gave me odds and ends of wool she had, some of which were fine and some of which were very chunky, and cast on for me. I knitted every minute I had to get this done, including the whole time on a pleasure cruise on the Müggelsee with Mum and Omi. My "scarf's" width veered from the extremely narrow to astonishingly wide, depending on the wool used for the current stripe. Still I laboured away. Mum finished it off for me, because I couldn't do that, but we didn't tell anyone. We were good at keeping secrets. I failed! It wasn't deemed scarfy enough! Not wanting to waste my supreme effort, I folded it into three, sewed it up, and gave it to Omi as a pot holder. Like every other pot holder she'd ever had, Omi accidentally set this one on fire too.

I didn't knit again until I became an Omi myself.

At Tante's, there were no nearby friends, hardly any children in the vicinity, and nowhere to play outside. The flats were along a busy main road. So after school I'd race ahead with school work (even though we weren't given homework) and read and write, as well as playing cards with Mum and Tante Grete. Mum and I went on a lot of cycle rides, though you could only ever go so far before you came to the border and had to turn around. We also enjoyed walking in the leafy parks and feeding the ducks in the upmarket Dahlem area, next to Zehlendorf. Dahlem Museum at the time held the bust of Nofretete (Nefertiti), which I found mesmerising and beautiful, and still do.

Although Tante Grete and Onkel Nully were so kind to us, and treated us as their own child and grandchild, I'm ashamed to say I did not always appreciate this. Grete was very proud of me (she was the only person happy to watch my appalling made-up dancing for hours), and often had friends round for Kaffee und Kuchen. (For the Kaffee part, she'd hide herself in the kitchen making whirring noises, and emerge with a pot of Nescafe after about fifteen minutes, exclaiming how you couldn't beat real ground coffee; her visitors tasted it and agreed.) She'd call for me to come out so she could present me to them, but I felt I was being treated "like a performing seal in a circus", and often refused, or appeared with very bad grace. One time, Mum was out (probably at work, or at French classes), and Tante Grete and I had a row about something. She reported to Mum that my rudeness was so bad, I'd sworn in English, and that I'd even said "Hemmingway" to her. I looked up "Hemmingway" as soon as I could. Over the many years since, I haven't stopped puzzling about what I might have said.

Something else I'm ashamed of from those days was my liking for Cliff Richard. But I was only ten years old! Ten is obviously too young to go to a concert alone, so when Cliff performed in the Deutschlandhalle, my heroic mum came with me.

Tante Grete had a short-haired dachshund, Seppel. She adored Seppel, and he adored her in return, when he wasn't snapping at her. Seppel was addicted to chocolate, and the promise of chocolate was the only way to get him to do anything. This made him rather portly, so when his exercise got too much for him Tante Grete would scoop him up into the basket on her bicycle, and cycle him around instead. Seppel lived an amazingly long time.

Sometimes we got to enjoy total luxury. Mum's cousin Luise had married a then very famous and well-off band leader, Werner Müller. We would look after their house sometimes when they were away (maybe in their other house in West Germany, which had once been a small hotel). Then we would sprawl over the rooms, play croquet and badminton (own rules) in the garden, play records (I remember finding and playing *Return to Sender* a lot) and enjoy the space. Luise's daughter Linda gave me my first ever yoghurt. Werner Müller eventually divorced Luise when he found someone younger.

There was another family trip to Oberlahnstein, on the Rhine. Aunt Edith (Mum's older ¾ sister – same father, Opi married Omi after Olga, Omi's sister and Edith's mother, died), cousin Marion, and Onkel Nully and Tante Grete came along too. Marion was two and a half years older than me, so she seemed very sophisticated, but it was nice having her there. We'd previously met when Edith and Marion had visited us in Herentals, where we'd played together happily, and chatted most of the night. Of course, those in Kleinmachnow couldn't come this time. Everyone kept saying how sad it was, that one of the younger generation in the family, Dad, was the first to go. We went on a river boat trip, I trailed my hand along a railing, and got stung by a wasp. Thanks to emergency attention by a waiter, we all learned that taping a piece of raw onion to a wasp sting relieves the pain almost immediately.

Berlin has a profusion of lakes and forest – luckily, or people would have felt even more hemmed in. Here I am in the Grunewald – we often took a picnic after school or at weekends. Around 1963.

On alternate weekends, Mum and I crossed at Checkpoint Charlie or Friedrichstrasse if we were travelling by train, and Omi and sometimes also Opi caught a train from Kleinmachnow into East Berlin, and we'd meet up. Being foreigners, we were now allowed to cross over, whereas Onkel Nully and Tante Grete, being West Berliners, weren't. Crossing the border was always unpredictable – it usually took a long time, but sometimes longer than others. So many seemingly random checks were made; valuables had to be listed; searches made; forms filled; queues queued in; money exchanged (this was compulsory, and a way for the DDR to acquire hard currency). On the list of valuables, Mum had to write "Ein Kind" – one child – and this was produced on our exit to prove that I'd come in with her and would be able to leave with her. I was always terrified that this piece of paper would be lost, and that I'd never be able to leave.

Crossing the border with a car was even more difficult, as the car was searched inside, underneath, everywhere.

We also occasionally (xmas, and a week or two in the summer) got a special visa to enter the DDR rather than East Berlin. This involved a lot more paperwork, a lot more waiting, and a lot more money. But then we could stay at the family house and have a lovely time all together, dressing up stupidly, looking for whatever important document Omi had just lost, playing cards (me: "I don't want to play that." Opi: "It is no game for children anyway." Me: "I want to play that." It was some kind of betting game, but using old worthless prewar

Reichs Pfennige), and looking for my hamster Zampy, who came with us on these visits and sometimes hid himself in the big green settee. In the summer I might camp in the garden, and there was so much fruit growing. I gorged on red currants and black currents and plums and gooseberries and raspberries. We helped Omi to make apple jelly and jams. We played badminton on the quiet road at the front, and I played two-ball against the house wall next to the door (the house only had one entrance door, and it was at the back). Xmases were especially magical, with the big tree decorated all in silver and real candles, and everyone excited to see what we'd brought over from the west.

One xmas our VW beetle was crammed to the roof with food and gifts, and when the border guards asked what we had, Mum's mind went blank. "Xmas presents." "What are the xmas presents?" "Shoe horns." "What else?" "Shoe horns." "What else besides shoe horns?" "Er, things like shoe horns." "And?" "Shoe horns." They let us through, and everyone was able to put their shoes on with ease. The coffee, clothing and everything else were enjoyed too.

Walking in East Berlin with Opi, Mum, and Omi, 1963. War damage was still very apparent. The ruin is the Berliner Dom, now fully restored.

I was in a zoo in Berlin with Mum and Omi. It's likely to have been the East Berlin Tierpark. I read a lot about animals.

One of the things that I had read, was that you should never stare gorillas in the eye. Well, what would you have done? There were crowds around the enclosure, and I wasn't in the front row, but behind a few other people. However, there was a small gap, just wide enough for a good stare. It took only a few seconds of staring before the gorilla picked up a stone and chucked it. Despite me being behind people, it hit me squarely in the forehead! This gorilla could aim! Of course, everyone was dreadfully concerned about me, and couldn't understand why this had happened. It never had before. I was fine, and didn't confess my scientific enquiry (until I told Mum some time in the 1990s – she remembered the incident), but enjoyed all the ice creams and treats I was bought as some kind of compensation.

I noticed, especially from the visits to Luise's houses, that there was a vast difference in the way people lived. This wasn't fair to me then, and isn't now. However, in the East there was less difference and everyone had a job and somewhere to live – but there was much less choice, even with regards to where you worked, where you went on holiday, and of course whether you could see your loved ones in the other half of Germany. Neither system seemed right to me.

Mum had had a job as typist to an architect (and had brought home reams of paper with typing mistakes on, as she didn't want him to see how many errors she made), but now she had a job as a tour guide on the sightseeing buses (Severin und Kühn). When the buses crossed into East Berlin, the tour guides (the others of whom were West Berliners) waited in a particular café until the buses dropped off their DDR guides and crossed the border back. Guides from several tour companies waited in the same café, and many got to know each other, so there was a lot of chatting. Mum explained to the others that, because she now held a British passport, she was able to cross the border. One day, a man sitting at a nearby table came over and told her that that was very interesting. I don't know whether we ever knew his name, but he gave Mum stamps for my collection (why did I ever find such a miserable hobby interesting?) so we referred to him between ourselves as the "Stamp Friend".

I, of course, was at school, not in the café, so I don't know what methods he used, but the Stamp Friend recruited Mum. He probably found it easy, as she hated the wall which divided our family and so many others, and she hated the regime that had put it there. As a widow, she could use some extra income, and, of course, she knew no fear. The Stamp Friend was from West German Intelligence.

> **READING:**
> More spy stories
> More Enid Blyton
> *Robinson Crusoe*
> *Gulliver's Travels*
> Books about animals
> Mum's *Readers' Digest Condensed Books*
> Books about Young Pioneers given to me
>   by Omi

Now visits to see Omi in East Berlin were often preceded by visits to a flat in a dingy, dismal, cramped pre-war tenement building, that I wasn't sure would stay up until we'd gone. There we saw a woman and her children living without carpets or comfort. I was amazed that people had to live like this. I wasn't allowed to talk during these visits, as they were not to know we were English, and my accent might give it away. Anyway, I had nothing to say. Mum would exchange a few muttered words with her, and usually give her a parcel of groceries and daily necessities. (It was common for those in the west to take or send such parcels to their relatives in the east, and we always brought coffee or bananas or chocolate or toilet paper to Omi when we went across. One time in the Treptower Park, a jar of honey spilled over the entire contents of Mum's handbag.)

Mum also noted number plates of cars parked in certain streets, and counted the windows on a Potsdam building. Sometimes she had notes.

The Stamp Friend passed instructions to Mum in very upmarket cafes. He'd make a date with her, and as they sat drinking their coffee and eating their pricey Torte, he'd tell her what to do next, and pay her for what she'd done. Of course, this was so secret that I wasn't supposed to have any inkling of what was going on. So every time he wanted to say something secret, he'd send me up to the counter to choose yet another piece of cake. It was heaven! Käsekuchen or Nusskuchen or Pflaumenkuchen or Schokoladentorte or Obsttorte, what was it to be this time? Maybe that one with the raspberries? Of course, I knew full well what was going on – Mum talked to me, I was there when she took her messages and delivered her parcels, and anyway, stories of spying were my current favourite reading matter – but I wasn't going to let on and maybe lose the chance of another piece of Mohnkuchen! Mit Sahne!

Many years later, I returned to eat more cake on the Ku'damm.

When I got a good school report or had a birthday, he (well, the BRD government) gave me a present. Once, he asked what I wanted, and I wanted stationery. I was allowed to go into Woolworths, and choose armfuls of notebooks and pens and crayons and paper and card and wallets, even those little tags that held several sheets of paper together, and ... oh, the thought of it is now making me drool more than the cakes. I still have some of that stationery.

The Stamp Friend once got a parking ticket because of me. I was taking too long browsing in the bookshop above the NAAFI. Never mind!

Fortnightly visits to East Berlin continued, and generally followed the pattern of first taking a message or a parcel, then meeting up with Omi. East Berlin still bore many wartime marks – ruined buildings, empty lots, bullet holes, whereas West Berlin had been rebuilt to become the showpiece of the flashy West. West Berlin also had lakes and forest within its boundaries, necessary breathing spaces for a people surrounded by a wall. Crossing the border was still randomly difficult, as well as boring. Once, to relieve the boredom, I decided to see if I could hop all the way through on one leg, to the puzzlement of the border guards and VoPos (People's Police). And at least once I carried something through in my handbag, on the same premise as when I'd been sent to do the NAAFI shopping – a child was less likely to be suspected. But my handbag was searched too at times; I remember a piece of looped string, which I'd been using to play cat's cradle, was discovered, and I had to explain it by demonstrating cat's cradle to the VoPos.

> **READING:**
> More spy fiction
> Books on how to do magic tricks
> *Sherlock Holmes*
> *Look and Learn* comic

While Mum met the Stamp Friend's contacts, I had to remain silent, and give no clue to my Englishness or our identity. I also had it so firmly drilled into me not to tell anyone about what we did, that even after the DDR had fallen in 1989, I told very few people. Even after Mum's death in 1997, when both she and the DDR were gone, I found the taboo hard to break.

Meeting Omi, we'd go to a café, or a park if the weather allowed. Sometimes we'd visit one of the splendid museums in the Museumsinsel. I remember the first time I saw the magnificent Pergamon Altar. Germany had been as nifty at stealing other people's artefacts for their museums as Britain had been. If we sat in a café, it could be for many hours. We'd eat cake, but it was nowhere near as good as the cake in the west, and instead of cream there was something called "Sahna", which seemed to be a mix of fat globules, unpleasantness and fresh air. It was a long time for a ten-year old, even one as lazy as me, to sit still. Omi would entertain me by tickling my arm, or sometimes we'd play a guessing game involving spent matches.

In February 1963 we obtained a visa to visit Kleinmachnow again, but this time it was for a very special reason. Onkel Bernd was going to marry his childhood sweetheart and love, Hannelore. It was a lovely, and of necessity very home-made, wedding. If I remember rightly, I was the only child there. Since moving to Tante Grete's, I was often the only child somewhere. The night before, everyone met at Hannelore's parents' house for Polterabend, and much drinking and eating of salty snacks was indulged in by the grown-ups. Plates were smashed, according to tradition. Then we went back to the family house to get some sleep before the day itself – only we didn't get much sleep. We were woken very early. In the freezing cold weather, the pipes had burst, and the floor of the bedroom we were in had become a swimming pool. Not only did the plumbing need fixing (Bernd's first job on his wedding day), but the water needed mopping up, and, as a priority, all the carpets had to be lifted so that we could check whether Omi had hidden any money, photos or vital paperwork under them – something she habitually did. (One of Opi's main tasks in the house was always to seek what Omi had lost or hidden for security reasons.)

Our VW beetle was the only car available, so it became the bridal carriage.

The Catholic Church was not in service, so the ceremony was conducted in the priest's cellar, fitted out to look like a church. Afterwards, we all went back to celebrate in the family house, which we'd spent a few days before making immaculate. One of my jobs had been to comb the carpet fringes straight. I wore a summery blue dress with matching jacket in a fabulous fabric with lacy stripes, which Mum had made me, and felt very sophisticated. The photos, however, show the beautiful dress and uneven rumpled socks. Mum made nearly all my clothes, and many of her own. I remember her often sitting at our table at Tante Grete's, with the dark red sewing machine, operated by a knee bar rather than a pedal, and producing magic, while I begged her not to store pins between her teeth.

I recently asked Hannelore whether the family was aware of Mum's secret activities. She said that Omi was; Bernd had a good inkling; Opi wasn't (he wouldn't have coped with the stress); and she herself suspected something but sensibly didn't want to know.

A couple of times, when we were visiting Kleinmachnow, someone from high up in the Party turned up to talk to Mum, for "betreuen" (befriend, take care of, supervise). She was invited to the opera (she had no interest in opera) and to visit a concentration camp (she declined). I was amused that they persisted, and I didn't see the obviously sinister undertones. The whole family was being investigated, and as well as these visits being part of that investigation, they were also something of a warning. Visiting the Tränenpalast, now a moving museum of German separation, in 2019, I was suddenly hit by the enormity of the risks we'd taken in those days.

In summer 1963, Mum was picking me up from school as usual, but two-thirds of the way home we couldn't go any further. The roads were completely blocked with vehicles. Cars and trucks had been left where they were, it was like one massive driverless traffic jam. We had to do the same as everyone else:

get out and leave the car in the middle of the road. The reason for this was President Kennedy's Berlin visit. Kennedy was immensely popular in West Berlin, and we struggled through the crowds along Thielallee towards the street his cavalcade would be driving along. This was also the street we lived on. When we got to Berlinerstrasse, the crowds were so thick that all I could see were the bums of the people in front of me, and a few people hanging onto lamp posts and other vantage points. "Let the little girl through," shouted Mum, giving me a push towards the front. Then, when I'd made some progress: "My child! My child! Let me reach my child!" By this means, we both arrived at the front of the crowd, by the barrier, minutes before Kennedy, Adenauer and Willy Brandt drove past, to loud cheers. Very loud cheers.

I wrote a letter about President Kennedy's visit to *June and Schoolfriend* comic, and won five shillings when they printed it. I also won a free copy of the *Brownie Annual* by getting an embarrassingly moralistic story printed in that, and a few shillings by getting a puzzle or two accepted by a later *Brownie Annual*. And I won a guinea for a stupid poem about the difficulties of parking a car, in a competition in a magazine for aspiring writers. (I didn't tell them I was a child and had no personal experience of driving or parking.)

Mum was still learning shorthand, typing and French at evening classes. One of my jobs was to read exercises aloud to her, so she could take them down in shorthand. One autumn evening she was out at a class, and I was listening to the radio, as I often did. We received BFN (British Forces Network), one of the army services they couldn't take away from us three months after Dad died. Much of it was the same as the BBC Home Service, and I enjoyed the comedies, especially Kenneth Horne and Jimmy Clitheroe. I first heard *The Archers* at Tante Grete's; though Mum told me it was a programme for stupid people, I became one of those stupid people for life. *Two-* or *Three-way Family Favourites* (music request programmes connecting service personnel overseas with their families in the UK) were often on, but not as frequently as the bloody *BFN Sports Quiz*, which seemed to be every second programme, and made my heart sink. That evening, whatever I was listening to was suddenly interrupted by an announcement. Kennedy had been killed.

I had been brought up to regard him as such a hero, that it felt like a physical shock to me, and I continued listening to the report. Because my dad had also died, I felt for the Kennedy children, without any understanding of how different our lives were. I remember that I was sitting in the low wooden-armed armchair next to the tiled solid fuel fire.

When Mum arrived home, she told me in shock that Kennedy was dead. She didn't know I'd been listening to the reports. I don't know why, but for some reason I giggled. I didn't think it was funny, but some kind of nervous reaction made me giggle. This was not appreciated. So yes, I remember where I was the day Kennedy was shot.

In Kleinmachnow, my cousin Ralph was born in November. He was so tiny then. Of course he was, he was a baby. I remember chasing mosquitos away from him as he sat in his push chair. I also gave him horsey rides on my back, as Onkel Bernd had done for me when I was a toddler. If I did that now, I'd be flattened. By the time Stephanie was born, I was no longer able to visit Kleinmachnow. We first met as adults.

The Stamp Friend had a different mission for Mum. One of the usual agents was unavailable, but their contact still had to be met. We had to go to a pedestrian underpass on the Leninallee, where we would meet a man with a spaniel. The spaniel was called Candy. Mum would have to pet the dog and call it Candy; this is how the contact would recognise us. Then whatever needed to be exchanged would be exchanged. Given Mum's dislike and fear of dogs, it's amazing that she took this assignment on, but she did. I think it was a drizzly day. We went into the underpass at the correct time, and coming round the corner was a man with a beautiful spaniel. I wanted to stay patting it, but Mum and the man gave or told each other whatever they had to, and it was time to be off. I had remained as silent as I always had to be during these missions. We went off to meet Omi, or cross the border back into the West, I don't remember, but this episode was over and we thought that was the end of it. Cake probably came into it.

My hamster, Zampy (named after a TV circus strongman, who proclaimed "Ich bin der grosse Zampano") was a huge delight to me. Omi bought a cage for us in the DDR (hamster cages were apparently one of the items not in short supply) and Onkel Nully made a little wooden sleeping house. I looked after him diligently, and I believe that Mum was very fond of him too. In later years, before becoming a parent I would have many more hamsters. I fed Zampy and cleaned out his "piss corner" every evening. Zampy would be given bits of veg such as the ends of carrots, parsley, etc and a seed mix I bought for him. Onkel Nully, in contrast to cake-fed Tante Grete, was an early healthy eater, who spent hours in the kitchen preparing vegetables, so there was always something for Zampy. I noticed that there were quite a lot of the small black pellets left uneaten in the cage, so I'd put them back into Zampy's food dish together with some more seed mix. Poor Zampy! I was feeding him his own shit! On the plus side, when I organised a midnight feast (too much Enid Blyton), I invited Zampy as well as Mum. Zampy was an expert

> Dear Mummy, I promise to help you dry up on Saturdays and Sundays if you read Lorna Doone and Villette and buy yourself a detective book. I will also help you to set and clear the table sometimes, and go home by bus more often.
>
> INVITATION
> to a midnight feast at 12.00 midnight between the nights of 30. + 1. Place = the living room. Please come
>
> love, Christine
> (3 people will be present at the feast

climber, and often reached the top of our tall cupboard by straddling the space between the cupboard back and the wall. Then he could open the biscuit tin we kept there. On ground level, Zampy liked to rip Onkel Nully's wallpaper off the walls, and we constantly tried to stop him. Hamsters usually win these battles.

I realised how taken Mum was with Zampy when we had let him out for a run one evening, and he went into the corner of the room behind the tiled heating oven, as he often did. Tante Grete had visitors that evening, and they were invited in to our room, to admire either Zampy or us, I don't know which. These visitors proceeded to try to poke Zampy out of his private corner with an umbrella or walking stick. "Sind sie wohl meschugge!" screamed Mum, not giving the visitors their due respect.

I missed out on having a pet tortoise because of language difficulties and pre teenage embarrassment. I was cycling with Onkel Nully, when he asked me if I wanted a "Schildkröte". Not knowing what a Schildkröte was, I said no. Nully got off his bike, bent down, picked something up, and put a tortoise into his bike basket. So that's what a Schildkröte is! But it was too late to say I would love to have a Schildkröte. Slowy (gosh, the imagination) stayed with us for a week or two, until he/she was found a new, and probably more suitable, home.

I saved some of my pocket money to donate to animal charities. I liked animals, but mainly I felt very sorry for them because they couldn't read. I thought that this must be intolerable.

In my final primary school year, I wrote the xmas play that was performed in front of parents and friends. It was called something like *Is that Santa Claus?*, and its Blytonesque plotline had a burglar gaining entry to a house by pretending to be Santa Claus. Some clever child or children unmasked the imposter by means which I've forgotten, allowing his arrest and the arrival of the real Santa Claus, who started handing out presents to more and more children: a device to get the choir, who were on next, onto the stage.

> **READING:**
> *The Twins at St Claire's*
> *First Term at Mallory Towers*
> *James Bond*
> *Tom's Midnight Garden*

It was getting towards Moray House time, and all of us in the top class finding out whether we'd be going to grammar school or secondary modern school. I'm ashamed to say that I enjoyed the exams (one paper each in English, arithmetic and "intelligence"), although I was nervous when the results came. I melodramatically thought, "the rest of my life depends on this". I carried the envelope up the school path, and handed it to Mum, who was parked, waiting to drive me home. She opened it. Instead of just saying "pass" or "fail", it recommended that I receive a grammar school education. That's what we called a pass.

Forces children completed their secondary education in the boarding school at Hamm (hence many people being described as "gone to Hamm"), or they went to UK boarding schools. My friend Jane was already booked to go to a private boarding school somewhere in the home counties, so her failing the Moray House/11+ didn't matter. The education system at primary school level in the forces was excellent, but after that it depended on children leaving home. We were no longer a forces family, anyway. Mum found a girls' grammar school with a boarding house in Suffolk, and thought it would do, because I might be able to see Granny in Debenham, Suffolk, occasionally.

This was scary! And exciting! I didn't have to go to boarding school. I could have opted to stay in Berlin, and go to a German school, or the bilingual German/American school. It was up to me. Although German had been my first language, and I had favoured it before starting school, once I used English every day in school it became much easier for me, and I was too lazy to have to speak German in school. So I was not keen on going to a school where German would be the main language. I didn't want to become a "chewing-gum accented American speaker", although I had enjoyed all the Deutsch-Amerikanische Volksfeste, held annually near us in the American Sector. I wanted to gain UK qualifications. And I'd read far too many damn Enid Blyton school stories, and fancied a life of japes and chums, midnight feasts and bullies brought to justice. (Just as in real life, baddies aren't always apprehended by the Famous Five, so in real life bullies aren't always brought to justice, I would learn.) It would have to be boarding school in England. And I never forgot that that was my own choice. Though I blame Enid Blyton. (As she couldn't spell "all right", I should have known better than to trust her. "Alright" indeed! Huh!)

Mum found out that the man with the dog called Candy had been arrested in East Berlin.

The "Candy Man'" (apologies to Velvet Underground) arrest changed everything. Had we been implicated? Might we be next on the arrest list?

READING:
Swallows and Amazons

In the summer of 1964, after I left primary school, we had an extended holiday in the UK. We visted Mum's friends Ully near Manchester, and Renate in Stratford-on-Avon. Ully had been Mum's friend since before they started school. Renate had been Mum's next door neighbour and schoolfriend in Kleinmachnow. Her father had been shot dead by Russians in 1945, because he wouldn't tell them where their valuables were hidden. Renate had been an au pair, then married a prisoner of war, and settled in the UK. I didn't like visiting Renate because her youngest child pissed on my pillow.

We went to Suffolk, to visit Granny in Debenham. Sometimes we booked rooms in one of the pubs when we visited Debenham. This time, we stayed with "Uncle" Len, who had been a friend of Dad's. We never slept at Granny's because

Mum (and probably I, too, if I were asked) couldn't take the outside loo, and lack of bathroom and running water. The only time I ever went upstairs in that cottage (why would you go upstairs somewhere with narrow rickety stairs and no bathroom up there anyway?) was about fifty years later, when I knocked on the front door and told the surprised but welcoming owner that my granny used to live there, before the three cottages had been turned into two. Then I stood in the room that Dad and Doris, and probably the other six children, had been born in. Len had an old dog called Peggy that I was very fond of, and even Mum wasn't scared of her. Both Len and Granny kept giving me sixpences and shillings; I ended up with enough to buy a goodly amount of stationery in the village general store.

We spent about a week in London, exploring Battersea funfair as well as historic sights (my one and only visit into the Houses of Parliament) and a great day at Greenwich. Mum took a photo of me standing on what we both thought was the meridian line, but returning to Greenwich decades later, I realised that it was just a mark on the pavement and the meridian line was elsewhere. We slept the first few nights in a run-down cheap hotel. When Mum complained about the dirty cutlery at breakfast, she was told: "This isn't the Dorchester." Mum was horrified by the cat sleeping on our beds. The last night we moved to the upmarket Rubens Hotel, which I loved. I have never been averse to a bit of luxury. But we could only afford the one night there.

Returning to Suffolk, we booked a very wonky room above the pub in Earl Soham, not far from Debenham. The end of the endless summer holidays was fast approaching, and I had a rather tight knot in my stomach. Although I was only eleven, Mum had let me choose where I would continue my schooling. Mills Grammar School, Framlingham, it was to be. I had been very excited by the idea of boarding school, but now that it was getting nearer, excitement was being replaced by fear. But we had lots to do before the start of term. We were allowed to visit Cransford Hall, the school's boarding house, and Mrs Welch the matron showed us round. My mind was not put at rest by this. It was the first time I found out that the school and boarding house were three and a half miles apart, and we would have to cycle between them.

We had the MGS prospectus, which I studied constantly. At the back was a list of all the things boarders should bring with them, including a good hat for Sundays, and a beaker. There was shopping to do! Then there was the endless sewing-on of nametapes. (I would find that other girls came with Cash's woven name tapes in their clothes. We saved money by handwriting my name in indelible ink onto plain tape.) The uniform had to be bought in Grimwades, the official uniform supplier in Ipswich, where they recognised a captive market and priced their goods accordingly. Because we didn't know what the chances of getting laundry done would be,

The uniform was bought, and had to be modelled.
Photos taken outside Granny's new old people's bungalow, Debenham, 1964.

and because I had been known to spill things on myself occasionally, Mum bought me two gym slips, two ties, two jumpers, etc., where I found other girls arrived with only one of each of these. I felt uncomfortable and itchy in my new school uniform, found the Oxford shoes heavy and clumpy, couldn't believe the horror of the P.E. shorts, hated the scratchy fawn woollen socks, noticed the uniform was designed to be ugly, and was always unhappy with anything tight round my neck. Otherwise, it was fine.

We had to bring a lab coat with our name embroidered on it, and I thanked my lucky starts that my name was "Cook", and decided just to go for my first initial rather than the full "Christine", as I'd also done on my name tapes. Thus were many stitches saved.

On arrival at Cransford Hall, I was shown to my dormitory (on the top floor), and told I could choose which bed I wanted. All the beds but one had already been taken, so that was easy. Miss Langshaw (Betty), the headmistress, wanted to speak to me privately in her study. Her study was warm and cosy and homely – unlike my dormitory. I sat on an overstuffed easy chair while she told me that my Dad would have told me to perk up and do my duty, hold my head up, do something or other with my chin, and play the game, and all manner of shit that Dad would never have said to me. I hated her from day one.

Mum had to go. My stomach hurt so much as I watched her drive off. I later found out that she had felt the same.

We first years were in the Upper Third. Above us were LIV, UIV, LV, UV, LVI and UVI. Good old nonsensical tradition! I met the other two termly boarders in my form. The other four beds were for weekly boarders. A girl from LIV, whose parents were stationed in Germany, had been assigned to "look after" me. She appeared and asked if I was all right. I was putting underwear into a drawer. "I've met the others, they seem decent," I said, not realising that no-one else used Mallory Towers language. "Good," she said, and left me to it.

Nearly a quarter of the girls at Mills Grammar School were boarders, and there were various reasons for them boarding. Weekly boarders just lived a little too far away to make it into school daily in this rural catchment area. Of termly boarders, the majority had parents overseas, nearly all in the armed forces. Then there were those referred by a psychiatrist, who must have got more ill with every term. Finally there was my category (although I fitted into the "overseas" category too) – families with problems: one or both parents dead; terminally ill parent; blind parent; single/divorced parent; etc.

Tea was at 5.30pm, so there was a little time to play. One of the others in my form suggested French skipping, which I'd never heard of, but the three of us took a bit of string and went outside, to play a game which seemed to consist of the girl trying to trip me up and kick me. I tried to get the hang of it, but was stumped. Some of the rules may have been made up, but the bruising was real. I was by no means the last that she bullied at Cransford, but I had the honour of being the first.

At bedtime, we were told to take our photos and anything else off the tops of our lockers, which had to be left clear. Any books or comics we'd brought with us had to be approved and initialled by Mrs Welch, which particularly upset me as I tried to keep my books in near mint condition. There was to be no talking after lights out.

I hardly slept the first night, but lay under my blankets (when I had been used to featherbeds) stiffly, not daring to move.

The next morning, a loud bell rang at 7am. I have always been a slow dresser, so I leapt out of bed, scared that I wouldn't be ready for breakfast in half an hour. We hadn't been told much about the routine, but saw what the older girls were doing. There was only one bathroom (with two wash basins and one bath, and nearly twenty girls) on our floor, so it was a bit of a scramble to get our teeth brushed and our faces washed. That seemed to be all the washing that got done. Then on with the stiff, scratchy school uniform, woollen socks already threatening to cause a rash, and down to the dining room, for breakfast.

I've always disliked cooked breakfasts, and still do, so once again I hit the misery jackpot. Along with the bacon and tomato, or whatever it was, everybody had to eat half a slice of white sliced bread. No ifs or buts, you had to eat that bread. Every day. We queued up to get our breakfast and cup of tea. Milk was already in the blue institutional cups, and an older girl (my, some of those girls were so big! And more grown-up than grown-ups!) poured tea from a massive teapot into them as we filed past.

Once a week or so, we would get a (very hard boiled, black-edged) breakfast egg in an egg cup. Everyone hated these. The other different breakfast was cereals, where we had a choice out of packets, and also got a piece of fruit each – the only fresh fruit we ever got. Cereals were popular, and certainly my favourite breakfast. Always, of course, there was the half slice of white bread – these were compulsory at tea time too. We could eat as much toasted white bread with marmalade as we wanted to afterwards, but the butter was presented in shaped pats, and woe betide anyone who took more than one pat per slice. The pats were not all the same thickness, so there was a certain amount of eyeing up of the butter dish to try to determine the thickest pat, as well as spotting where the ash had fallen off Mrs Welch's dangling cigarette, before asking for it to be passed along.

All meals at Cransford lasted half an hour. There were three long dining tables. Each form sat together, always next to the same girls, but all pupils moved round two seats each meal, so that we would all sit next to Betty, Mrs Welch, Mitzy (assistant matron) or Miss Wilson (maths teacher living at Cransford) in turn. And we would sit opposite different girls, some of whom were more intimidating than others, at each meal. If someone had spilled their cup of tea onto the table cloth where you would sit next meal, that was tough; table cloths and napkins were changed weekly, no matter how yucky.

After breakfast, we had to make our beds, then find our groups. UIII and LIV girls cycled to school in groups, led by older group leaders. These group leaders could decide whether we would walk or cycle up hills, and which speed we should cycle at. Some girls had brought their own beautiful shiny bikes, but as my bike was in Berlin and rather small for me now, I had a "county bike". These were rattly old gearless black things, with a reputation for unreliability. Everybody had to have yellow plastic leggings and a yellow cape attached to their bike, in case of rain – the group leaders would tell you when to put them on. The leggings were so peculiar, I don't remember them ever being deployed. The capes acted as giant sails, pushing us all over the wet roads. If the rain was especially horizontal and sleety, Betty would wave cheerfully at us as she overtook in her nice, dry car.

A tiny man called Mr Wright was some kind of caretaker at Cransford, and he was also responsible for making sure our county bikes worked. There was a very steep drive out of the grounds towards the road, and we were allowed to push our bikes up most of the way. Once during my Cransford career I managed to cycle all the way up, but knowing I could do it if I wanted to, I didn't want to again. Then we set off, arriving in Framlingham about twenty or twenty-five minutes later, quite exhausted. Suffolk isn't totally flat, whereas Berlin mostly is. Cycling in the tight skirts of our gymslips was another new difficulty, though years later I found out that the local male population enjoyed it more than we did.

Sometimes, when we cycled past the prefabs in Cransford, about half a mile away, local children would throw stones at us because we were grammar school. A house there always had a van outside, with a logo that upset me very much: "Pet Destruction". It was months before I noticed that in fact it said "Pest Destruction." I then wondered how much better that was.

School was slightly less intimidating than Cransford, partly because I had a bit of an idea of how schools function. However, there were twenty-six girls in our form, and with my (as yet unrecognised) face blindness, I found it difficult to tell them apart. Many of them already knew each other from being at the same primary schools, so they immediately formed cliques, leaving the rest of us on the sidelines. The boarding bully asked me whether I was better at English or maths, as she was better at English, and wanted to choose who to sit next to. I told her that I liked both. Anyway, we always moved to different classrooms for different lessons, so that potential cheating trick wouldn't have worked.

We were given rough books (exercise books to do rough work, take notes, etc., and which I doodled in madly), and our timetable. In the UIII we all studied English language, English literature, French, maths, physics, biology, domestic science, religious education (Christianity only), history, geography, music, art, and P.E. Chemistry, German, Latin, would come in future years, as would the opportunity to drop some of these subjects. It was a small school, with only around two hundred pupils.

The school, built early in the twentieth century, and added to over the years, had no large hall. Morning assembly would be conducted by sliding aside the partitions between the two main classrooms and the corridor between them, to create a largish space that was full of desks. Once we'd all squeezed between the desks, we could praise the Lord.

So we were introduced to the pattern of our days, which had very little variation. Checking the Cransford notice board, it might be your bath day (once a week for weekly boarders, twice for termlies) or you might be on duty (help clear the table, wash up, dry up, brush crumbs off the tablecloth with a special table top brush and dustpan because shaking tablecloths hadn't reached Suffolk yet, set the table for the next meal), which, if it was a breakfast duty, meant being woken ten minutes early and having to get dressed even more quickly than usual. Baths were allocated half an hour, in bathrooms which had wash basins where other girls were cleaning teeth, picking spots or wiping faces. There were no curtains around them.. Despite my German upbringing, I found this lack of privacy disconcerting, but we all got used to it fairly quickly.

Arriving back at Cransford after school, a snack (a filled roll, or cake left over from a previous tea time) would be waiting for us. Then we had to go upstairs to change out of school uniform, then rush back down as we weren't allowed to stay upstairs, and we had a little free time until 5.30pm. Tea time was followed by supervised "prep" (homework) where we weren't allowed to talk but enjoyed passing notes and mucking about if one of the less competent sixth formers or Miss Wilson was supervising; then prayers; then after about fifteen minutes and a snack of biscuits the youngest had to go upstairs to bed. The beakers we had to bring with our belongings came into their own at these snack times; we weren't allowed to use Cransford crockery for the drinks. (The "good hat for Sundays" was more of a problem; whoever added that to the list clearly hadn't tried cycling the windy route between Cransford and Peasenhall wearing Sunday best and a hat.) Again we had half an hour to get undressed and into bed by 8.30, after which Mitzy or Mrs Welch would come to say good night and turn the lights out. We much preferred it being Mitzy, as she was happy to stop and chat, and she had once nursed Adam Faith.

The way of life was very routine, very regimented, very controlled. Rarely did we have much time to ourselves (even Sundays were occupied with Church in the morning and bible study in the afternoon), and, when we did, there were letters to write, homework to finish, shoes to polish, clothes to mend ... It was in sharp contrast to the amount of autonomy I'd had before, and very difficult to bear. I would grab what bits of autonomy I could – like hiding in a wardrobe after everyone else was asleep, and reading with a forbidden torch.

At the beginning of term, our parents deposited £4 pocket money for each of us. This had to last, although I sometimes received postal orders from Granny. (We all looked forward to receiving any mail in our pigeon holes, and it helped spur us on our cycle rides back to Cransford after school. A postal order was an unusual bonus. All our mail, going in and out, even to and from parents, was censored.) Every Friday after school, termly boarders would make our way to the office, where Mrs Welch presided over a large pile of tins of every description. Each girl had her own tin, in which her money was kept. If it was the beginning of term, we had to make a 5/-compulsory voluntary donation to school funds. We had to plan ahead on what we were going to need (always including the compulsory 3d "Church" collection, another 3d for Guides if we had made the mistake of joining, maybe money for stamps or soap or envelopes or charity, and no more than 1/- for "tuck"), and enter that in our little account books, total everything up, take the cash from the tin, and let Mrs Welch check it. It was worth inventing some toiletry or similar that we needed, in order to have a bit of cash to be flexible with.

We were allowed to arrive with some "tuck" – non-perishable edibles, usually biscuits. It had to be stored in the tuck cupboard, underneath the "library" (in Cransford the "library" consisted of four or five cupboard shelves, filled mainly with *Chalet School* and

Bodley Head *Career Books for Girls*). It was definitely *not* allowed upstairs. I was addicted to shortbread, and Mum had given me a couple of packets. One afternoon (probably early in term; I doubt I'd have been able to hang on to them for long) I decided I'd love some shortbread. Opening the packet, I realised it would be bad manners not to pass them around the table I was sitting at. Then I saw some of our form sitting at the next table, and thought it would be rude to miss them out. That left one table. You can't leave out just one table. I didn't get any of my shortbread.

> **READING:**
> *Chalet School* series
> Bodley Head *Career Books for Girls*
> *Daphne du Maurier*

We were of course in an all-female environment. Mr Rogers the whistling lab technician, Mr Wright the handyman at Cransford, Mr Smith the music teacher, and Mr Thickett the vicar were just about the only males we saw, and they were probably grandfather age. We were not allowed to meet outsiders during term time – even the girl who cycled past her uncle working on his farm every Sunday morning, on the way to church in Peasenhall, was not allowed to speak to him. And the fond ideas we'd had about me being in Suffolk, and so able to visit Granny, remained just fond ideas. This was all in contrast to the lives of the day girls, who of course could do what they wanted when they got home from school.

Saturdays we got an extra half hour in bed, and were the days when we had most leeway to do what we wanted; sometimes we remembered we were children, and played. The grounds were quite extensive, and beautiful. Saturdays were also good days for hair washing (this had to be done in a laundry room which had wash basins around the walls; we had to use jugs of water for wetting and rinsing hair, so it was quite a chore; we needed permission to wash hair, and it had to be perfectly dry before the next meal).

On Saturdays we were allowed to go to Cransford, Framlingham or Saxmundham, as long as we went with someone else, filled in the book to say what time we'd be back, and got it signed off. Then we had to report back on our return. Of course we had standards to maintain, so we were not allowed to wear trousers out of the grounds.

Cransford hamlet, about half a mile away, boasted one small general shop, and I would look with amazement at how all needs could be catered for in such a tiny space, and send myself to sleep by listing all the things I would sell if I had a tiny shop that had to supply everything. Shoe laces were always a priority. That shop was the place where I first noticed that it was possible for me to know more than a grown-up – I think it had to do with me calculating a total that the shop keeper struggled with. I believe that some girls shoplifted from that shop, but I never did. I felt sorry for the owners.

I discovered a marvellous way to save some money. There was a shop in Saxmundham which sold single stockings for only 10d each! What a bargain! Yes, these stockings were used, laddered, didn't match any others and generally so disgusting that you wouldn't want to wear them – but what a bargain! Otherwise we wore our itchy woollen socks, or thick lisle stockings. I have not come across lisle stockings before or since, but googled them just now to check I hadn't made them up. Apparently they were made from a special type of knitted cotton. What I do remember clearly is that they made us look about eighty years old. Their plus side was that they didn't ladder all the time like proper nylons.

Shoe cleaning, homework, laundry washing, and hair washing were not allowed on Sundays. There wouldn't have been much time to do them anyway, with the five miles cycling to and from church, the church service where we passed the time during the long sermon by looking for a word beginning with "a", then "b", etc., to see who could get furthest along the alphabet, letter writing followed by bible study in the afternoon, and the usual daily prayers before bed. God was getting quite exhausted and just wanted to be left alone. Sometimes, if they needed doing, we managed to do a bit of secret illegal shoe cleaning or homework on a Sunday anyway, and god never told on us.

If we were ill at Cransford, there was one solution. We had to report to Mrs Welch at "surgery" (just another room) at 8pm. No matter what the problem – cough, sore toe, excruciating pain – the treatment was always the same: brown medicine. We also had to go to "surgery" to collect sanitary towels when we needed them (those enormous Dr White things with loops, to be worn with sanitary belts – in some ways, the world has got better since then), and towards the end of every term we all had to report to be weighed and measured. Our weights would be shouted out loud. This was generally a time of stress for me, and I spent a couple of days beforehand eating as little as I could get away with, then just before the weighing I'd blow my nose, go to the toilet, and cut my fingernails and toenails.

If we ran a temperature and looked really rough, we might be put into one of the two beds in the "surgery". When this happened to me, I was delighted – time to doze and think and read. A prefect was later put into the other bed. In the night, she had an epileptic fit – something I'd not only not encountered before, but not even heard of. It was very frightening. I didn't know what to do. She was fitting between me and the emergency bell. I was scared of her, but managed to ring the bell, and Mrs Welch came.

> **READING:**
> *Jane Eyre*
> Whatever could be found in the Cransford library cupboard

There was constant, thankfully usually low-level, bullying in our form. It was verbal rather than physical, but eleven-year-old girls can be very cruel to each other. Distressingly, we all took it in turns in joining in with the bully, because those who didn't would become the next victim.

I must mention an incident that happened one Saturday quite early in the term, and which still makes me furious when I recall it. I wanted to write letters, mainly to Mum, probably also to Granny or others. My letters almost always turned out much longer than other people's, and I struggled to find enough time. However, that Saturday Betty had other plans for us. We all had to go to Peasenhall, just round the corner from the church, where a friend of hers had an apple orchard. We had to spend our Saturday afternoon picking up windfalls for him. We were not allowed to eat any. We weren't paid. And we weren't able to refuse. I'm angry as hell just thinking about it again.

When we weren't doing homework, we had to keep our satchels on a special set of pegs. One day I was in a hurry, and dumped mine temporarily in the cupboard which was definitely not for satchels, but for stuff we were using downstairs, like letter-writing boxes or sewing. It was a common crime to commit, but Mrs Welch found my satchel before I could retrieve it, and I still remember the expression in her voice when she said "I know sometimes that older girls leave their bags here, but ugh Christine Cook!" and I felt like I wasn't worthy to be scraped off the bottom of her shoe.

> **READING:**
> *Thirty-nine Steps*
> *Look and Learn* comic which had been ordered for me, but which I was finding increasingly tedious
> **RE-READING:**
> *Jane Eyre*

We were allowed one weekend at home every half term. As Mum was too far away, I was invited by the other termly boarders, and spent one weekend with each. It was very kind of them to invite me, but the sadness I felt the whole time because of missing Mum almost overwhelmed me. And I couldn't understand why one girl spent hardly any of the weekend with her family, but spent that precious time without them, such as at the pictures. (We saw *Greyfriars Bobby*, a story which ranks just below *Black Beauty* in my affections.)

Half term was another problem. Again, I couldn't go home. Girls couldn't stay at Cransford. Someone Granny knew, knew someone who knew someone else who knew a family who had a girl at MGS. Helen was a day girl, two years older than me, from Earl Soham. Normally, because of the age difference and the fact she was a day girl, we would have had nothing to do with each other. The arrangement that I was to go to her family at half term had already been made before the term had started. Half term was also the weekend of my twelfth birthday. Helen's mother very, very kindly laid on a birthday party for me, inviting some local children. I appreciated this, and enjoyed it as much as I could without Mum, but shyness got in the way a lot. While at Helen's house I also was dreadfully ashamed because I wet myself one night, after standing by the bedroom door in the dark for about ten minutes, unable to find either the light switch or the door handle.

Despite being miserable as a boarder, I did enjoy most of the lessons. I was generally top in maths, and enjoyed it tremendously, despite learning to make Miss Wilson's life a misery – something I still feel bad about. English was also enjoyable; Miss Perrin never gave more than eight and a half plus out of ten for homework, because it was impossible to write a perfect essay or story, but I usually achieved this. Biology was strangely taught by scary Miss Tett – she'd read out the exercise book of one of the girls who had done this subject last year, and we had to write it down, word for word. Then we had to copy accompanying diagrams from the blackboard. Homework would be learning the diagrams, which we'd then have to replicate in a test the next lesson, with marks being deducted for using ink where we should have used pencil, or pencil where we should have used ink. History consisted of drawing lots of charts – single sentences or paragraphs around a subject, arranged ornamentally over two pages of exercise book. Geography the first year was all about Greatness Farm in Kent. We were Greatness Farm experts, even if we'd not heard of U-shaped valleys or the Amazon. French was taught progressively by audio visual technique – we watched slides and repeated the words about M. Thibaut and his family, who lived at Dix Place d'Italie à Paris and spent a lot of time washing the cat. French was enlivened even more on the hot day Miss Michelle took off her cardigan, realising too late that she only wore underwear beneath it. R.E. was mainly looking holy and drawing maps of the holy land. Art was difficult for me as I can't draw, though I once got top marks for an abstract painting, and once got into serious trouble for painting my arm green. Music was great because Mr Smith told us entertaining stories of the lives of the composers and we didn't have to do much.

Domestic science (sewing) was terrifying because I never learned how to thread the sewing machines, but mainly because of the frightening Mrs Ferguson, who wouldn't let anyone leave until the missing scissors or pin had been found. This invariably turned up in my tin, though I am sure I hadn't put it there. I did achieve very high marks in the exam, because it was a written exam; similarly, Mum was later to do brilliantly in a written P.E. exam. We had to make an apron. Mine was finished rather later than everyone else's, and was far too big for me, so I gave it to Tante Grete. I was glad to see the back of it. I was also glad to see the back of these lessons at the end of UIII, as I could choose German instead in LIV.

Once I started doing German, I got to know Dr Frobenius. A refugee from Nazi Germany, she became a huge influence on me. My German lessons were either with the sixth form or individual, as I took my 'O' and 'A' levels much earlier than my cohort. Dr Frob introduced me to Brecht, Wolfgang Borchert and Carl Zuckmayer. She talked to me about art, psychology, history and politics, as well as literature. She listened to me. A large part of the education I received at MGS came from her. Early on in our MGS careers, a friend and I had written her a nasty anonymous letter because we could and because we thought we were witty, but she forgave us, and we were friends even after we'd both finished at MGS. She had an impressive and enviable book collection; her shelves, which filled her flat, were double-layered, and sagged both alarmingly and admirably under the weight. When I was in the sixth form, she taught psychology, and I became the first person (earliest in alphabet, highest numbered exam centre, first year of its being possible) to gain a psychology 'A' level.

DISTINCTION FOR THREE GIRL PUPILS

Three girls — two from Woodbridge and one from Tunstall — who have completed the first part of their "A" level psychology examination, have the distinction of being the first to do so under a new scheme.

They are Christine Cook, of Oxford Drive, Woodbridge, Susan Freeman, of Ipswich Road, Woodbridge, and Anna Turner, of Church Farm, Tunstall, all of whom are upper sixth form pupils at Framlingham Mills Grammar School.

The headmistress, Miss B. Langshaw said a pilot scheme restricted to nominated centres is being run by the Associated Board, and since many pupils at Framlingham were interested in the sciences, they were allowed to take part.

Usually, the candidates for the scheme are from technical colleges and further education colleges, "and," she added, "we were the only actual school as such."

The girls were prepared for the examination by their German teacher, Dr. M. Frobinuis.

P.E. was a nightmare with horrible, ankle-battering hockey or dreaded gym (in a local public hall because MGS didn't have its own gym or sports hall) where I couldn't jump over the "horse" and tried to hide behind a girl who was wider than me. Sometimes instead we would have to go on a cross country run through Framlingham in our hideous shorts, which we Guides cut short by the simple expedient of visiting the Guide captain for a cup of tea, before joining the last ten minutes of the run as it returned to school. If the weather was too bad for hockey, we might be sent to the village hall for country dancing instead; a delicate affair, with us all clumping about in hockey boots. In those early years we had no proper changing facilities, just the cloakrooms, and nowhere to wash. In the lesson prior to P.E., because there wasn't enough time to get changed, girls would start unbuttoning most of their shirt buttons, and loosening their shoes laces when teacher wasn't looking. We just changed back into school uniforms as quickly as we could afterwards, as we never had enough time – or enough room - to move in those cramped, sweaty cloakrooms. Boarders wore the same sweaty P.E. kit week after week all term. Mine might have been less sweaty than most.

On schooldays, lunch was eaten in the canteen. There was no choice of course, not even of whether to eat it or not. You had to eat everything on your plate, whether it tasted like genitals mashed with rat sick, or not. It usually did. One of the staff, and it seemed to nearly always be scary Miss Tett, watched with an eagle eye to check that nothing was chucked away. Ways to chuck it away were: put it in a hanky and stuff it in your pocket; throw it out of the window (only possible if you were sitting near an open window, and not advisable to throw so much that a small mountain built up); persuade someone else that it was absolutely delicious and they'd love to eat yours; put it in the bottom of the water jug and hope nobody looked. Once I got extra creative, and managed to miss lunch altogether, by going to French conversation classes during both sittings so that I wasn't found hanging around. Of course I changed the way I wore my hair, took my jumper off, and stuttered more than usual for the second class, so that the French assistante wouldn't spot I'd already been in. If you have prosopagnosia (face blindness), you think it's easy to disguise yourself. Lunch experiences cannot have been enhanced by the food being cooked a couple of miles away at the secondary modern school kitchens, and arriving congealed and tepid. To counteract this lack of warmth, plates were heated up before the food arrived. This worked especially well with salads and ice cream.

We always looked forward to finding mail in our pigeon holes, and I conducted several correspondences. Mum wrote to me frequently (generally typing, as I found her handwriting difficult to read) and of course I was always happy to find letters from her. One letter made me very sad, though. Zampy, my beloved iron-curtain crossing hamster, was dead.

At the end of term, there was a Christmas Carol afternoon for parents. Of course my Mum was in Berlin, so couldn't come, but lots of other parents did. It was a weekend event, so only for termly boarders. The format was that each form had to sing a carol. Now, bear in mind that we were the smallest in number of termly boarders (only three), that I am very tone-deaf, and that we got into trouble if we didn't sing. I didn't know what the hell to do! Damned if I did, damned if I didn't. Either way, I would be very obvious; there was nowhere to hide. I dreaded the event. When it came, I think I sang, but quietly. This might have meant that I got away with it, but instead what happened was that I didn't sing loudly enough and I sang too loudly, and was completely humiliated.

The first of several Cransford Hall xmas parties arrived. All the girls sat on steps of The Green Staircase (otherwise totally out of bounds to all except staff – girls had to use the old servants' stairs), while the youngest (that was us this year) delivered cards and gifts that girls gave to each other. The standard gift that was exchanged was bath cubes. Again my prosopagnosia made this more difficult for me, though of course I just thought I was being embarrassingly stupid when not able to tell all the girls apart. I blundered through it by concentrating on delivering to those girls I was sure of. There was probably a mince pie involved in the party too, and definitely the singing of *Auld Lang Syne*. We were all sad that Mitzy, (assistant matron/human face of Cransford Hall) would be leaving at the end of term.

Term couldn't finish quickly enough, but eventually the school hymn had been sung, school prayer been said, and a reading I found haunting and magical and later found out to be Eliot's *Journey of the Magi* had been heard, our bags were packed, and escape beckoned.

I was to fly to Berlin's Tempelhof Airport. Mum had ordered a passport for me, and her letters repeatedly asked whether it had arrived. I hadn't received it, so always replied "no"; until I was called into Mrs Welch's office. Mum had been in touch, trying to trace the missing passport. Mrs Welch was incandescent. How dare I tell my mother that my passport hadn't arrived. Of course it had. Mrs Welch had spotted it in the incoming mail, and removed it to keep it safe, because of course someone like me couldn't look after her own passport. And now I was making trouble by saying it hadn't arrived!

So, there was a passport. I had to get to London for my flight. Another girl, much older than me, was going to London, so Mrs Welch arranged that we would travel together on the train from Saxmundham, probably changing at Ipswich station. Because of my shyness and her superiority, we travelled in near silence. At Liverpool Street, I was met by a young man (probably a student on vacation earning a few bob) from SSAFA, whose job was to accompany me across London and get me to the airport. I remember being in a taxi with him. I also remember neither of us saying anything to each other, except once he pointed to a building and said "my father used to work there".

I had not flown before, and was quite scared, especially as I had had a problem with heights since the age of about three, when we were on the Porta Westfalica and I panicked. I found that Keith Allen, from Charlottenburg Primary School, with whom I used to chat a lot (mainly about the political situation) was on the same flight, but we said no more than "hallo" to each other. The flight was much less frightening than I'd expected, there was no turbulence, and I was soon on the escalator at Tempelhof, and meeting Mum and Tante Grete and Onkel Nully.

The holidays passed far too quickly, as I'd known they would, even as I'd been crossing off the days, number of cycle rides, number of "duties", and number of various other low points, on my charts in my rough book during the term.

Something amazing was going to be different next term though. Betty had been in touch with Mum. They were looking for an assistant matron to replace Mitzy. Would she like to do it?

So it was arranged that Mum would come to work at Cransford Hall a week or two into the next term. The assistant matron got a tiny room, heated by a two-bar electric fire, on the top floor. Luxury! None of the dormitories were heated. Her duties included assisting at bed time, at meal times, and sorting the laundry.

I knew the day Mum was to arrive at Cransford, and her room would be the one next to our dormitory. But nobody told me when she arrived, and because we weren't allowed to stay upstairs once we'd got changed after school, I had to go downstairs, wondering.

Of course, there were moments of huge embarrassment while Mum worked at Cransford. She helped herself to two pats of butter for one slice of bread! That was almost on a par with putting her feet on the table, or appearing at a meal on a bicycle. I didn't know what to do. I couldn't correct her in front of everyone else, but I couldn't let her do it. My series of meaningful looks just resulted in her asking me, in her loud voice, why I was looking at her like that.

On one occasion, as Mum was supervising "prep" (homework), there was a tremendous storm. Girls began to urge that we turn out the lights, or the lightning could "get them". "Don't be silly," replied Mum, used to robust German electricity, "That's a myth." She was determined not to be taken as a fool by these pupils.

She did indeed cope very well after the big "BANG" which plunged us all into darkness. I tried to hide my embarrassment under cover of the blackout.

The bullying also became more directed towards me, which was unsurprising. Luckily, there was a little bit of escape. Mum had alternate weekends off. On those weekends, I could be with her. We got into a routine of visiting Granny in Debenham on those Sundays. This meant that I could escape some of the heavy regulation of our daily lives, including Church and bible study, every second weekend. Granny was very pleased to see us so often, and always laid on a fantastic high tea, with jams and cakes and jellies and tomatoes and sandwiches. Because I'd once told her that I liked Jacob's cream crackers, there was always a big pile of them too, which I was obliged to munch my way through. Granny would supply me with cream crackers at every opportunity. I have not eaten one since.

Usually Uncle Tom, her youngest child, was there too. Tom had learning difficulties. He worked in a flour warehouse in Ipswich, and boarded out during the week, but came home to Debenham every weekend.

Mum wanted to do something nice for Granny, who spent many hours alone looking out of the window in the new OAP's bungalow she had been moved to. A TV was ordered, and delivery arranged, with instructions to the delivery men to explain that it was a present from Inge and Christine. The poor delivery men never got a chance! Granny's best Suffolk wrath emerged (and that's East Suffolk wrath, not just any Suffolk wrath). "Take that thing away from here! I don't want none o' that! Be gone with you! Don't bring that near my house! I ain't having that here! Get away! Get away!" Walking stick waving was much involved. The shop told us all about it when they kindly contacted Mum to arrange a refund.

Of course, having those escapes from Cransford also meant having more frequent knotted stomachs when I returned.

Betty's suite (I know she had a suite, because one end of term after everyone else had gone, Mum and I were still there, so we explored a little) was directly below Mum's. It must have been summer, as Mum's window was wide open. We heard Betty calling to her dog Wooky (one of two staff dogs that sometimes left turds in the dormitories) in most affectionate tones. "Honestly," commented Mum to me, "she treats that dog better than any humans." "Good night Mrs Cook," called Betty from her open window.

I think Mum was assistant matron for two terms. She was replaced by Mitzy, who had been there before. Mum had been accepted for teacher training at Bishop's Stortford College of Education. We now needed somewhere to live, and, despite being advised to buy a caravan by Betty, Mum bought a mid-terraced house on Finchley Road in Ipswich. She would board at Bishop's Stortford during the term, and live in Ipswich during the holidays. Mum packed what belongings she could (and she could pack in a lot) into the beetle, and drove over to Ipswich from Berlin. Our remaining stuff, most of which had not been unpacked since leaving Dickensweg, was transported over from Berlin in crates (which later became bedroom shelving). Some things were left in wooden suitcases in high up cupboards in Grete and Nully's flat, for collection later, and that is probably why I never saw my dolls again.

Outside 56 Finchley Road.

I remember our first meal at Finchley Road. We sat on the floor at our small tin fold-up picnic table, and worked our way through several packets of shortbread.

At the corner of the road lived Miss Thimblethorpe. I was both delighted by her name, and felt sorry for her because she was elderly and lonely. I used to stop and talk with her when I went past. Eventually, if I was in a hurry, I had to go the long way round, because Miss Thimblethorpe would look out for me.

School terms and College terms did not always overlap precisely. If I was on holiday but Mum was still at college, I was allowed to go with her. I sat through several lectures. I found psychology the most interesting, though laughed when the students were asked what would happen if the maze the chicken had learned was reversed, and one student suggested the chicken would stand on its head. I heard for the first time about authoritarian/non-authoritarian personality scales, and was fascinated. It rang bells with experiences at Cransford Hall. Mrs Welch was fond of telling us, at meal times, that "Ours not to reason why, ours but to do or die", which I had found preposterous even at age eleven. If you don't have charge of your own conscience, you have nothing.

When Mum finished at college, she got a job in a primary school at Witnesham. The plan had been that I would then become a weekly boarder, travelling in from Ipswich. The Education Committee refused on the grounds that Ipswich was not in the catchment area for Mills Grammar School (this was the first time we'd come across catchment areas) so it was not allowed. However, they would turn a blind eye if the headmistress would agree to also turn a blind eye. We were full of hope. After all, I had been allowed to continue at Charlottenburg Primary by means of a headmistress's "blind eye". I told my friends that I was going to become a "weekly". I was excited and delighted. I remember Mum going to see Betty to discuss it. And I remember Mum coming out of the discussion to tell me that Betty had refused, and I had to carry on as a "termly". I remember that I dropped my beret in the rose bushes, and got scratched with thorns retrieving it.

There I was, desperately unhappy to be stuck with termly boarding into the foreseeable future.

Of course, there was fun at times. Other boarders had joined the initial three, so the bullying was slightly more diluted (although much worse for the one person all the others turned on), and we found ways of enjoying ourselves. There were seven or eight termly boarders as well as half a dozen or so weeklies.

One way we tried to inject variety was by sleeping in strange places – in a bath, or on the floor. One morning we didn't wake up until Mitzy came in to rouse the girl on duty. "What on earth are you doing down there?" she asked, staring at us with our pillows and blankets on the floor. Sometimes I can do quick thinking. Not that morning. "I don't know, Mitzy", I replied, trying to look extremely surprised at finding myself there.

(In keeping with the Bizarreness of Cransford, when Mitzy left for a second time she was replaced as assistant matron by

Sarah, a girl who had been in our form but expelled for bad behaviour.)

In my memory, the dorms were always freezing cold, although in reality it must have been summer once a year. Our beds had three blankets on them. We were allowed a "hot" water bottle, filled from the tepid/warm bathroom tap. We supplemented the covers with dressing gowns, and wore socks in bed. Getting up could be particularly nasty, and we might try to put some clothes on before getting out of bed. Downstairs, there was a radiator in the under-stairs alcove, and I can still picture the clusters of girls clinging to it like limpets.

One of the reasons I had chosen boarding school over a school in Berlin was the promise of midnight feasts. These were actually permitted right at the end of term, if we got agreement from Mrs Welch. However, official midnight feasts had none of the excitement of the illicit ones, where sometimes it was just one dormitory or sometimes a couple of dorms would club together. These involved whispers, muffled giggles, and much careful creeping about. We were not allowed to have food upstairs, so our purchases had to be secreted on our persons and smuggled to our dorms, to be hidden in drawers of underwear or at the backs of wardrobes.

In the summer term, Cransford girls had the option of sailing in Southwold on a couple of Saturdays. Being a tight-fisted physical coward, I neither wanted to spend my money nor risk my life in this way. For a small charge, we could go to Southwold on the sailors' coach, and I enjoyed this. Our dorm had tasked Judith and me with buying some midnight feast supplies while we were there. We bought most of what had been agreed. The problem was bread. The two bakers, the general shop and the supermarket had all sold out of the rolls we were to get. We returned to them all, asking for loaves. Alas, loaves all sold out. The next possibility we thought of was Ryvita. But I was too embarrassed to return to the shops a third time, asking for a third option. Never mind, I had a good plan. I parted my hair on the other side, took off my glasses, and spoke with a funny made-up accent. Thus brilliantly disguised, we obtained Ryvita and the midnight feast was saved, although the Ryvita turned out to be soggy and leathery.

Although it was strictly forbidden, there was plenty of talking after lights out. Conversations could go on into the early hours, involve games and hilarity, and make life worth living. We always had to be on the alert for staff, though, and we were caught more than once. In keeping with the bizarre nature of Cransford Hall, punishments for this included sleeping in the corridor, and once we had to draw lots for who would be moved to sleep alone in the "Brass Room". When it came my turn to pick a straw, the lengths of all of them were shown to me in Mrs Welch's hand, so I could identify the short straw. I picked it. I enjoyed my spell in the comparatively luxurious Brass Room (it had a brass bed). I have always liked my own company, the bed was lovely, and I had lots of space. I have no idea why I was shown which straw was which, but this supposed punishment was great! I think I was there for a few weeks; during this time I was reading illegally smuggled in *James Bond* books, and they were found under my pillow when I had forgotten to hide them more thoroughly. So now I was in double trouble!

> **READING:**
> *James Bond*
> "Golden Age" crime fiction

Other things we weren't allowed to have were torches or transistor radios. I had been given a radio as a birthday present, and brought it along, to listen to on cycle rides, or under the blankets at night, very quietly (where I also sometimes read with my bike light). I listened mainly to Radio Luxemburg. I was so delighted with this present that I mentioned that Mum had given me a transistor in a letter to a friend. I was called to Betty's study. "Where is your transistor radio?" I didn't know how she knew I had it, but reluctantly retrieved it. She confiscated it until the end of term. Mum found out that she'd read my letter and guessed that I had brought the transistor to Cransford with me.

School life was peppered with the occasional loud crash. In the bathroom called "Luggage" (because some luggage was stored in racks there), Marilyn and I found a heavy old green iron radiator that wasn't attached to the wall. "Look, it wobbles" we laughed, as we swung it to and fro. We swung it too far. It overbalanced, and, as it crashed towards the floor, Marilyn tried to catch it. Her hand was trapped. I managed to find help to lift the radiator off her, and she hopped around with the pain. We put things right before staff found out what had happened. Strangely, Marilyn has completely forgotten this incident.

Another crash came when Poppy, a brilliant musician and the pianist usually called on whenever a pianist was required, tried to do her share in tidying up St Michael's Rooms – the hall in Framlingham that was used for drama, country dancing, gym, etc. She tried to put the piano away. All by herself. The crash was thunderous, accompanied by almighty, persistent tinkling. The tinkling died away to dead silence. Then a stereophonic "Oh Poppy!" You haven't lived until you've heard the sound of a piano crashing to the ground.

These were the days of terror of nuclear attacks. The Cuban Missile Crisis, which no-one was sure humanity would survive, took place less than a year after Dad's death. Both sides of the Iron Curtain pointed deadly missiles at each other. Life on earth would never be secure again.

In order to cope with the possibility of the end of life on earth, the WRVS (Women's Royal Voluntary Service) came to Cransford to give us a talk about what to do in the event of nuclear attack. Thankfully I have not yet had to put their – no doubt well-meant – advice to the test, as I'm not sure I have ever had *that* many cushions.

Mills Grammar School was completely white - as white as you can get, as was the rest of rural Suffolk in those days. (Ipswich was more multicultural.) The "Debating Society" (the number of times it met ran to at least one) thought it acceptable to debate the motion whether or not Britain should have a "colour bar". I am glad to say that shocked me, even then.

I was also shocked after Enoch Powell's "Rivers of Blood" speech. The class bully and I were talking about it (in the bathroom called "Luggage", not that that's relevant), saying that we shouldn't ignore these things. I assumed she meant what I meant: that it was important to see how wrong and dangerous the speech was, because we are essentially all the same. I was deeply shocked when I realised that in fact she meant that she agreed with him.

Once we were in UIV, so thirteen years old, we were considered to be old enough to need contact with the opposite sex as part of our social education. But it had to be supervised! And it had to be excruciating! I was probably a late developer in that respect; I was also shy; I really didn't want to go to the dances at Holbrook. But it was compulsory to sign up on the voluntary sign-up sheet. Holbrook was Royal Hospital School, Holbrook: a huge school for sons of the navy, dressed in navy uniforms, near Ipswich. The grandiose buildings already intimidated as our coach approached. We had spent all day washing our armpits, filing our nails, brushing our hair, choosing our best dresses and maybe applying a little makeup if we thought we could get away with it. Now these efforts were to be put to the test as we stood on one side of the room, waiting to be "picked" by one of the boys, whom I could only tell apart by the amount of grubby vest they had visible. As with sports teams, so with Holbrook. I was usually one of the last to be picked. I missed much of what went on anyway, as, in my efforts to be devastatingly attractive to the opposite sex, I had left my glasses behind. The evening then consisted of dances such as the *Dashing White Sergeant* past the close scrutiny of staff from two schools. This, at a time when free children were enjoying discos and discovering the Stones. One Holbrook master yelled at me that I had two left feet. Only two? He clearly didn't know about the abortive Hanover dance classes.

In the summer, there would be a variation from the dances. I remember playing badminton with the Holbrook boys. Badminton was a sport I could sort of do, and I enjoyed it and used to play it with Mum in the Grunewald, in the road in front of the Kleinmachnow house, or in Tante Luise's garden. But because my glasses were ugly enough to make me cry, I had left them off, so could only slash wildly at fresh air, where the shuttlecock might possibly be, as it landed on the other side of the court.

The boys came to a summer garden party at Cransford Hall. Again, they had to pick partners from us, and once chosen, we had to look after them by fetching them plates of food, etc. A combination of short-sightedness and prosopagnosia resulted in my having to make a random guess as to which of the boys was my partner. As luck would have it, I presented a plate of goodies to the class bully's partner by mistake. She accused me of trying to steal him from her. I had no more interest in stealing her Holbrook partner than I had in stealing her personality. I just wanted it all to be over.

I have recently found out that, a year or so later, some termly boarders in our form climbed out of their first floor dorm window at nights, to go to meet boys. I was in a different dorm so I knew nothing about this, but at that time didn't want to meet boys and certainly didn't want to climb down from a first floor window! I am amazed at their bravery!

Poor tormented (by us) Miss Wilson, the maths teacher who used to eat a slimming biscuit after her full meal, retired. No longer would I crawl under her desk to tie her shoelaces together. Her place at Cransford was taken by a young, charismatic Welsh teacher of Latin, who wrote letters to her fiancée while she was supervising prep – this was how we found out that her first name was Tegwyn. She was clearly always cold too, as she walked around Cransford Hall with a nylon quilted dressing gown on top of her day clothes. The first time she took evening prayers left us astounded. She said the prayers as if she were talking to a real person with whom she had a deep and loving relationship. Her lips trembled as she praised god. She spoke from the heart. "I think she believes in god", one of my friends commented afterwards. Some girls developed a crush on Tegwyn, and a number of us were so blown away by her different, personal approach to god that we chose to follow it up. I "got religion" enough to go to Church in Ipswich, even during school holidays, for a year or so; thankfully I left Cransford before my intended confirmation date, and in time to let reason reappear.

A set of two or three showers was installed in one of the bathrooms during my fourth year at Cransford. They could be used – at specific times – without permission! As with everything Cransford, though, there had to be accompanying weirdness. It was forbidden to wash our hair in the showers. Despite this absolute prohibition, hair was found in one of the plugholes! Who could have committed such a heinous crime? A meeting of all the girls was called in the Noisy Room (the room where homework was supervised and evening prayers were said), and, in front of the whole assembly, each girl was asked individually and in turn and on her honour whether she had ever washed her hair in the showers. This is the sort of thing that can happen if you forget that pubic hair exists.

I was enjoying learning French, and Mum booked a weeklong trip to Paris for us both. It was great. We flew a short hop over the channel, from one tiny airport to another, and stayed in a small hotel Boudon ("Chez Boudon, c'est bon") near Montmartre, and did all the usual tourist stuff, and then some. I loved the Place du Tertre, but was too scared to go up the Eiffel Tower, sadly, and hated myself for that. (I have been up it several times since.) I was fascinated by the bouquinists selling their books and prints by the Seine. I felt sorry for men selling watches out of their overcoats, and tried to persuade Mum to buy one because everyone was ignoring them. I had my portrait drawn, so badly that Mum objected, but the "artist" claimed it must look like me as it had eyes, nose and mouth. We went to Place d'Italie, to see whether M. Thibaut and family really lived there – it was a bakery, so we bought some delicious pastries. We walked round Versailles a whole day, and Mum laughed when a fly flew up my nose. I didn't. Any hotel breakfast we didn't eat, we made into sandwiches to sustain ourselves during the day. Neither of us ever liked waste. Thus it was that we found ourselves sitting at an upmarket Champs-Élysées café, surreptitiously munching on jam sandwiches when the waiters weren't looking.

Out of the blue, before a summer holiday, Betty lent me a copy of *The Screwtape Letters*, and said she thought I should read it. I wondered why on earth she'd suddenly lent this to me. After looking at it, I assume that she thought I was possessed by the devil. I was reading it in the bunk at night in the cross channel ferry, forgot to pick it up in the morning, and spent the rest of the summer panicking about what I was going to do about this. How could I get another copy in Berlin? How could I get an identical copy anywhere? Argh! I have avoided C.S. Lewis and his wardrobe ever since.

"Activities Week" had been introduced at school. This was a week I looked forward to, and not only because it came at the end of the summer term. There was a varied programme of events. As long as we all did something all week, we could choose any of them. My favourites were day trips to Colchester and Norwich, and learning to crochet with Miss Tett, who was a much better teacher of crochet than of biology. "Deportment", where the way we sat on chairs was endlessly criticised, was more MGS and less fun.

Mum and I still went to Berlin every summer. But something happened that stopped us driving there. In future we would drive to Hanover, then fly from there.

The past hadn't gone away. While she was in Ipswich, Mum received a visit from MI6. Following the "Candy Man's" arrest by the Stasi, MI6 were suspicious because, despite all the secret jobs Mum had done, and all the visits to Kleinmachnow as well as East Berlin, she had never been arrested or taken notice of by the Stasi. There was a probable explanation for this. Mum could have been a double agent, working for the Warsaw Pact countries. MI6 had come to find out.

I was at Cransford when they called at 56 Finchley Road, but what Mum told me was amazing. MI6 knew just about everything there was to know about us. And not just us – our family, too. For example, they knew that before the war Onkel Nully, a railway carpenter, had worked in Argentina. They knew that Omi, Opi and family lived in a privately-owned house. They knew about Dad, of course, and our English family too.

I think they questioned Mum on a number of occasions before they were persuaded that she had only ever spied against East Germany. They advised her never to enter the DDR again, both to allay their suspicions, and also for our safety. We stopped going to East Berlin or Kleinmachnow, and we stopped driving to Berlin from West Germany by land. If we wanted to go to West Berlin, where our belongings as well as Tante Grete and Onkel Nully were, we'd drive to Hanover, park, then use a government subsidised flight over the DDR to Berlin Tempelhof. We couldn't see Omi or Opi, Onkel Bernd or Tante Hannelore.

Just as I had gone to Bishop's Stortford a few times with Mum when our terms didn't match up, so I went to the primary school in Witnesham once or twice, whilst Mum was doing her probationary teaching year. I was allowed to help with the little ones, and loved it. I was also allowed to eat some school dinner, and loved that rather less.

Betty asked whether we would host a girl from the French exchange; there were more French girls coming over than there were English participants. The French exchange was for the whole school, so involved all ages. I would enjoy hosting a French girl that I could do things with, as, being at Cransford most of the time, I had no friends my age in Ipswich. Once, I had been invited to his son's teenage party, by the man who ran the corner shop, and kissing games were played when the adults weren't around, but otherwise I was mostly on my own. However, when "our" French girl arrived she was 19 years old. "Perfect!" Betty explained, "she is the right age to keep both of you company." Martine didn't want to know about stationery. She wasn't interested in my childish interests or Mum's adult interests. All she wanted was to go dancing. She slept at Finchley Road, and spent the rest of her time finding discos and dances and doing all the nefarious things nineteen-years-olds on their own do. We were bed and breakfast. I learned no more French, but I did get introduced to the concept of tights, when Martine spent ages asking where she could buy some, and I tried socks, stockings, trousers ... but didn't suggest tights because they weren't in our Ipswich universe. When the penny finally dropped, it was marvellous. Such things exist! That would be more comfortable than stockings and roll-ons!

Sometimes, during school holidays when we were around fourteen or fifteen years old, a small group of boarders would meet and take a train from Ipswich to Liverpool Street Station for a day out in London, mainly shopping. We'd try to buy "trendy" clothes, and went to Carnaby Street as well as C&A in Oxford Street. Frances had a family friend who knew/had known (or whose mother knew?) George Harrison (or was it George Harrison's mother?), and it was very exciting when we were invited to her flat, and doubly exciting when she showed us her wardrobe, which seemed to feature mainly short, red garments.

At school, the length of our skirts was strictly controlled. We'd have to kneel on our desks, while a teacher with a ruler went around checking that no-one's hem was more than two inches from the desk. Then we all stood and rolled our waistbands up and up until we achieved the satisfactory mini-skirt look again.

After one of these days out, we all got out of the train a station too early, at Manningtree, because our brains were very poorly engaged. Staff at Manningtree station tannoyed the parents who were waiting to pick us up at Ipswich station. They had to drive over to meet some sheepish, embarrassed teenagers.

When the Witnesham year was over, Mum looked for another teaching job. Betty suggested she apply for a job at MGS, to help Dr Frob teach German. Mum got the job, but MGS being MGS, it was decided that Mum should not teach German, but maths, for which she had an aptitude but no training or qualifications; the German classes would be taught by an English woman with an English accent. That all makes perfect sense.

Once more, I would have to suffer the embarrassment of my mum working at my school, although she wouldn't be teaching me. It was good news, because Mum was now able to buy another house, and one in the MGS catchment area. The end of my boarding days was in sight. First, the Finchley Road house had to be sold. This took longer than we wished. Once we thought it was all over, as contracts had been signed, but at the last minute it transpired that the buyer was a mentally ill serial house purchaser who could neither afford the house nor be held to the contract. Finally, Mum sold it by making a small loss on it.

Our new house was in a brand new (Deben Rise) estate in Woodbridge, near enough for me to become a day girl. Many other MGS pupils lived in Woodbridge, and travelled by bus. Downstairs were a big through living-room, a kitchen, a big under-stairs store cupboard, and an attached garage. Upstairs were the bathroom, the airing cupboard, and three rooms. Mum and I shared a bedroom. The smallest room became her sewing room, and the biggest room was for me. It was 1968, so I chose bright orange carpet. We put a huge notice board on the wall opposite the window, and I covered it with pictures of pop stars, etc. Together we built a long, low bookcase, that sat under the window. I had a writing bureau for homework, another bookcase, and Dad's old army camp bed softened with Mum's Nazi wartime sleeping bag and a cover and cushion she made for me out of swirly orange fabric. It was wonderful!

We had a TV in the living room, and the furniture from Finchley Road, which slowly got replaced as the years went by. Some of it ended up with me in Nottingham. Aunt Maggie (Granny's sister, and an expert sponge cake baker) kindly came with us when we went to choose carpets. The kitchen was our first ever fitted kitchen, with cupboard fronts in that shade of blue that all kitchens had in those days. The back garden was smaller than the long, narrow one at Finchley Road, but it was much nicer to be in.

The houses opposite were still being built. That space was used for a bonfire on our first 5th November there. There was a kind of barrier between our private estate and the neighbouring council estate. Don't want those two sides to mix! I found I enjoyed the company of those on the "other" side, however. Soon, houses filled the empty spaces in the estate. As well as locals, a lot of US families from USAF Woodbridge moved in, including, later, cousin Judy. One American woman used to shout out of her window for Kimberley and Michael every single day.

> **READING:**
> Blue Pelicans
> Alex Comfort
> James Joll's *The Anarchists*
> Leonard Cohen
> Hunter Davies's *The Beatles*
> *Penguin Modern Poets 10*

I had done very well in my mock 'O' Levels, when I had had nothing to do in Ipswich other than revise. I decided that that could probably see me through my 'O' Levels. Day girl status seemed to coincide with rebel status. But look at the year it was. It was inevitable! Most of my education now came from reading for myself. I learned more quickly than I ever had. I had a copy of the Penguin catalogue, and for St Nicholas Day (December 6th, when I would leave my shoes outside my bedroom door, for them to be filled with treats), I asked for any of the ticked books in the catalogue.

Frances was another ex-boarder MGS day girl. Now that Mum was teaching at MGS, she'd usually give Frances and me a lift, so we wouldn't have to catch the 8am bus from up the road. (I have memories of first listening to the Beatles' *White Album* on the radio while waiting for that stupidly early bus. That album still feels new to me.) Frances' parents, being a lot better off than us, were also very kind, giving us help and more. Frances once stayed the night at ours, and complained of feeling cold the next morning. She'd lain on top of, rather than under, the cosy feather bed. Frances and I often went to see plays at the Ipswich Rep theatre together. I remember enjoying most of those plays very much.

I also have a fairly hazy memory of an evening party on a beach, with lots of people my age, and a wonderful bonfire we'd built. Our fun was dampened when the fire brigade arrived and put it out. There was nothing near that could have caught fire, but we didn't have a permit.

> **READING:**
> *Beachcomber*
> *Down with Skool*
> Poetry

Mum and I watched the moon landing in 1969 in our living room, where we'd set up garden beds in front of the TV. I remember a pleasant drifting in and out of consciousness as I struggled to stay awake, and in front of me men were walking on the moon!

In the summer of 1969, I had my first holiday on my own. It was booked through an organisation whose object was to promote international friendship. People from various (mostly European) countries shared a house (meals provided) to row furiously with each other at Les Sables-d'Olonne, on France's west coast. I travelled there by ferry and train. On the train I met a Lebanese man who invited me to Beirut. (Once I returned home, I'd persuaded my mum enough that I got a new dress for hot weather, and we went to a travel agent to find out how to get there. The travel agent tried to tell us that it would be more expensive because we couldn't use the Suez Canal. I tried to explain that there was no need to use the Suez Canal. The travel agent insisted that the Suez Canal would be a problem in reaching Beirut. I insisted it would not. But my studies of Greatness Farm, Kent meant I had a better grasp of geography than the travel agent. I eventually lost interest in a trip to Lebanon – despite Joseph's extremely polite letter to Mum –

when I met someone else. More later.) Les Sables was indeed sandy, and had excellent exciting waves. I was cheated at the photo shop when I asked the shopkeeper to put a film into my camera, and he charged me but gave me my camera back empty. I spent a lot of time reading on the beach, and the Roger McGough book I took with me still has French sand in it. I shared a room with well-off Patricia, who couldn't wait for the holiday to be over, told me stories of sexual exploits and insisted we hold a séance. (The séance was boring as nothing happened, but made me feel uneasy.) Guests generally stayed in their nationality groups, and there seemed to be a distinct lack of international friendship.

When I got home, it was to find that I'd passed all ten 'O' Levels. And that Opi was dead. Mum had been in Berlin while I'd been in France. At this time, East German pensioners were allowed to make visits to West Berlin. Opi had forgotten to take his tablets with him. He died on his birthday after eating a banana.

Despite my lack of sporting ability, I did manage to win the school Junior Athletic Cup. I had already been presented with the tiny, tarnished, wobbly Hope Cup for Best 'O' Level Results, and wasn't expecting any more glory. Then a week or two later, at assembly, Betty announced that she was presenting the Hope Cup, and called me up. I was sure I already had the joy of this budget silverware, so, puzzled, didn't move, but the girl behind me muttered "Go on, Christine", and pushed me forwards. I went up to collect a second cup. A day or two later, again in assembly, Betty announced that she'd accidentally presented the Junior Athletics Cup to me, and could she have it back. But I had been a sporting champion for a few days.

I loved poetry. I sometimes visited the Orwell Bookshop in Ipswich (which scared me with its very hairy inhabitants the first time I visited, but I persisted) and felt that I was home. I subscribed to a number of small magazines. I wanted my own small magazine, I wanted other people to read my poetry and to read other people's poetry. I started *Leaves*. I advertised it in other small mags. Brian Patten agreed to let me print one of his poems. But how to get *Leaves* printed? Mum helped. After school, Mum and I would use the school duplicator, in the tuck shop/sick room/duplicator room, secretly. We used school paper. This went on for months, until there was an enquiry in the MGS staff room about disappearing paper. (Then I had to pay to have it commercially duplicated until I bought a beautiful wooden flat-bed duplicator, which was extremely labour-intensive and worked like silk screen printing. The wooden case it is in is reminiscent of Onkel Nully's wooden suitcases.)

As well as poetry magazines, I was seeking out all manner of alternative print; anything I could buy in Orwell Books, or find postally. I collected various student magazines, *International Times* (*IT*) and subscribed to *Zigzag* for music. Once you found one thing, it would lead onto others. I had to search hard, because the sixties hadn't really reached Woodbridge.

Our form with Miss Stewart in the grounds of Mills Grammar School (now happily demolished). Summer uniforms, 1969. I am kneeling in the front.

Sixth form study periods were spent in the library. Because I refused to apologise to a prefect who was a few months older than me, and because my explanation that if I said "sorry" when I wasn't, I would be lying, was seen as further provocation, I was made to spend every study period at a folding desk outside Betty's office. I remember spending my study periods reading various revolutionary magazines while I sat out there. Betty told me I would stay outside her office until I apologised. After many months and curious looks from several visitors to the school, she told me to stop sitting there. A small victory, but beautifully savoured.

A couple of other victories over Betty at this time were uniform-related, presaging my uniform struggle at the library forty years later. When I was told I should have bought a dark blue sixth form tie, I replied that it was an unnecessary expense, and if the light blue ones were good enough for the rest of the school, then they would be good enough for me. And when I was reprimanded about having red lining in my duffle coat where I should have bought one with dark blue lining from the official supplier, I explained that my Mum couldn't afford to shop there – an answer I was proud of, as Mum was working at the school.

> **READING:**
> *Peace News*
> *Freedom*
> *IT*
> *Catch-22*
> Brian Patten
> Carl Jung
> Kretch, Crutchfield, Ballachey's *Individual in Society*
> A.S. Neill's *Summerhill*

As a challenge to myself, I thought it would be fun to walk home from school one day, a walk of about eleven miles. Mum usually gave me a lift. I set off via Parham towards Wickham Market, having a lovely time. At Wickham Market, I was horrified to realise that I didn't know which road to take, although I was driven along this route five days a week. Two roads looked familiar. We sometimes drove the Parham way, and sometimes the Easton way. Instead of taking the Ufford and Woodbridge road, I chose wrongly, and headed back towards Framlingham on the Easton road.

I did and do frequently get lost; it doesn't usually bother me, as I find it makes life more interesting. I believe that people with prosopagnosia often have difficulty with directions and finding their way. I also seem to be able to tangle things up just by being near them: hair, wool, ribbons, shoelaces – none of them stay untangled in my presence. Hair and earrings are a particularly potent mixture. I have no idea whether or not I can blame this on prosopagnosia. It's rather more likely just a tangly failure on my part.

Around this time, I became vegetarian, and have remained so for the rest of my life. I had decided to stop eating meat as soon as I could when Dad was still alive, and I discovered that that cute piglet we saw at the side of the road was the same thing that I found on my plate many Sundays. I learned about land use, and how more people could be fed if we didn't use the land to feed livestock first. This was my main motivation, added to by a plain disgust at eating corpses, sympathy for animals, and the fact that becoming vegetarian would be accepted as a reason for taking packed lunches instead of eating school dinners.

On visiting Granny, she offered me a plate of ham, and I told her I didn't eat meat. She was alarmed: "Be careful me girl. You could become one o' them vegetarians."

The war in Biafra was raging and I was distressed by the suffering I saw on TV. I found a bunch of people I could join in with to rattle collecting tins at the people of Ipswich.

I had come across, and joined, the Peace Pledge Union. YAPPU was its youth branch, and they held a summer camp in a farm in Melton, next place along from Woodbridge. I was allowed to attend, and was probably the youngest there. I was given a chicken incubator all to myself to sleep in. Women slept in chicken incubators or in spots around them, and men in nearby Nissan huts. I enjoyed my week there very much, heard some interesting discussions, learned about new authors and different lifestyles, was told about the beauty of the Yorkshire Moors, and was slightly overawed by everyone. I came home with a whole new lexicon of swear words. I went to a handful of

YAPPU meetings in London, and had my very first experience of leafleting (general anti-war leaflets) at Euston Station. More, much, much, much more was to come.

I went on my first ever protest demonstration in Grosvenor Square, London, against the Vietnam War. This wasn't the 1968 one where lots of people were injured, but a later one.

Through *Freedom* or a similar paper, I made contact with Ben and Libertad. They lived in East Bergholt, all the way over in West Suffolk, but my hitch hiking thumb would get me there. I spent a few weekends at their house, talking and listening, but mainly listening. Lib was the daughter of refugees from Spain. I had not heard of the Spanish Civil War before.

I had wanted to leave MGS and take my 'A' Levels at Ipswich Civic College, but the Education Authority would not agree because I was in an establishment already where I could sit 'A' Levels. I said that I wanted to study sociology, which was unavailable at MGS but available at the Civic College. They replied that sociology was unnecessary. I was stuck at MGS for another two years. I already had my German 'A' Level, so I "studied" French, psychology, English, and Economics and World Affairs for my other 'A' Levels. The inverted commas are because I did not make too much effort, preferring to concentrate on my own reading. English with Mr Jones and psychology with Dr Frob were, however, very interesting.

> **READING:**
> George Orwell
> Aldous Huxley
> Blue Pelicans
> James Baldwin
> Kropotkin
> Coates and Silburn on Nottingham
> *The Communist Manifesto*
> *Alternative London*
> *The Pacifist Conscience*
> Adrian Mitchell

We also had a weekly talk under the heading "General Studies", which was another exam we would all sit. (I did very well in that exam. One of the essays I wrote was about poetry, and I referenced a number of poets I had invented.) I only remember two of these talks. One was given by my friend Sue's mother, and was the only sex education we ever received at MGS, apart from copying a drawing of a rabbit's testicles. Betty insisted on sitting in, and no-one had the courage to ask questions. The other was about perception in birds. A man turned up with a wooden owl, and discussed whether or not birds would think it was a real owl. So, at this point, we had been taught as much about wooden owls as we had about sex. I hope no-one confused the two.

Around the 1970s: Dropping out and selling books

Small poetry magazines used to swap copies with each other, and one magazine I came across was called *Together*. I got in touch, and the editor, Keith, and I exchanged some letters and magazines. He was a Cambridge student, and when he and his friends planned a party in April 1970, I was invited. I arrived with Mum's wartime Nazi sleeping bag in a suitcase. That suitcase had been very difficult to close with the big puffy sleeping bag in it. So it was lucky that I never had to close it again, Keith having offered alternative sleeping arrangements.

I visited Keith every weekend. Of course, I couldn't afford the train that often, so I hitch hiked. I got to know those roads between Woodbridge and Cambridge well, and had some wonderful times, including the sports car and my hair blowing in the wind (it was a bugger to comb through afterwards). Due to not wearing my glasses, I accidentally once tried to hitch a funeral. The accidentally hitched bus and the ice cream van did both stop for me, though. Often I'd get lifts from American servicemen, whom I would ask if they'd ever killed anyone. I never had to wait long for a lift. There were some dodgy drivers and tricky situations, but I extricated myself from them all safely with the confidence of youth. Only once did this involve running away. Mum, of course, was not told any of this.

The Cambridge term finished, and Keith's university career was over. We spent the summer hitch hiking around, going to festivals and visiting his family in Maidstone. We were at Phun City, where I do believe the calls of "Wally" at festivals started. Phun City ran out of money, so it was made a free festival, with all the bands being asked to play for free. The only band which refused was Free. We went to the Isle of Wight festival, got muddy and tired, and saw Hendrix.

We volunteered briefly at a Christian Action project in London, which provided tented accommodation for young backpackers. We were to roam the parks to find rough sleepers, and direct them to the project, in Wandsworth. We slept in a sports club cloakroom in the grounds. The man running the project lived in a converted lorry, which I thought was marvellous.

Sometimes, Keith and I would go to London for a weekend. We'd stay on a mattress on the floor in the Maida Vale flat of (Lady) June Campbell Cramer, who had submitted poems and artwork to Keith's magazine, *Together*. (*Together* was printed at the Cambridge Arts Lab, so we sometimes went there too. After sleeping there one night, I became tremendously itchy.) June's flat was a mecca for all that was fine in music. (It was the flat from which Robert Wyatt was soon to fall.) Regular visitors included Daevid Allen, Didier Malherbe and others from *Gong*, as well as people such as, if I remember rightly, Jeff Dexter. Overawed, I stayed pretty silent. Kevin Ayers emerged from the bathroom I'd been waiting to use.

When we were in London, we sometimes went to "happenings" and things at the Roundhouse. These were amazing, and worth being a baby boomer for.

I was also overawed when we bumped into Hoppy (John Hopkins) in Woodbridge, and brought him back to my room for a cup of tea. He was so interesting, though I don't remember much else about him other than he sat next to the wooden sewing box that nearly caught fire on another occasion, when we closed the lid with a candle burning on one side, and a paper flower on the other.

Keith had no plans other than that we wanted to be together. Somehow I persuaded Mum that he could be a lodger in our house, sleeping on the army camp bed in my room. One of the benefits I proposed to Mum was that he had once made a small wooden table. Keith got a job landscape gardening with Notcutts Nurseries, at £15 a week. I was horrified to find that women were paid less for the same work. Keith helped Mum, not by making small wooden tables, but by assisting her to prepare for her following day's maths lessons. She was still teaching maths, and still untrained to do so, though she was starting an Open University course. Before Keith had arrived, Mum and I used to sit side by side on the sofa, marking together, and having good laughs. One girl solved every problem with the word "let" – if she had to prove that x was the centre of the circle, she did so by writing "let x be the centre of the circle." Perfect!

Now I was in UVI, the pinnacle of Mills Grammar School. Betty promised to modernise, and let prefects be chosen by ballot from the pupils, instead of being imposed by her. But she wanted to regulate who could be on the ballot. Every girl standing to be a prefect would have to sign a document to promise to obey all the school rules. Because I found many of these rules daft or unfair, and because I had no great ambitions to be a prefect anyway, I refused to sign. I thought it would be marvellous if we all refused to sign, and the others agreed this was an excellent idea as, one by one, they all signed.

It was our form's week to take assembly for the whole school. I offered to read a poem. I had to submit the book and page number to Betty for approval. On the day, I took a different book, and from the same page number in that book I read Yevtushenko's *Telling Lies to the Young is Wrong* to the school. Betty was furious, but the poem had been read.

> Telling lies to the young is wrong.
> Proving to them that lies are true is wrong.
> Telling them that God's in his heaven
> and all's well with the world is wrong.
> The young know what you mean. The young
>   are people.
> Tell them the difficulties can't be counted
> and let them see not only what will be
> but see with clarity these present times
> Say obstacles exist they must encounter,
> sorrow happens, hardship happens.
> The hell with it. Who never knew
> the price of happiness will not be happy.
> Forgive no error you recognize,
> it will repeat itself, increase,
> and afterwards our pupils
> will not forgive in us what we forgave.

Neither my head nor my heart was at school. I did participate in a couple of extra-curricular activities, however. I joined in a twenty mile sponsored walk along the beaches to Walberswick, in aid of Shelter. Keith came too. And I agreed to be in a team for a fund-raising school quiz. I was the only one at the quiz who had heard of the Wright brothers. The school was constantly fundraising for itself – usually for a minibus, later on also for a swimming pool. (The swimming pool was eventually built after I'd left, in the middle of Walnut Tree Lawn – a lawn in the middle of the school buildings that was so extremely special that the only time we were allowed to put our dainty feet on it was when the official photographer came.) Not many years after that, the school was demolished.

When I turned eighteen in November 1970, Mum let me have a party in the house. We had to cover all the carpets and furniture with cloths, making the house look like it had been shut up for the winter, or it was pretending to be a ghost. The car came out of the garage, and posters went up at wonky angles. I had invited lots of people from all over the place, and they came. It was wonderful. Someone called Martin came; I called him "Martin with the Empty Shoe". I don't know why, maybe because he was from Shoeburyness? Mum disapproved of Sue, but it was Frances and her theatre club friends who broke the garage door. I'd protected the trolley, where I'd put the bottles, with green crepe paper, so the dye came through and stained it blotchy green. Mum eventually covered it with wood-effect Fablon (sticky-backed plastic). Most of the 1970s were covered in wood-effect Fablon. Mum came back home late in the evening, and wasn't utterly delighted with what she found. Lots of people had come quite a distance, and ended up sleeping all over the living room. Someone had opened the back garden gate. It banged against its posts all night long.

These were volatile days, with me having little interest in school, and frequent rows between us all at home. The relationship between Keith and me was always fraught. However, I can vividly recall the evening the three of us were watching TV in Woodbridge. *Monty Python's Flying Circus* was on. We were all enjoying it. The Ministry of Silly Walks sketch came on. We all three burst out laughing, and found it difficult to stop.

I have always loved comedy. As well as Monty Python, other favourites have been Dave Allen, Peter Cook, *Do Not Adjust Your Set*, Monty Python follow-ons (*Ripping Yarns*, and particularly, *Fawlty Towers*), Marty Feldman (unrecognised genius, in my opinion), *The Fall and Rise of Reginald Perrin*, Spike Milligan, and more. *The Goodies* were a sort of baby Monty Python. Much later, there were *Father Ted*, the *I.T. Crowd*, *One Foot in the Grave*, *Red Dwarf* ... the list goes on. And that's just TV. Some of the best comedy is/was on the radio, with *Hitch-hiker's Guide to the Galaxy* coming top of the lot.

All the time since Dad's death, Mum had avoided non-platonic relationships with men. True, when she was on the sightseeing buses she'd accepted an invitation from an American pastor to look at his room in the Hilton, but I think he was not best pleased when she turned up with ten-year-old daughter in tow, who was fascinated by the chocolate on his pillow. Now I'd see men come to visit. Some of them only once, but Reg became a regular. He had a boat, and Mum would help him paint and clean it, and otherwise maintain it. After some time, this relationship fell apart when Mum realised that she never got to actually go on the boat, just to work on it.

School was finally over forever, except in my nightmares. It was traditional to ring the school bell as we left for the last time, but Sue and I refused. We also refused to shake Betty's hand.

Physical Education.	Christine sometimes works with interest.	FLAN.

Times absent *19*

GENERAL REPORT *Christine's undoubted ability should ensure her success in the 'A' level examinations. However, her understanding of the problems of responsibility lack maturity.*

J.S.I.C. (?) Form Mistress.   *B Langshaw.* Head Mistress

Next Term will begin on .... and will end on .... 19 ......

Finally I could leave school. I think that Betty Langshaw was as happy to see the back of me as I was to see the back of her. Just one final report ... 1971.

I did gain from Mills Grammar School, despite everything. I learned about Eliot and Brecht; I care about apostrophes; I use too many semi-colons; I met Dr Frob. Most importantly, there were the other girls. Sue and I stayed friends until her far too early death, at fifty. Poppy and I have been friends all along, and thanks to modern technology I have been reunited with others. What a wonderful bunch of strong, idiosyncratic, glorious, caring, witty, fabulous women they are!

In the summer, Keith and I went to more festivals until we argued so much at one that we never went to any more together.

We went to Nottingham, to volunteer at the St Anns Community Craft Centre, a place whose concept I adored. They did work in the community for free, and lived on gifts given by the community. A free shop. No money. We visited some old people and did their shopping for them. One of them wanted arrowroot biscuits. This is the only time I have ever encountered arrowroot biscuits outside of fiction. I had ambitions of joining a project like this. It was a great concept, although I discovered I had a total lack of skills to contribute.

We thought about joining a commune, and arranged to go to London to meet a bloke who wanted to set one up, and already had some interest. We stayed in his bedsit in Shepherd's Bush, but went to a pub to discuss communes. He thought everybody should go to Israel to experience a kibbutz. I knew nothing about Israel or Palestine other than how to draw maps of the "Holy Land". As the evening wore on, he got more eloquent, but also spent more time in the gents. Nothing came of this, and anyway, Keith had already been abroad and not liked it.

Mum wanted me to go to university, but I felt I'd had more than enough of formal education. She promised to give me the dependent's part of her war widow's pension if I went. I filled in the UCCA application form. This form then had to go to Betty for signing and whatever, before she sent the bundle of them off. My friends started getting acknowledgements that their forms had been received. I heard nothing. It was getting near the deadline. We asked Betty. She hadn't sent my form off. I'd passed all my five 'A' Levels, but I only got one offer of a university place, thanks to Betty. This was to study politics, economics and sociology at Essex University.

So it was that in autumn 1971 Keith and I arrived at Essex University. Yes, he came too, and lived secretly with me in my tiny room. Essex was a modern university, and student accommodation on campus was based in tower blocks, with flats (floors) being either for men or for women. We managed to cram a load of stuff, including many books, into that tiny room. I decorated the walls and ceiling with our footprints cut from paper. Luckily, my room was directly opposite one of the shower rooms, making it easier for Keith to flit in and out unobserved. The other women in the flat accepted that he was there, except for the mature student who kept asking who he was and what was he doing. The communal kitchen still wins the all-time prize for utterly disgusting. We mainly ate in the canteens, as food was subsidised. Keith was living off savings from landscape gardening, and I had a proper decent old fashioned student grant, from which I even managed to save a little.

What I didn't do at university was study. Sure, I attended a few lectures. Anthony King taught politics. He was a good lecturer, but the course was more focussed on the workings of British government than on political theories, which I'd have preferred. A Dr Bliss taught economics. Nobody could understand what he was talking about, to the extent that it led to protests (well, it was 1971 Essex). I can't remember who taught sociology, but I did read some of the set books and found them very interesting. However, I completed few assignments, and my attendance at seminars became less and less regular. What was I doing instead? I was sleeping. I was enjoying the paternoster lift in the library. I was eating cream doughnuts. I was attending the poetry society. I was attending the conservation society. I was supporting the miners' strike by giving up bedding for the pickets to use. I was listening to music: Incredible String Band, Jefferson Airplane, Love, Grateful Dead, Simon & Garfunkel, Fairport Convention, Pink Floyd, Al Stewart, Arlo Guthrie, Leonard Cohen ...

And I was very frequently stoned.

Somebody had rented a room in the flat above ours, and dedicated it to growing marijuana plants. This was a clever scheme, until the cleaners burst their way in.

Milk was sold in triangular cartons. People living in the higher flats found it fun to fill these with water and chuck them at passers-by on the ground, so when walking around you had to be constantly alert.

On one occasion, someone had doctored all the payphones, so that they worked without money being inserted. The queues at these phones were exceptional, as we all called people we barely even knew and had nothing to say to.

Steve from Woodbridge, who had worked with Keith and liked to read Krishnamurti, was at the university doing some landscape gardening. He came to see us. I am still appalled by how the students mocked his working clothes, muddy boots and accent once he had gone. This really put me off university, even a supposedly radical one like Essex.

Two terms were all I managed. The backlog of assignments was too big, my interest was too little, I had no ready answer to the note from the administration asking where I was, and anyway, we had a new plan for the future.

I had persuaded Keith that we should set up an alternative bookshop. Shops like Compendium in London, and good old Orwell Books in Ipswich, were happy to give us advice. We needed a lot of advice; there was of course no internet to teach us, but we learned what we needed to from those who were already doing it. Where should this bookshop be? Suffolk was out of the question – the only town big enough to support such a shop already had one. We hitchhiked to Maidstone, but Keith's parents were definitely not keen on us doing it there. While in Kent, we went over to Canterbury to see Frances, from school, who was studying there. Her boyfriend came from Nottingham, and suggested we should have a look because it had cheap property and lots of students. He even suggested we should explore the Arkwright Street area.

We hitch hiked up north (as I considered Nottingham to be), and on arrival aimed for a hippy contact/help place, that we'd seen advertised. That place no longer existed. It was now evening, we were in West Bridgford, and we had nowhere to sleep. We asked a long-haired bloke walking along the street if he knew anything about this contact/help place. He and his family put us up for the night in their house, and told us about a commune where we could ask for help the next day. We stayed in a shared room at Wretched Stirrup until the owner sold the house some weeks later; then a friend of the commune let us and a few others share his bedsit.

During this time, as well as learning more about running a bookshop, we were looking for shop premises. The Meadows area, across the river from West Bridgford, was due to be redeveloped. Arkwright Street ran through the middle of it. It was a lively, fascinating street, with plenty of second-hand shops, specialist shops, greengrocers, Selectadisc record shop, and everything you might ever want – including old 78 records – leading all the way to the railway station and city centre. Number 261, at the river end, was available for rent, owned by the council. The council offered it to us for £5 a week (shop and living accommodation above), so we said "yes please", even though we hadn't been able to look inside.

> **READING:**
> John Fowles
> *Master and Margarita*
> Horovitz's *Children of Albion*

We went to Woodbridge to collect what we'd need, and moved to Nottingham, where I have lived ever since, by hitchhiking with a typewriter and a small thin rolled up mattress.

261 Arkwright Street had previously been a jewellers', and many of the fittings were still there. Walls and ceilings crumbled alarmingly in places. The only indoor plumbing was a cold water tap in the first floor kitchen. The toilet was outside, and when sat on it we would be visited by the Alsatian from Sign Design next door. Everything was dirty. The sash windows didn't close properly, and let in filth and fumes from the street. The only heating was by coal fire (Keith carried coal upstairs from the cellar in cardboard boxes) and the old Grobbendonk paraffin

heater Mum had given me. This was immensely better than a bedsit shared with four other people!

As well as the kitchen, there were three rooms upstairs. People from the former commune were given the two top floor rooms. We had the first floor room, and carpeted it with rugs, scraps and offcuts in a sort of jigsaw. A jewellery display cabinet from the shop became our bookcase, and the mattress at the other end of the room was our bed. A nasty greasy sofa and a couple of fireside chairs had been left by previous occupiers. Many of our belongings were housed in cardboard boxes.

Downstairs, there were a back shop and a front shop, with the staircase between them. There was also a low-ceilinged, clutter-filled cellar, that was rather horrid to go into, but sometimes we had to, to get coal or change a fuse. Opening the door to the cellar from the back shop, there was a switch which looked like a light switch. Turning this on caused a massive jewellery polishing machine to judder into life inches from your nose.

The front shop would be for books, and the back shop would house joss sticks, cards, clothes, Rizlas, bags, craftwork and other paraphernalia, as well as a notice board and "free corner" – take what you want, bring what you don't. (The free corner became the habitual sleeping area for Prodnose, a filthy black and white stray we befriended. More than once he was mistaken for a free afghan coat.)

We got quite a lot of free book shelving (ostensibly on loan) from paperback publishers such as Penguin, Corgi and Pan. Friends helped us to make more. We'd never heard of rawlplugs, so there were some disasters, especially in the kitchen where I'd put milk, oil and vinegar on a shelf and got instant – though floor-based – salad dressing. Our initial stock cost about £600, which came from the portion of war widows' pension Mum had given me, and savings I'd made from my student grant and Keith had made from his Notcutts wages.

The shop was to be called "Mushroom", after Keith rejected my initial suggestion of "Dung" (I liked its resonance).

We were on a main road, and knew quite a lot of people who knew other people, so word of mouth was the main way we advertised. This was supplemented by A4 publicity leaflets we designed ourselves, which we'd hand out in the city centre to anyone with longish hair or jeans with patches. The 10p joss stick packets drew serious crowds.

A friend designed and made signs for the outside of the shop. We opened in September. The first book sold was by Spike Milligan. We took about £10 the first day. We enjoyed doing it.

The window display was always lacking something. Probably the wow factor. Usually, it consisted of unpaid invoices and other paperwork waiting to be done, a few dead flies, and crockery waiting to be washed up. (We'd eat at the desk at the front of the shop.) Underneath all that would be some books and leather bags.

It would obviously be a considerable time before we could make a living at this. We had to have some kind of income, even though the rent was so low. I babysat (although I had no experience of babies, I was sure they would stay asleep – and they did!), which also sometimes gave me the opportunity to wash my hair in a proper bathroom. Otherwise, we'd use the public baths over the road on Muskham Street, but instead of showers they had staff banging on the doors telling you you'd taken too long. I cleaned houses, although I hated it. But even more hated was cleaning the offices of Turney Brothers leather factory, at Trent Bridge. I had to do this twice a week, and those two days seemed to come round much more quickly than the other five. This was a spookily Victorian place, strange to be in alone. Sometimes Keith or other friends came with me. I had gone off on a dream during the floor polisher instructions, so never used that. In the boardroom I found the first pocket calculator I'd seen, and spent too long playing with it. I noticed that the wall above the radiator in the boardroom was grey and grubby, so started to wipe it. Realising that I couldn't wipe the entire wall, I changed tack and wiped a psychedelic pattern into the grime instead. I'm proud to say that I not only got the sack, I lost the cleaning company the entire contract. Though I came away with a wooden letter rack and enough Flash cleaning powder for several years.

I also tried teaching German. My student was a very nice guy, but obviously not getting value for money as, although I could speak some German, I had never learned grammar, syntax, anything other than "that sounds right" or "that sounds wrong". Keith got some better paid work, teaching maths at a cramming college near the castle. He kept that job for some time.

Once settled in Arkwright Street, I soon populated it with hamsters. At one point, after successfully breeding them, I had about fifteen. The floor in our room was covered in cages, and bars were rattled and wheels squeaked all night long. Percy Hamster got inside the nasty greasy sofa, which Keith had been insisting we keep, and wouldn't come out. The only way to retrieve him was to take the sofa apart. When that was gone, I thanked Percy from the bottom of my heart. The well-used Nazi sleeping bag was chewed to shreds by hamsters, bringing it to a fitting end.

The Arkwright Street kitchen was extremely basic, with only cold running water, warm running mice, and an incredibly ancient gas cooker on which you could reverse one of the burners to turn it into a grill. Cutlery was kept in a four drawer filing cabinet we found; crockery was stacked in a homemade bar that had been left behind; food was on shelves which didn't fall down once we'd been introduced to rawlplugs, and the work surface was a marble slab which had been left behind and put on a (very) low bench. Despite this, we made bread, lots of cakes, agar agar jellies and trifles by the dozen, and lots of brown rice meals. This kitchen was also our bathroom. How I hated having to boil kettles of water to carry across to the sink to wash my long hair. I'd use the public baths when possible; they cost 10p a go, 11p after the introduction of VAT.

If one of us was out working or shopping, the other would be running the shop alone. Over the road was Fine Fare, where we often bought food. Dave worked there, and became our friend. He regaled us with tales of when he and a friend entertained themselves by knocking on people's doors, saying, "Ey up Duck, we've come for yer toilet door". If both of us and Dave or another friend were there, we'd often take the opportunity to go upstairs one by one and get stoned.

Cheesecloth was ubiquitous.

At home in Woodborough Road, Nottingham, with veg and cheesecloth.
Early 1980s, photo by Pat Shammon.

The shop gradually got better and better known. Everybody could detect which books had come from us because they smelled of joss sticks. We were open Tuesdays to Saturdays, giving us a two day weekend.

We had some police visits. Once, to search one of the top floor rooms, as the lodger there had been suspected of stealing library books. Once, because a young girl who was a regular customer had stayed out overnight, and the police suspected that we'd harboured her. They pointed to the piece of foam we had on the floor for customers to sit on while they drank tea or coffee, and claimed that she must have slept there. And once they came because our pay-as-you-use-it electric meter had been burgled – and they had to call for help because they'd locked themselves out of their panda car.

First there was *Alternative London*. Then there was *Alternative England and Wales*. We were asked to supply information about Mushroom for it; also head and shoulders photos of ourselves. We did as asked, and were immortalised on the back cover.

Nottingham

Nottingham's pride is its claim to be the best-dressed town in England. It has no real slums and a history of prosperity based on cigarettes and other light industry which carried on right through the last slump. Also it's a town where women are more liberated than elsewhere—even if only in small ways like ordering the drinks—because they're as used to earning as the men. It's not an attractive town—rather suburban with a modern centre ; most of the interesting old buildings are due for demolition. Surprisingly, it is the base for some important things like the Bertrand Russell Peace Foundation and recently *Peace News* moved here from London.

Contact. The People's Centre is a general help info centre staffed by an unlikely mixture of radicals and auntish do-gooders— most of their work is like CAB since there isn't one in Nottingham, but they can also put you in touch with squatters and political groups. Mushroom, 15 Heathcote Street, is a gentle hip-run headshop open Tuesday till Saturday only because the owners have to get a job on Mondays to support it. They sell alternative publications; have a food co-op; sell home-made crafts without charging commission and have a give-and-take clothes exchange. They are also helpful with information and have free ads—see p.132 and 115 for People's Centre.

Every autumn there's an enormous fair when the whole town turns out and showmen buy and sell their equipment.

Nottingham described in Alternative England and Wales, *1975.*

I remember the first week we took £100. We felt as if we were millionaires! We'd made it! I also remember when we found something had been shoplifted. That was so depressing. I would think about how many hours cleaning I had to do to make the amount that was stolen. In all the years I was at Mushroom, I never caught or spotted a single shoplifter, not because they didn't exist. Keith's dad was an accountant at the local paper in Maidstone, so he did our accounts for us, but we kept the books well so there wasn't that much for him to do. How could I forget the *Simplex D* account book? VAT was introduced instead of purchase tax early in Mushroom's life, but we were well below the threshold for needing to bother about it for some years. After that, there was the *Simplex D* VAT book.

The *back* of Alternative England and Wales, *definitive catalogue of the "underground"*.

We were in a group of friends who were together, stoned, regularly. The father of one of them was the vicar in a village near Newark. We would join him in looking after the vicarage when his father was away. I remember the wonderful kitchen, with a range, and the upstairs rooms where we could roam freely.

Eventually, the time came to move the shop. Lots of properties around us were being demolished. Again, it took some time to find somewhere suitable. We rented 15 Heathcoat Street, near what was the Co-op Film Theatre, and is now Broadway Cinema. However, we continued living at 261 Arkwright Street, above the old shop, for a considerable time. Returning late at night, and unlocking the front door, the police would often appear and ask us what we were doing at this apparently derelict building. The Meadows were being demolished around us, and we found more and more mice in the kitchen. When it finally came time to leave, we had a splendid party, one of the main features of which was encouraging people to write on the walls. The building was going to be knocked down; we wouldn't need to clear up after this party.

> **READING:**
> *Alternative England and Wales*
> Jane Austen
> *Ring of Bright Water*
> Gerald Durrell

Mushroom continued to do well in the more central Heathcoat Street location. However, the premises were a bit smaller than at Arkwright Street, and it was always difficult to fit in everything we wanted to. It was handy being in the city centre, as I could do our food and other shopping during quiet periods. Returning from the shops along the alleyway between the Film Theatre and our shop one dark winter's day, I was attacked from behind. For money and more. Because it was winter, I was wearing so many clothes that he couldn't do anything quickly, and he couldn't find my money in the plethora of pockets. I used this as a method to delay him, until some people appeared at the top of the street after what seemed like ages, and he ran off. I couldn't get the feel of him off me for a long time, though.

Early in our relationship, Keith and I had spent a week in Amsterdam, sleeping in the Vondelpark, as everyone interesting did back then. That was the only time we went abroad together (excluding Ireland in 1979). He'd seen abroad, and not liked it. However, we did have holidays in the UK, predominantly staying with friends wherever they were. This was mainly Cornwall, Robin Hood's Bay, and Derbyshire.

Mum and me in her back garden, Woodbridge.

Mum married again in 1976. When we arrived in Woodbridge for her and Ken's wedding, she was so happy. It's a shame that boys behaving badly spoiled the day, but we have photos of people smiling, and the marriage was a success. I never got close to Ken, but he made Mum laugh and I was glad that she wasn't lonely. After Mum retired (before she was sixty), she and Ken used to travel to the Algarve every winter, staying longer and longer every year, first in a camper van, then in a big caravan.

We did have somewhere to live after Arkwright Street, thanks to Mum's generosity. She put down the deposit for 604

Woodborough Road, a mid-terrace house on a slope, so there was one more floor at the back than at the front. The kitchen had been down in this damp semi-basement, connected to the rest of the house by rotting stairs. We had a council mortgage, which had various conditions attached: we had to move the kitchen upstairs and add a ventilated cupboard, and outside we had to make good the flaunching. No, I'm not going to tell you what flaunching is, but it was made very good.

A new house to decorate on a budget, we threw woodchip at it wildly. We put temporary curtains, that stayed there for years and years, in the front room. We had a bath! We even got a shower (that leaked from day one) fitted above it, to take the misery out of hair washing. A lodger called Steve had the front room with the beautiful temporary curtains at first, and we slept in the first floor bedroom and used the top floor room as a living room. Rarely did we make it all the way to the top in that tall thin house, and anyway the hamster was in the first floor bedroom. Mum gave me her old gas fridge. I think gas fridges are wonderful, and it kept our food nicely chilled until a nasty gas fitter condemned it in the 2000s, simply for being a gas fridge. Why aren't more things powered by gas?

I used to cycle on my own quite often, on my one-speed sit up bike, which was somewhat reminiscent of the old "county bikes" of Cransford. I usually went towards the Vale of Belvoir (Harby, Hose, etc) and pottered around Radcliffe on Trent. I might do fifty miles, and I enjoyed the time alone, with sandwiches in my basket.

In 1977, the year of the Queen's Silver Jubilee, many people planned street parties and celebrated. Others decorated as many places as possible with "Rot all rulers" stickers. In addition, this was the year I bought a new, multi-speed bike. After much research, I bought it from a bike shop on Alfreton Road, which was on the Queen's route for her official Nottingham visit. I emerged proudly from the shop with my exciting new purchase, and started cycling down the road. I noticed rather late that the road had become closed to traffic and was lined with loyal subjects, all of whom were watching me trying to get used to my new bike as I wobbled along the road. Maybe they were wondering where I fitted into the royal family. I managed a royal wave without falling off.

One time in 1978 I decided to cycle further, and I cycled to Woodbridge. The trip took me two days. I couldn't find the people who were going to put me up for the night in Cambridge, so blew the budget and stayed the night in a B&B pub. The cycling was no problem and I enjoyed it immensely, but the vibration caused awful problems to my right hand, so that I couldn't feel or hold anything. I obviously couldn't write. Nothing helped until, eventually, time did cure it. Ever after that, I have always worn padded cycling gloves when on a bike – the fear that I would never be able to use my hands again had been very real. I wasn't able to cycle home at the end of the weekend, but could get my bike and me back to Nottingham by train.

Having to find accommodation on an overnight ride gave me an idea. I set up "Mutual Put-You-Ups", which was later taken over by the Cyclists' Touring Club when I couldn't carry on running it. The idea was basic. If you were willing to put your address on a list as offering accommodation, then you could have a copy of the list and stay at the others. It worked.

When I wasn't cycling, Keith and I were nearly always together. I did, however, go away on my own for a week to a retreat at Caldey Island, off the coast at Tenby. I wanted to "get my head together". In those days, the Cistercian monks welcomed visitors on a "pay what you can afford" basis. They welcomed me, despite my non-belief and inability to afford anything. I went by coach to Tenby, stayed a night in a B&B, and then a boat took me and another guest two miles across the water to the island.

The island was stunning in its peacefulness and beauty. I walked a lot, and also spent a lot of time watching sheep and lambs find each other by recognising each other's baas. I had a round room in a tower, which I loved. Indoors and outdoors were freezing cold (I think it was February), and I wore many layers under my trousers. I read a lot. I sat in the beautiful wood-panelled guests' day room and chatted with other guests, one of whom gave me a pile of postcards with Turner paintings on them. Sherry was served before meals (I was astonished, but refused it), and we ate in a dining room with one or two monks. The monks were vegetarian while on the island, but carnivorous while away, which I found nonsensical. After eating, we helped to wash up. For some reason, the washing-up sink was too small, outdoors, and supplied with barely lukewarm water.

I was very upset when I found a seagull trapped on some barbed wire. I tried, but couldn't help it, so I ran all the way back to the guest house, and told a monk, expecting help. However, he just told me how we must accept what happens and bow to god's will.

After a day or two, the guest who had been in the boat with me was no longer around. When I asked after him, the monk replied that sometimes people don't come with good motives. This is something I still wonder about.

Believers or not, we were all expected to sit in during some church services. The church was small, plain, and beautiful because of that. I have always enjoyed the theatre of the Catholic church (in my childhood, I had sometimes attended with Omi), and I did again, although I was not tempted to participate.

Getting the new Woodborough Road house ready of course fitted in with running the bookshop. We were now selling fewer craft goods and the like, because we just didn't have enough space. Private space at 15 Heathcoat Street was limited too. Behind a curtain at the back was just room for a washbasin and somewhere to sit. This thin curtain (actually an Indian bedspread from stock) was all that was between the customers and whoever was getting stoned behind it.

One day, we noticed that a woman was paying by cheque from a bank next door but one to our Woodborough Road house. Maybe she lived near us. Keith got us invited round to her house on the strength of that. I moaned that we had enough friends and were busy enough, and someone banking near your house was not a ground for friendship, and I had stuff to do at home and didn't want to go out. Pip became one of my closest, longest friends. I am so pleased she banked where she did. When Pip and Andy's son died of sudden infant death syndrome at six months, we tried to support them as well as we could, though that must remain inadequate after such a devastating loss.

Mushroom at 15 Heathcoat Street.

Mushroom was now a member of the Federation of Alternative Bookshops, and we'd go to meetings around the country at other bookshops. This was very interesting, because as well as seeing what the bookshops looked like and stocked, we all got to exchange ideas. FAB morphed into FRB when it was decided that being radical was more important than being alternative.

We had started to be able to pay ourselves a small amount by now, and not have to clean, teach or babysit. The shop would get jam packed on Saturdays, and needed to expand. We were able to move into 12 Heathcoat Street, over the road. This was much bigger, and also had offices at the back. We sanded the floor with a hired sander. I think it took more than a whole night. We got a portable Calor Gas fire to heat it. We got more book shelves. We had a green-painted oval table with cup hooks screwed into it to hold joss sticks; candles went on top, and on the table we put on top of that. It all looked lots better, even if there were still sometimes the odd invoices in the display window.

In pre-internet days, many contacts were made through our notice boards. In this way, an @narchist group was formed, and some of the people from those days are still friends. We didn't do an awful lot besides having meetings and sometimes producing publications or organising national conferences where people might sit silently for some time, afraid to say anything that might be oppressive to others. Strikes and anti-fascist activity were supported.

The ABC trial took place in 1978: two journalists and a former soldier were prosecuted under the Official Secrets Act for informing the public about what we ought to be told. We joined in the campaign about this, using Post Office Telecomms' yellow bird Buzby. "Buzby says: who's tapping your phone?" stickers could be found in phone boxes for years afterwards. We did do more than put up stickers; it's just that the stickers are what I remember. (The three were found guilty only of Section 1 charges, and received non-custodial sentences.)

Mushroom continued using the system we'd used from the beginning, of writing all books sold in an exercise book, and re-ordering from that. Money taken was written on a scrap of paper, with sale or return, VAT and non-VAT columns, and the cash itself went into a wooden bowl. Totals were transferred to our trusty Simplex books at the end of the day.

Up until now, Keith and I had run the shop alone, with odd bits of help from friends. That was all going to have to change, as our first baby was due in February 1979. We recruited for more members of the collective, and four or five additional people joined us. One of these turned out to be a psychological bully using techniques similar to those I'd experienced at Cransford; thankfully, he was eventually asked to leave by the whole collective.

> **READING:**
> Kurt Vonnegut
> Leonard Cohen
> Anne Tyler
> Patrick White
> Ursula LeGuin
> *One Flew Over the Cuckoo's Nest*
> Brian Patten
> Books about hamsters
> *Hannibal on Holiday* and other books about
> Hannibal the Hamster
> *Richard's Bicycle Book*
> Milan Kundera

I had an easy pregnancy, and flourished with it, although I vomited in the corner shop. I'd changed to the homeopathic doctor as he was the only one we knew of who would support a home birth. The same health care professional previously prescribed copper ointment, rubbed onto my legs, to treat facial cold sores.

By now, we didn't have a lodger, and the downstairs room was our living room. The hamster and guinea pig shared our bedroom. Wanting a home birth, I thought that the midwife might object to a hamster and guinea pig in the delivery room, so Mock Harpo and Barnaby were moved downstairs. Other preparations we made were: getting a gas fire installed in the bedroom, buying sponges and nail brushes and assorted stuff off a list, and collecting loads of baby clothes and a beautiful wooden crib, which were all given to us by friends with older babies. Everything was going textbook perfectly. And I was reading the textbooks. Early on February 8th, I could feel something happening. We called the midwife, and soon I was well into labour. It was excruciating of course, but I didn't need an epidural, and was still able to make what I thought were witty comments between contractions. The homeopathic doctor appeared too, and said how much he liked the print of tree roots we had on the wall. Everything was calm and perfect. Everything stayed calm and perfect, except that when Robin was born, he didn't breathe. The doctor and midwife tried to make him breathe, but couldn't, and soon a flying squad arrived and whisked Robin off. An ambulance came for me; I was given chamomile tea (it was just right then; I usually hate it) and carried down the narrow stairs on a stretcher, then whisked off to the City Hospital, where Robin had also been taken. On arrival at hospital, I was put into a side room and told that Robin had started breathing after twenty minutes. Mum was called, but couldn't make it up straight away. I was in suspended animation. I was taken to the neonatal special care unit, and was allowed to put my hand into the incubator where Robin lay, all wired up. He'd been paralysed with curare, and looked perfect and beautiful. I wanted to wrap him in my heart. I had to go to theatre to have some placenta removed.

Robin lived for two days. Only. My son. My Robin Edward. My baby.

After he died, we were allowed to hold him, and photos were taken. We organised a funeral, led by a clergyman who was prepared to do a non-religious funeral. A friend played guitar. Lots of people came to the funeral. We appreciated their support. I felt as if I might disintegrate at any moment. Mum was there, apologising that she hadn't come sooner.

When I left hospital, we moved into Pip and Andy's for a little while, so that we weren't alone. They were uniquely able to understand us. But I felt we shouldn't stay there too long, or I'd develop a phobia of going home.

We went to visit friends in Wales who, it turned out, had problems of their own. I have never seen so many animals in one house, and I have never seen so much cat shit in one house. I was frightened to move in case I touched some.

We were also invited to Cork by an ex-customer, who was now lecturing there. His flat was large, airy, overlooking the river, and devoid of cat shit. There was a small crisis when we arrived and no-one answered the bell ("See, I knew it was wrong to leave home"), but then Grace from upstairs let us in. George and Grace drove us to see many places in her little 2CV, including a tour of the Ring of Kerry. I fell in love with Cork and Kerry. And dried apricots.

I don't remember if and when I went back to work. I do remember being asked in the hospital, after Robin's death, whether I needed any nappies. I do remember the pain of my engorged breasts. I do remember not being able to decide what to do with all the baby stuff – keep in case another one came along, or give away and then maybe need. I couldn't think straight about it.

When we visited Woodbridge, Ken told us we'd moped about too long, and it was time to pull our socks up and forget about the baby. I expect he was trying to help. Everyone has their own way of grieving, even if, like me with Dad, they haven't worked out how to do it. I would like to ask anyone reading this never to tell another person how to grieve.

I do remember lying in the bath and being alarmed by a lump in my stomach. I asked for a pregnancy test, and the doctor told me it was negative, I was just willing myself to feel pregnant. The lump grew. Either it was a tumour, or I was pregnant again. At about three or four months, my second pregnancy was confirmed. We told as few people as possible. I was worried sick. I couldn't make myself live the super-healthy lifestyle I'd lived for my first pregnancy. Walking along the streets, I'd look at all the people and marvel that they must have all survived birth and babyhood.

Around the 1980s: Motherhood, single life, direct action, Bob

After I had been knowingly pregnant for about three months, I went to the hospital for a routine check-up. All was deemed well. We went to visit a friend off Mansfield Road. On the way, I felt some wetness. When we arrived at hers, I was obviously haemorrhaging severely. We called the hospital. They told me to sit down and have a cup of tea. I did this, then realised how stupid and dangerous this advice was, so called again. The emergency ambulance was at the door very soon.

I was wheeled about and doctors and whoever poked me and moved me. I didn't know what was happening. I'd expected them to put right whatever was wrong, send me home, and I'd have the baby in a couple of months, when it was due. Obviously, this wasn't on the cards, and the truth gradually dawned on me. "Am I going to have the baby now?" Yes, they were preparing me for emergency C-section. About two months early.

When I was in the appropriate area, I found caring and competent staff. They introduced themselves to me ("Hallo, I'm Mr Something. I'm the anaesthetist, and I have lots of experience and will take good care of you." That sort of thing.) The surgeon was Mr Vasey. Did I have any questions? Yes, would this affect any future pregnancies I might have? I shouldn't have more than nine. That was probably all right, then.

As I was having a Caesarian, I cheered myself up by thinking that at least I wouldn't have to go through labour. Then labour started.

The last thing I remember hearing before I went under was talk about anaesthetics. When I came round from the anaesthetic, Keith was there, and told me we'd had a beautiful baby girl. We hadn't been able to think of a name previously. Now, my head full of talk about anaesthetics, I knew her name instantly. "She's called Anna."

I wanted to see her, but she was behind me, and I wasn't able to move. I asked if she could be brought to me, and the nurse in the room said no, she had to stay by the radiator because she was so tiny. Another nurse came in. I made the same request. "Of course," she said, and brought my beautiful, longed-for darling baby Anna to me. She was so very, very tiny. But she had no trouble breast feeding. The nurses would say, "Look at little baby Cook, she knows how to do it."

Anna had to go into the neonatal unit briefly, I think it was for observation. I was alarmed, but told not to be. I was allowed to go down in a wheelchair to see her, and had all manner of mixed feelings when I saw she was directly opposite where Robin had been.

> **READING:**
> Penelope Leach's *Baby and Child*

Anyway, Anna was well, and after the standard ten days we both went home. Despite all my reading and regular antenatal classes, I still found the responsibility alarming. Pip and our next door neighbour and other friends with children helped with advice and suggestions, and I gradually relaxed. But gosh was I tired! Keith helped with nappies and baths and everything, but soon had to go back to the shop, and I spent days alone with Anna (and the hamster). It took ages to prepare to go out, those cloth nappies needed such frequent changing, and the massive coach-built pram we'd found for a fiver was difficult to get up and down the steps. I tried to sleep whenever Anna let me, but there was food to prepare and laundry to do. The laundry was mostly unsuccessful, as I tended to scorch it whilst it dried on the fire guard.

I wrote to Mr Vasey a year later, to thank him. He'd emigrated to Canada, but replied.

Anna slept in our room in the beautiful wooden rocking crib we'd been given for Robin. She made some very strange noises while she slept. We called her the little grrrk. I was always the one who saw to her in the night because I was breast-feeding, and because I was the one who was woken by her cries. Each feed was accompanied by a nappy change. Happily, Keith had agreed to washing machine purchase when I was first pregnant, so I didn't have to hand-wash the nappies and babygrows. Day and night blended into each other.

If I were to describe everything about Anna's early life, that would be a book in itself, and probably one that would only be of interest to a handful of people reading this. However, she was my life, and I loved her more fiercely than I would have thought possible. (And I still do.) Rev Todd, who had conducted Robin's secular funeral, came to see her, and asked if he could bless her. I couldn't see that that could do any harm, so he did.

In April, Keith, Anna and I went by train to Cambridge, to celebrate our ten years together. We sat on the banks of the Cam reminiscing while a duck pecked our sandwiches from us. On the train, Anna's massive poo burst through the disposable nappy I'd used because we were out and about. I complained to Peau Douce, who made the nappies, and got a bag of free ones, money to launder my dress, and various other goodies.

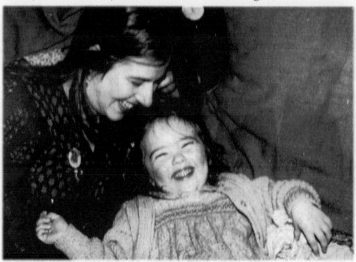

With toddler Anna, around 1982. Photo by Pat Shammon.

I will never forget the magic moment when Anna turned from a baby into a fully-fledged human. I'd put her into one of those fabric bouncing cradle seats that all babies had, and dangled mobiles made from milk bottle tops and other bits of tin foil and colourful wrappings in front of her. I saw her focus on various bits, smile, and try to touch them. There is no way to express the joy and love I felt, and the amazement that this little person had grown inside me. Later, one of these mobiles would fall on her face and set off tears on her part and guilt on mine; the mobiles were light, but it must have been very startling.

I volunteered for the Stillbirth And Neonatal Death Association, to befriend more recently bereaved parents, and be a shoulder to cry on. Looking back, I think I did this too soon. I was certainly very out of my depth with the Catholic woman who'd been given a hysterectomy during her dead baby's birth, so now had not only lost a baby, but couldn't have any more, and was having religious problems on top of it.

Mushroom continued to do well without me. I think I probably went to some collective meetings, but don't remember much because my attention was with a tiny new human. I was more interested in how often she did a poo, than in which drawer the stamps should be kept. We took Anna to Maidstone and to Woodbridge. When she started learning words, her first ones were "already" and "all right". She adopted an empty pillowcase I'd put under her head, in case of sick, as her favourite smelly rag – her "burra". She enjoyed flicking the dangling handles on her chest of drawers, being read to, and refusing vegetables I'd spent hours pressing through a sieve.

It was quite a lonely time for me as I saw very few adults, but also a wonderful time, as I watched my daughter change almost hourly. I spent some time with Pip. She had had her third son two days after I'd had Anna, but, unlike me, was able to go home almost immediately. The plan had been that I'd look after her older son while she was having this one; Anna scuppered that arrangement.

The first time that Anna slept through the night was alarming. We woke up, actually rested, at a reasonable time, and immediately thought something dreadful had happened to Anna. I was constantly scared that something dreadful might happen to her. But no; she'd just needed a decent night's sleep as much as we had. She slept through most nights after that, from a young age. Thank you, Anna!

In 1981, we were invited to join a Yorkshire holiday at a Quakers' place. It was organised by a peace group. I very much enjoyed being with other people much of the time, and not being the only mother. The week went quickly, the cleaning up required at the end was daunting, and we as a group kept in touch and visited each other frequently for a while. This was also the time where the relationship between Keith and me plummeted.

It took us about a year to split up fully. There was bitterness. Eventually, Keith moved out. He continued to love, see and look after Anna regularly.

When she was old enough, Anna started at the Family First nursery for one or two days a week. Leaving her there at first was a complete wrench, but gradually we got into the habit, on nursery days, of running down the road with the McLaren pushchair in front of me, to try not to be too late.

I found a lodger for the top floor room, and made my bed on the floor in the living room. The room on the first floor was Anna's. No lodger stayed very long. Kev, who was an excellent babysitter and good friend, stayed longest. I charged babysitting instead of rent.

Kev provided entertainment as well as babysitting. He had been brought up in care, and visited social services to ask to see his notes. When they refused to let him take them away to read at home, he grabbed them and ran off. The police turned up, to search his room for documents. He had painted his room black and put in a 10W light bulb. The floor was knee deep in documents. The relevant ones were not found – they were not even in his room.

Changes were being made to provision for young people. Thanks to Thatcher, housing support was being withdrawn from them. I asked Kev where the now homeless young folk hanging around the square had gone. "Er, they're mostly upstairs," he told me.

I had been with Keith since the age of seventeen. Now, at twenty-nine, I was on my own – scary, but freeing. I made up for lost time, and embarked on a number of ultimately unsatisfactory relationships, but had some fun as well as tears on the journey.

With Anna at nursery part time, I went back to the shop part time. This was good, and I enjoyed being back with people and books although Anna was always foremost in my mind. Mushroom was expanding: the premises of the old second-hand bookshop next door were to be rented too, and the wall between the two shops would be knocked through. This created a big shop.

I also got more involved in political activities. For some reason, during my life with Keith, there seemed to be little time for this. Now I was more able to follow my inclinations and conscience.

I got my ears pierced, and began my collection of wonderful earrings. Then I got one ear pierced another couple of times. As I had too many earrings, Anna made me a set of false ears.

I went to festivals again, with Anna, and a rucksack on my back, a big bag dangling from each pushchair handle, and a suitcase in one hand. You need a lot of stuff when you are camping and have a toddler! My school friend Sue and her partner now lived in London with their baby. They had converted an old ambulance to sleep in. I would get myself and Anna down to London, then go to one of the East Anglian fairs in the ambulance with them. These fairs were wonderful, smaller-scale, friendly, surreal and exciting events. I'd pitch the tent someone had given me next to the ambulance. One evening I was sitting next to the tent and ambulance with the others, when I heard crying. I was sure it was Anna, but it wasn't coming from the tent. I could see the front of the tent. It was still zipped up. What was going on? Round the other side of the tent, Anna, in her babygrow, was wandering around crying; behind her, a massive hole had been ripped in the back of the tent. That's how to get out if you can't operate a zip! I mended the rip as well as I could with tape, safety pins, and whatever came to hand.

We also went to Glastonbury, usually with my partner at the time, and often getting in free as we were with the CND hot air balloon contingent. We didn't work on the hot air balloon, but could get into the festival with them. The Year of the Mud was especially memorable. We'd get a drink, sit ourselves down next to some of the muddiest areas, and watch people slide about.

At a festival near Tewkesbury, late 1980s.

I got a grant to have the Woodborough Road house repaired, so Anna, Kev and I moved into a borrowed house on Hungerhill Road for a few weeks. This worked well, but I dropped a heavy door, which I didn't realise was unattached, onto my foot. Thus when we went to London to protest Reagan's visit, I was hopping and hurting rather more than I would have wished.

The house was much improved afterwards. It had been rewired, there were new windows with actual window sills, and the plaster had been repaired. Previously, there had been a constant rain of small white bits from the ceiling onto the heads of those who sat below, which used to enliven meetings of Mapperley CND when they met at my house. I painted my room black and red, and decorated the kitchen walls with pasted-on posters, mementoes of campaigns and actions.

I made friends with a mother of two girls in Mapperley, and together with our children we went to a massage course at the Women's Holiday Centre at Settle.

I joined a Mencap befriending scheme, and met Josie every week. She wanted to learn pottery, so we attended evening pottery classes. I was upset when one of the other students said they admired my patience; Josie was better at pottery than me; they should have admired Josie's patience instead. Josie and I continued meeting regularly until she moved away to be with her sister.

With my then boyfriend Colin and his children, we went on the "holiday of a lifetime" – a horse drawn caravan in Ireland. It conjured up completely idyllic images of children dancing along in the wild flowers in the greenery at the edge of the lane, while the sun shone, the Guinness flowed, and the happy horse trotted along merrily, glancing at us in delight from time to time. Bells probably tinkled. The bit about the Guinness was right. Children cannot gambol beside a caravan on a road when cars are overtaking at full speed. And the horse didn't glance at us in delight, it generally refused to move unless it knew it was approaching a campsite at the end of the day, when it would suddenly bolt off, leaving anyone sitting at the front to cling on for dear life, and anyone who'd been knocked off the seat and managed to catch onto some horsey, harnessy bits to cling on even more grimly. Whilst keeping the bottle upright. (I am not a horse expert.) The caravan was also cramped when it rained and we couldn't go out: we were in Ireland; there was rain. No bells tinkled.

When the holiday came to an end, we went to catch our return ferry, and were stunned to be told that we couldn't board because, although we had return tickets, we didn't have the double-secret magical tickets we needed in addition. We had to get on that ferry. We had three small children and all our money was spent. We had no alternative. They continued to refuse us, so we made ourselves comfortable in the waiting room. We had to spend the night somewhere, and with children the streets weren't an option. We were to leave; they were shutting. We refused. The Guards were called. They were armed. We explained that we had nowhere else to go, and asked to see the manager. We were shown into the manager's office. Once there, we said we would stay, unless we were allowed onto the ferry. I thought our manager's office sit-in would last all night, but before long we were let onto the ferry, and sailing for home.

We had frequent picnics and camping expeditions at Lambley Dumble, often as an anarchist group activity. It wasn't known who owned this piece of land by the stream and near some woods, but it was a fabulous place to spend a sunny day or a warm night. We'd light camp fires, pitch tents and say hallo to the dog walkers who might pass by. Nobody told us to go away.

The ground under Nottingham is riddled with caves and tunnels, mostly human-made. I remember two particularly interesting explorations, both with a group of friends, and both undertaken spontaneously without preparation. We managed to get into the old railway tunnel, which started in the hole at the Victoria Centre (previously Victoria Station), and walked until we emerged near the Mansfield Road/Gregory Boulevard roundabout. I think we had one candle, and had to be very careful of not stumbling on debris or being spooked by rats.

Around that area by the roundabout, just inside someone's garden, is the entrance to a narrow cave/tunnel system, and we explored that too. The front part of it had been used as a wartime air raid shelter, and still had "Ladies" and "Gents" toilet signs. Continuing, we often had to wriggle through narrow passages, emerging eventually into a large cavernous area, decorated with Indian bedspreads, statues and mystical ephemera, in a garden in Mapperley Park. The lights were on in the house; we had to suppress our giggles as we climbed out of the garden.

During the 1984-5 Miners' Strike, I went on some pickets and threw what I could into collecting buckets. I poured beer on to someone who dismissed the cause. But my main contribution possibly was to go to my top floor window as the scabs and police vans drove along Woodborough Road below towards Gedling Pit, and chuck Anna's last few nappies, which I'd never got round to washing, at them.

CND was gathering strength. I joined PAN (Peace Action Network, for direct action) and Nottingham Women For Peace as well. The week was full. We were frightened of nuclear war, and I still didn't have enough cushions.

It was around this time, early to mid-eighties, that I developed pelvic inflammatory disease, which was agony. After I had an ovary removed, the pain was gone. When I came round, I could see from the ward window right into a staff canteen window, where surgeons were eating egg sandwiches. (That's what we patients surmised was in them, anyway.)

Meanwhile, at Mushroom, things were not happy. Keith was obviously uncomfortable working with me. A personality clash crystallised into an ideological dispute. In those pre-internet days, Mushroom played a big part in setting the radical agenda locally. Thus I found it important to stock material from various sides of a debate, and this included class-based politics. *Class War* was not my favourite paper though I enjoyed reading it, but it did matter, what it said shouldn't be swept under the carpet, it should be available to be read and discussed, if not liked. Mushroom decided to ban it, at a meeting I was unable to attend. When I opposed this, I was then sacked – told I had resigned, left out of meetings, not paid, not spoken to if I turned up for work anyway. Mushroom had been part of my entire adult life, and had been my idea in the first place. This was dreadfully upsetting.

I had no income for myself or Anna, and could not obtain social support because in the eyes of the law I'd walked away from a thriving business. I did a bit of baking, and a few stints in a community café, to earn a few pounds, but really, really didn't want to go back to the early Mushroom type of scraping for money by cleaning or anything I could find. And this time I had a child to support. I went to the Citizens' Advice Bureau, wondering what I should do, and was told I should save money by baking my own bread: "here's a recipe". I decided I needed to take legal advice. Legal aid was still available in those days.

The case dragged on for years. At least I could now get social security because I was taking legal action, and hadn't just "walked away" from an income. Mushroom employed scabs to replace me. There were public meetings, enquiries, vitriol from both sides. I once had to represent myself in court because my lawyer wasn't available, and there was a refusal to postpone. It went on and on and dominated my life. My spirits were kept up by the number of supporters I had in Nottingham. Eventually, at the last minute, more or less on the way to the court, Mushroom agreed to pay me a reasonable amount of compensation. A huge part of my life had still been ripped away, however, by people I had previously considered good friends.

We tried to set up "Black Raven Books", operating out of suitcases; but it's difficult when you don't have premises, and it was difficult to put my heart into setting up another bookselling operation from scratch.

I investigated various interests, and took woodworking classes, making myself a desk, a stool, and more. I put energy into *Nottingham Anarchist News*.

And, of course, I had Anna. When she started school, at Walter Halls just behind our house, she had an arm in a sling, having broken it falling down stairs. I mistook another parent for the teacher, and talked to her at length about Anna's arm. The arm healed, and Anna was naturally brilliant at school, ending up better at maths than the teachers. I volunteered at school, listening to children read.

I participated in several anti-war direct actions. At Upper Heyford, I was one of around thirty who were arrested for sitting in the road to block the entrance. The charge was obstruction. Seven of us agreed to refuse to pay our fines, in protest. As with the others, this meant a short jail spell. I was sentenced to five days on December 9th 1983, and spent them in Risley ("Grisley Risley") Remand Centre. Those five days were long days, but I was helped by my boarding school experience. My fellow inmates were different, but the regime felt all too familiar. I was lucky because, knowing I was going to prison, I had my bag packed with sufficient clean underwear, toiletries and books.

A sit down protest at a nuclear base, possibly Upper Heyford. Some of these people are still my friends. Bob is on the far left, but we were not yet together.

After I was taken out of the cell underneath the Guildhall, I was driven up to Risley in a police car by two police officers. My greatest worry was that I might need the toilet on the way up, because they wouldn't stop. Being processed on arrival took some time, and was as humiliating as they could make it. Duty of care had been exercised by asking me whether I was suicidal. I was taken to a landing and put into a two person cell, with bunk beds. There was a work surface with chairs along the other wall. A jug of water stood on this. The short walls were occupied on the one end by a barred window, on the other by the door. In a corner sat a chamber pot.

When the door was next opened, another woman was led in. She was in a state of shock. She definitely had not expected to be locked up. She had been involved in some kind of pub brawl or similar, but she seemed quiet and not at all threatening. I can't remember her story properly, and wouldn't know how true it was anyway, but somehow it was something she'd been caught up in, and it wasn't her fault. She made me laugh when she pointed to the bars on the window, and innocently said "This is awful. It's like a prison here. Oops. Of course. It is." We were both "new girls" who didn't know the ropes. Just like at Cransford, you were supposed to know what to do, and get bawled at if you'd guessed wrong.

My cellmate needed the toilet, so she rang the emergency buzzer by the door. There was no response, so she tried again. Eventually the hatch was lifted, and we were shouted at not to cause a nuisance, there was a pot if we needed it. The door was certainly not going to be opened. There was no privacy between each other, other than looking away.

My contact lens solutions had been taken off me because we weren't allowed "medications". This was excellent, because it meant that every morning I had to join a queue similar to "surgery" at Cransford, and wait to be allowed to use my solutions. This cut into the time I was supposed to be working – in my case, scrubbing a long corridor with a small brush (I'm not making this up) – so that often most of the morning was gone, and the scrubbing brush and I only had a nodding acquaintance.

I got on fine with the other inmates. I was lucky though that I was in a cell and not a dormitory, where I heard later that other non-paying protestors were bullied. I was lucky also in requesting a vegan diet – my food was envied by the meat eaters. I was given much Marmite.

Some of the stories I heard there were very upsetting. I have forgotten most, but remember the friends who were in, expecting lengthy sentences, separated from their children, for shop lifting. Ironically, they were wearing their shoplifted clothes in prison, and showing them off proudly. I remember also the older woman who had a child with mental health problems. This child repeatedly played truant, and its mother was imprisoned for failing to send it to school, thus taking away the only person it could relate to. There were many drug cases. There was also screaming and swearing and shouting when there was some kind of altercation between an inmate and a bunch of screws who, if I remember rightly, wielded a syringe.

At night things got lively. Women shouted to each other through their open windows, or they banged on the pipes that ran through the cells. Those with very loud voices yelled at the men in the men's prison opposite, and we heard men yelling back. Looking down, I could spot lots of "shit parcels" on the ground. How else to avoid all-night intimacy with the contents of the chamber pot?

I received tons of mail, and appreciated it very much. Five days is no time at all. But it didn't pass as quickly as it would if you were on, say, a lovely five day holiday in Cornwall. Coming towards the end of my sentence, a small part of me panicked that They had total control over me and could choose not to release me if they wanted. However, all was good, and after five days I emerged back into a world where you could lock your toilet door. Keith had been looking after Anna, and I couldn't wait to see her.

We got good publicity, and sponsorship, from the jail stays. I thought it was worth doing.

One of my favourite actions was when we invaded a USAF base whose perimeter was difficult to breach from most sides. But a train ran alongside it. When we were at the correct place, one of our number pulled the emergency cord, and the rest of us jumped out of the train, onto the base, to the shouts of a passenger: "You can't do that! Come back!"

On another occasion I dressed with a false pregnancy. This was interesting. Although I was arrested along with all the other protestors, I was never "processed". I was simply overlooked. At one point an officer came into the coach where we were being held before and after "processing", and asked if anybody hadn't been processed yet. I managed to kick the person who turned to me and started to say, "what about you, Chris?" hard enough to stop them.

Protestor stupidity could be very entertaining. The classic one is where somebody gives a false name on arrest, but, on release, signs for their belongings with their real name. My favourite might be the efforts made to enter RAF Newton, in Nottinghamshire. I was the cycle messenger on this action, so had a front row seat to watch the protestors throw carpets over the barbed wire, and carefully help each other over the top – a couple of metres from an open gate.

We usually organised ourselves in "affinity groups", and planned that we would all look after each other during an action. It appeared that the definition of Affinity Group should be "a bunch of people with a particular aim who are never in the same place at the same time."

At one event, one of the participants was from Amsterdam. She forgot to take her hold-all away with her, and for many, many years the "Dutch Bag" sat on top of my fridge, waiting to be reunited with its rightful owner. Respecting privacy, I never looked inside. Eventually, I was off to Amsterdam on a few days' break, and decided that it would be my mission to reunite the Dutch Bag with its owner. Before carrying it through customs, I knew I had to check what was in it. I found dirty socks and withered onions and garlic. Still, it was someone else's property, and must be returned – especially after

Returning the famous Dutch Bag to its owner.

I'd been hanging onto it for so long. One whole day of the trip to Amsterdam was occupied with following leads and tracking down the correct address, but eventually there was a huge feeling of triumph as the Dutch Bag was reunited with its bewildered owner. Returning the Dutch Bag took us to interesting parts of Amsterdam we would otherwise have missed. When I got home, the top of my fridge looked strangely bare. There was a hole in my life where the Dutch Bag had been.

The various actions all blur together a bit. There was a lot of sitting in roads, and invading air bases, all to try to disrupt the perpetrators of the nuclear threat. After arrest, you would be held some time, often in a large facility like a sports' hall. We knew our rights. After some time, we had to be given food. Often the predominantly vegetarian anti-Apartheid protestors would be given meat sandwiches and South African apples. (In those days we all boycotted South African produce. We also held our own action to try to stop the Co-op from selling South African goods, when we printed leaflets purporting to be from the Co-op, offering any South African goods free, saying the "caring, sharing" Co-op no longer wanted to support Apartheid.) One of the actions at Molesworth was in deepest snow, and I wouldn't be surprised if everyone's abiding memory of it is of wearing so many clothes you could barely move.

I got comfortable with doing radio and TV interviews during this period, and also wrote about what we'd done, and why. I narrowly missed exposing myself on a platform in front of a crowded hall when a friend pointed out that, with the light behind me, my dress was completely transparent; when it came to my turn, I said "I hope you all won't mind me remaining seated, but I'm more comfortable that way."

In our meetings, some people emphasized the need to talk to, befriend and even hug people who opposed us. Thus I thought it was a response to this call when I saw a good friend talking to locals holding up a "Go back to Russia" sign. When I got closer, I could hear what he was saying. "Why are you holding that fucking stupid sign?"

I only slept at Greenham Common once or twice, including one night before an action, in my own tent, which I shared with two other women I hadn't realised were in a relationship together. However, I went down for the day several times. I found some of the residents a bit cliquey and superior. But I was hugely impressed by the use of an old fridge as a watertight document cupboard.

In a minibus travelling over, I accidentally sat on the hummus. On one occasion, the plan was to decorate the fence with photos and symbols of what we might lose if cruise missiles were used. Walking along the perimeter, looking at all the baby clothes and other objects displayed was very poignant. I'd meet women I knew, like my doctor, who I hadn't realised felt the same way I did. On another occasion, the plan was similar, except that the decorating was a decoy, and the real action was cutting the fence. As the police were all inside, they couldn't stop us on the outside!

Sitting in the road blocking the entrance at Greenham could be an ordeal, as there was no end to singing of "You can't kill the spirit", and too much spider webby mumbo jumbo. But we did delay some lorries going in. It was scary at times. Police horses are big. There was a death later - Helen Thomas – but thankfully I wasn't there then.

READING:
> *Greenham Women are Everywhere*
> *At Least Cruise is Clean*
> *The Women's Room*
> Zoe Fairbairns
> Meulenbelt's *The Shame is Over*
> Ronald Blythe's *Akenfield*
> Thomson's *Woodbrook*
> *Rough Guide to Amsterdam*
> Marge Piercy

We organised local base protests. The USAF were using part of Chilwell base, near Beeston, Nottingham. We made many excursions there, looking for (one group found) the fabled tunnel, or simply trying to make our protest plain. Some of the protestors got to be on first name terms with M.O.D. police; maybe I would have, had I not been face blind. I often went in with a group of women friends; we dressed as from outer space (wire in the long hair meant I could bend it into extravagant shapes) and spoke made-up-ese if anyone in authority came near. We carried window cleaning equipment, and commenced cleaning the windows of the barracks.

Sometimes a male friend joined us on these Chilwell escapades. After arrest, one of my friends was hungry, so she climbed out of the window from the room we'd hurriedly been locked into, went to buy some bread, then climbed back in. The police were none the wiser, though probably surprised to find us making toast. They wanted to separate the man from the women, but we women were adamant that we would stay together. He, however, was more than willing to go. He begged to go.

A railway line ran through Chilwell Base. Always on the look-out for innovative ways to protest, I enlisted the help of engineer friend Bob to calculate how heavy the rails were, and thus how many people would be required to steal them. Discovering that we'd need more than forty people for one section of track, if we were able to lift it, meant that this action remained a dream. What would we have done with it?

All of this was small stuff compared to what was being organised now. A massive national protest/day of direct action was being planned. Reclaim Chilwell will always be a special day to me. Everybody, but everybody, I knew was there in some capacity. And all the groups were doing something different. Over there were women occupying a roof. Down here were groups tearing down the fence, which developed a kind of Mexican wave as officials inside pulled it back up and protestors outside pulled it down further along, working their way around the perimeter. Was that a Chinese dragon? Who's under that top hat? A friend picked up a traffic cone and was using it as a megaphone. That day, the base belonged to us. We were tripping over each other. Where was I? All over, but mainly with a bunch of women friends (most of whom had window cleaning experience at Chilwell already), inside a barracks building. One of us was arrested. Being held against a wall, she scathingly told her captor "It's all right. You don't have to hold me like this. I'm not going to run away." He let her go. She was off like the wind!

READING:
> Neville's *Playpower*
> Baumann's *How it all began*
> *Reclaim the Earth*
> *Preparing for Nonviolent Direct Action*
> *Protest without Illusions*
> *Only the Rivers Run Free*
> Brian Patten
> Goldman's *Living my Life*
> *Our Bodies Our Selves*
> Ward's *Anarchy in Action*

We were all energised by Reclaim Chilwell. However, afterwards my partner and I decided to express our anger at the lies perpetrated about it by the local newspaper. As we were expressing ourselves on its walls, he told me to "Run!" which I did. It was only unwise because I ran in the wrong direction – straight into the arms of the police.

These events all needed advertising. There was no internet. But there were buckets, brushes and wallpaper paste. We reckoned there would be no come-back as long as "not for fly posting" was printed on the poster.

Fly posting had its hazards, of course, and not just realising that you'd forgotten the posters once you'd walked a mile and loaded a brush with paste. One evening a friend and I were chased all over Nottingham by a high-heeled Tory Councillor, shouting "Stop these girls! They're post flying!" We were chased up and down Mansfield Road, and through the Golden Fleece. We tried a getaway in a taxi, but when we'd jumped in and instructed "Drive!" like in the films, the taxi driver turned to us and said, "You have to say where you're going." While we sat there, racking our brains furiously, we got caught up by our high heeled pursuer. She shouted through the window that she was a councillor and he wasn't to take us anywhere. We leapt out the other side, and the chase continued. To avoid police cars hearing her, we ran to Waterloo Crescent, a pedestrian avenue. She continued shouting as we hid behind some pillars, until a man came out of a house opposite and told her to "Shut the fuck up you stupid bitch!"

High heels must give some special athletic powers. This woman was about twice our age, yet she was able to chase us at a meaningful speed for ages. And I was consistently beaten by high heel wearing mums at school sports day parents' races. On lawns!

Another fly-posting hazard was: rushing around a street corner with a brush loaded with paste, only to bump into a large man in his best clothes. If you apologise desperately and try dabbing the paste off his clothes with a tissue, which then sticks to him, it doesn't make him any happier. Finally, it's very important that the person applying the paste doesn't apply it a metre higher than the person with the posters can reach.

It was fun participating in these actions and protests, but it was also scary at times. Although we had many a laugh, our intentions were deadly serious, as was the terrifying nuclear threat.

As well as the threat of nuclear war, I was also protesting capitalism itself. Much of capitalism, the funding of the atrocious, the rewarding of the appalling and the organising of oppression happened in the City of London. So we responded more than once to calls to "Stop the City", and organised coaches from Nottingham. We were going to make the City ours for a day. We held a party in a bank. We hung a protest banner from a high rise institution. (And, on descending in the lift, were hurriedly ushered out by the police who wanted to use the lift to go up and catch the people who'd hung the banner. We were in disguise, me as a *Woman's Own* carrying housewife.) I graffitied the Stock Exchange, and that's when I was arrested.

This was soon after my spell in Risley, and Christmas was approaching as my court date arrived. I worried about the outcome, but received only a small fine which I initially attempted to pay on an incredibly heavy paving slab.

The court refused the paving slab cheque, so I eventually paid in pennies instead, which were nearly as heavy!

However, after another peace action arrest, I decided to refuse to pay again, to show (mainly myself) that I hadn't been scared off. I got another five days. The strange coincidence was that I had been asked to be advisor to a theatre group, who were making a play about a peace protestor and an ordinary inmate sharing a cell. Jamie had been asked to advise from the other perspective. Now in real life we found ourselves sharing a cell. She was well known by the other inmates, and looked after me. She was expecting a long sentence for "organised crime". We remained friends for some time after her release, but in the end I couldn't handle her demands and her lifestyle.

At Birmingham Stop the City, I found it necessary to hide a tube of superglue. I wondered where a good place might be, then thought of somewhere probably no-one else might think of. It went into my shoe. It was an excellent hiding place! No-one found it! And about three weeks later I was finally able to prise the last bit of sock off my foot.

Engaging in these activities, and taking part in these actions, one would come across the same people repeatedly, in different contexts. The left, the peace movement, humanitarians, anarchists, women's groups, anti-racists, anti-fascists, vegetarians, environmentalists, anti-nuclear activists, Mushroom customers … there was much overlap; there was a kind of loose community.

One friend never gave herself any time off from being an activist. If I was walking around with her, I could suddenly be told to "Run!" because she'd just … I went to visit Poppy in Hamburg with her. The ferry over was half full of strutting British squaddies, and decorated with freshly applied anti-war graffiti. She was a dear friend, whom it was exhausting to be with.

Bob was someone who had been around many of the groups I was in, for many years. We knew each other as friends, but not close friends, for a long time. At one demonstration in London (possibly the one where he drove the minibus, and everyone else got out and disappeared as soon as we parked, with no discussion about where and when to meet again), we spent the day together. He shared sandwiches with me. If you think you know what's coming next, you're wrong. It was months before we got together. We'd been involved in organising a fundraiser gig for something or other in the old Yorker pub. At the end, after clearing up and carrying things out, two things happened. Firstly, people looked for the pub's hat stand, which had disappeared. "Ah. That hat stand. I helped two people carry it out to their car." Bob had unknowingly participated in hat stand theft, and cost us the evening's takings. The other thing that happened was that I got a bit tearful, and he kissed me.

Bob was to become my infuriating, messy, procrastinating, impossible, untidy, misspelling, generous, caring, funny, unpredictable and loving soul-mate. I would never have thought I would want to spend the rest of my life with someone who preferred naval history to Leonard Cohen!

I introduced Bob to Anna, and said that I hoped she would like him. "I already do", she said.

A week or two later it was Anna's seventh birthday. I'd booked a room in the International Community Centre, as there were a lot of children to invite. They all had fun, but I was dismayed to find that not all children were as well-behaved as Anna. As they unwrapped water pistols in the pass-the-parcel, they rushed to fill them, and then ran around the building, squirting various serious Trotskyist meetings.

Fulbeck in Lincolnshire had been proposed as a site for burying nuclear waste. As campaigners against the nuclear industry (on health and safety grounds) we were determined to do something. As people concerned about their back yards, Lincolnshire locals were determined to do something. This led to a strange alliance.

Groups of us from the peace movement trespassed onto the potential drilling site field, to see how we could stop these dangerous plans. We went late at night, being as quiet as we could. We emerged with two trophies. One was a long drilling rod, which taught us that if the person holding the back of the rod walks more quickly than the person holding the front, the person in front is liable to be pushed into a ditch. This drilling rod was hidden outside the site. The other trophy was a document, which might reveal top secret plans, enabling us to prevent nuclear disaster. Under light, however, it proved to be a recipe for slurry.

We had meetings with the local protestors. One, who called himself "Butch", proudly showed us his wig collection, which stopped him from being identified by the forces of law. They regarded us as some kind of elite vanguard, and had every faith that we could stop the drilling with our finely-honed commando powers.

The struggle continued. There was to be a public meeting with Douglas Hogg, the local MP, who would tell everyone how absolutely lovely buried nuclear waste was. Three of us decided to attend. Cat and I thought we might ask awkward questions, possibly even cause a little disruption. On the drive over, we were brought up short with a part of one of Bob's sentences: "after we've tied the drilling rod to the MP's car ..." What? What part of the planning for tonight had I slept through?

In the event, there was no possibility of tying the drilling rod to anything at all. As we arrived in Fulbeck, Butch and his team greeted us as heros and bought us a drink. Then another, and another. In no time at all, the intrepid elite vanguard was sliding down the walls at the back of the hall.

There was another public meeting. This time, it would be Angela Rippon (newsreader, and repository of vanloads of make-up) who would be defending the nuclear industry. The room was laid out with snacks, so I ate some. I noticed that as well as myself, there was also an elderly woman shouting angrily at Angela Rippon. This turned out to be Nina, Bob's mum. We all have to meet our future mothers-in-law somehow.

I wanted to take Anna on holiday, but obviously it had to be a cheap one. I found out that the first week of the Butlin's season was low priced, so for a couple or so years we had Butlin's Skegness holidays. I think Anna enjoyed them a lot, which meant that I did too. We had a chalet with a kitchen, so could cook our own food. Sometimes we'd take hot jacket potatoes on to the beach.

Anna learned a degree of independence in the exciting pool. When I took out my contact lenses, I couldn't see her. I had to be in there with her as a responsible adult, but really she was the responsible one, as she was the only one who could see. We also spent lots of time on the inclusive fairground rides, generally with Anna whizzing about on one ride while I stood in the queue for her for the next one.

One year Anna's friend Nina came too, and I had to explain to them that if they stayed up all night talking, they wouldn't be awake for the fun the next day. I remember not having a watch, so I carried a travel alarm clock in my bag.

I was a student during our last Butlin's visit, and found out that the booking clashed with a project that I was told was vitally important. When booking, you could name up to four (I think) people in one chalet, so I'd added Keith's name just to keep the option of an extra person open. When I realised that I'd have to return to my studies half way through the week, Bob agreed to come and replace me. I told him to say his name was "Keith" when he arrived. I then had a mental blip, and went to the entrance security gate and told the guards that "Bob" would be arriving. "Hallo, I'm Keith." "We're expecting Bob." "Ah. I'm Bob."

READING:
Everything about *The Archers*
Jaroslav Hasek
Douglas Adams
Maeve Binchy
Irish history
Flann O'Brien's *The Third Policeman*, and more

Computers were beginning to arrive. Jamie, of Grisley Risley, had sold me an Acorn Electron, which would play games if you weren't too bothered about the games being fun, and didn't mind waiting twenty minutes while they loaded into memory from a tape. This was cutting edge stuff! Anna and I played on it together. I found out there was something called Basic.

When CoDa (Community Data) had an introductory computer course, I was lucky enough to get a place, to satisfy lots of curiosity. I found it fascinating, and enjoyed every minute. Once I was late because Bob and I had been arrested the night before, when we'd been intending to spray paint a Tory election poster round the corner, but mistakenly spray painted a Carlsberg advert instead. We did the Tory one too afterwards. (That caused admirable confusion in the court later. Just how many posters were we being prosecuted for?) At CoDa, I learned about word processing, basic databases, basic spreadsheets, how annoying it is to display all the characters that just beep, basic principles of programming, what floppy discs look like when taken apart, binary, ascii, different types of printers ...

It was November 1989. Anna and I were sitting on the mattress in my room. The radio was on, with the news in the background. Suddenly we went still and stared at each other. Had we heard right? No, we couldn't have. He must have said something else, we weren't listening properly.

We continued to listen. It really did seem that the newsreader had said that the Berlin wall had fallen. But that couldn't be true. Some mistake? Or a dream? As we listened to this news, that seemed as unbelievable as the 1961 news that a wall was being built, my eyes moistened. Joy and incredulity.

It would some years before I had the time and the funds concurrently to be able to travel to Berlin, but Mum and Ken could and did. And I knew that I would when I could. A whole part of my life, which had been laid into storage, was accessible again. We listened to people celebrating and cheering. Sadly, Omi and Opi had died long before, but now Bernd, Hannelore and their family could be visited; and they could travel. They went mad with travel, making up for lost time, going everywhere and anywhere. Bernd took to making videos of their trips, which usually started with scenes of a toy aeroplane being dragged across a map by a piece of string, from Berlin to the destination. Thus are the great events of history translated into our everyday.

The anti-poll tax protests were taking place around now, and we were involved. At a demo in London, Bob was arrested, and I stayed the night in London in the flat of some people I'd met outside the police station, waiting for him. Bob, meanwhile, had been released and was tucked up in bed in Nottingham. When his trial date came, he was found not guilty on account of his good witnesses; I am pleased that I was one of those. The group of us celebrated by going to an Indian vegetarian restaurant and ordering every second thing on the menu. Although there were a few of us, this was too much!

When the CoDa course was finished, I wanted to find out more. I thought I'd be good at programming. And I saw a certain logical, philosophical elegance in the subject, that delighted me. (I don't think anybody has ever understood what I meant.) It was suggested that I have a chat at Trent Polytechnic, now Trent University. "You're in luck," said the lecturer I'd just gone to make enquiries from, about enrolling maybe next year, "the course has only just started, you should join now." So I did. I got another student grant, my previous one not disqualifying me, because I was now doing a vocational course; and I got extra for Anna. I was enrolled on H.N.D. Computer Studies. I was one of the oldest there, but found a group of mature students I was comfortable with.

I did very well the first year. Despite moments of panic when I thought I didn't have a clue what Jackson Structured Programming was, or what the sums in Systems were all about, the pennies dropped very suddenly and then it was a doddle. Finding the time to do all the assignments was less of a doddle, but never knowing whether there might be a crisis that would take me away from doing them, meant that I did them all as soon as possible – the exact opposite of the approach I'd had at Essex University. I liked programming, with its logical structure, best. It was like a puzzle, but a puzzle with a point to it. And I could make the computer do stuff!

The second year was a year of despondency. This was a sandwich course, which meant we had to spend the middle year on placement in industry. I was sent to a large company (CCN, now Experian) which specialised in credit ratings, other stuff like car registrations (programs to make sure there were no rude words in them), and direct mail (lists of people without mains gas might be interested in a Calor Gas mailshot). It was the stuff of nightmares, but more so because I got given very little of this ghastly stuff to do. Mostly I had to sit looking busy; occasionally I was called to send a fax. I passed the interminable hours wishing I was at home with Anna, and writing programs to work out how much longer I had to sit there, and how much I was being paid, minute by minute. I was wearing office shit too. A woman from Liverpool decided she was my friend, and we sat in the subsidised canteen together for many a lunch. I usually had a cheese salad or similar. She told me about a restaurant she'd been to: "You'd love it. They give you so much meat." I made friends with a German woman who approached me when she smelled patchouli on me. I got on all right with everyone on our team, but I was painfully bored and frustrated. Coming to the end of my year there, my team leader asked if I would consider staying on rather than completing my H.N.D., because I'd been such a good programmer! I was astounded but refused. No way!

I got distinctions in all but one module next year, and decided to get my H.N.D. on the stage, rather than have it posted to me. Bob was to look after Anna, who was only ten. He arrived late, having forgotten that his car needed petrol. Luckily Anna was allowed in on her own. I had to sit near the stage, with the others collecting their bits of paper. Afterwards, while all the young students were being congratulated by proud parents, I spotted Bob on the stairs and roared at him in a voice that caused the congratulations to pause momentarily. Then I remember being in a large hall with cheese on sticks.

> **READING:**
> Books on computing, goddammit

Happy and already chubby, with Mum and Dad in Germany, 1952.

In Berlin, with Opi, Omi, Bernd, Mum and Dad.

With Mum, Dad and Opi in Berlin, late 1950s.

Visiting Debenham the summer after Dad died. With Granny and Cousin Irene in Granny's back garden, when she still lived in the cottage, 1962.

Standing in front of BRP994 with Mum and Tante Grete one winter's day. Mum always bought VW Beetles. This picture is round the corner from Tante Grete's flat, around 1963. One day the snow was so deep, we couldn't get in the car and I missed school.

The "Stamp Friend" would send me off to choose more cake so that he could give Mum her secret instructions, about 1963.
I took full advantage of this.

A summer visit to Kleinmachnow, 1963. Omi always had heaps of old stuff, and she found black and yellow satin for me to dress up in. Then she, Mum and Bernd dressed up as well. Behind the family house, built 1936, and the Jentzsch family home until 2019.

A portent of the future.
Masky fun in Herentals,
late 1950s.

Hard at work as part of Ex-Libris, the Masked Booksellers, Green Festival 2012 and Booksale 2011.

Sometimes I just have to shout.

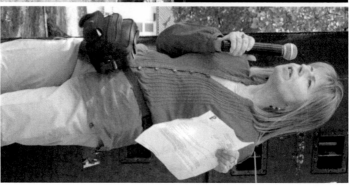

Messing about at the Edinburgh Fringe. Ampelmännchen were East German traffic light symbols, and we thought repeatedly crossing the road celebrating them was as valid as some of the stuff people do on the pavements during the Fringe. Bob had forgotten his Ampelmann teeshirt, so has tied cuddly Ampelmann toys to his plain teeshirt. 2000s.

At home with grandchildren Lily (with me) and Alfie (with Bob), 2014.

As Masked Booksellers, we sometimes hand over cheques. Here we are, helped by Jack and Alfie, giving a giant cheque to Stonebridge City Farm, 2019.

Lily learning to knit.

With Leon on a roundabout, 2019.

Thank you Mum & Dad.

Tripping the light fantastic in Torquay, 2013.

Around the 1990s: Ghastly jobs, libraries, too many funerals and a wedding

When I was seventeen, Mum had offered to buy me driving lessons, but I had refused because cars were nasty, polluting things (that I was always glad to have a lift in). As my HND finished, I also finally passed my driving test, after far too many dismal failures, which began on my first attempt when I couldn't remember which of the parked cars was the one I was driving. That turned me into a nervous twitching mass. I had, however, passed every part of my test several times, just not on the same occasion. I bought a very old mini.

Anna and I enjoyed city breaks in Paris, as I had done with my mum. I showed her as many of the sights as I could. One hotel we were in seemed a little posh, and I wasn't sure whether it would be permitted to bring food in to make our own snacks. If it was permitted, the sight of me with stiff arms, trying not to let the baguettes up my sleeves show, must have been even more bizarre. Anna helped us seem normal to staff by having a pile of souvenir Eiffel Towers balanced on her nose when breakfast was brought into our room.

The awful truth hit me that the subject I'd been studying out of interest was now supposed to be my career. I went through three or four programming or programmer/analyst jobs, each lasting less than two years, and each immensely boring and depressing. I don't cope with routine easily; if I know how the day will pan out before I get up, there seems no point in living it. I don't cope with idiots easily either, and there were plenty of those.

The first job was for a software house that dealt with the progress of materials through factories. As if this wasn't enthralling enough, its owner and director was a shouty short-tempered self-obsessed arse, who thought he was saving money by using programmers as litter pickers, and whose wife, employed as secretary, couldn't stand him. As I was one of the few women there, she chose me to confide in, resulting in an extremely uncomfortable situation. The software was flaky; when it was being demonstrated to me, it kept throwing up unexpected numbers. A random number generator is one of the most difficult things there is to program. As the team leader struggled to make the correct number of widgets appear on the screen, muttering, as they all do, "it doesn't usually do this", I congratulated him on coding a random number generator. I found out that witty comments are not the best way to impress on a new job.

I spent some time on the customer helpline too, where we all had to improvise because only one person knew the system properly. This was where I heard about the client who was advised to load his floppy discs, and replied that he couldn't get more than two of them into the drive at once.

My colleagues were all about ten or fifteen years younger than me, male, and interested only in sexism and money. At the xmas meal in a hotel restaurant, they delighted in throwing food about as if they were six years old. The better employees were randomly and suddenly fired, disappearing like pregnant grammar school girls.

The company was about to move to larger premises, further away. I found another job. My favourite moment in this job was on my last day, when a client (KTS Wire, I believe) rang to complain about something not working properly in the system, and I replied, "You surely can't expect me to defend this stuff, can you?"

To start with, being Next Release Analyst at Copystatic Systems was a step up. The office was in the city centre, meaning I could do chores in my lunch break. I had responsibility, as I was the person who sat between the programmers and installers, making sure that the various modules of the software, and their upgrades, compiled and worked together properly under both Unix and Vax operating systems. I could have done some programming and testing too, but I could never be bothered to find out exactly what the software was doing, so managed to stretch out my analyst work to fill the hours. I wrote automated systems, so was able to spend a large part of my day watching them unfold on the screen, pausing, muttering, and making notes if anybody came near my desk. (I met my successor in this role socially after I had left. He proudly told me that he had managed to squeeze all the Next Release work into an hour or two a day, giving him time to programme too. Clever, clever him!)

Some programmers made the same mistakes repeatedly, giving me another way of passing the time. And then I'd go to chat with Mary, who was writing the manual.

This could have continued, just, but once again a managing director/owner showed us what a turd he was. There were new, purpose-built premises, near the M1 junction. The octagonal pavilions looked almost cutting edge. My desk was in the centre of a pavilion, so I had no window. And no ventilation. The glass roof above me did let in light; also blazing heat in the summer; and it let any heat out in the winter. The owner wanted to smarten the image up even more, so he banned thermos flasks and bottles. If you wanted herbal tea, that was tough. As he froze our wages, he put on display what could only be described as a hardboard dolls' house, with the various rooms labelled with software module names. It was supposed to show potential clients what a fabulous system it was. Rumour had it that this dolls' house had cost £20,000.

Instead of doing my chores at lunch time, the only thing I could buy in the village shop appeared to be wooden fruit. It took much longer to get to work, and much longer to get home. I was angry. I was also very disturbed by who some of the clients were; I had been campaigning around Irish issues, yet now I appeared to be working for the RUC.

My last programming job saw me back in Nottingham, in the science park near the university. I'd managed to negotiate a four day week. But in other respects, this was another horrible job. I had asked to work with 'C' and Unix, my preferred programming language and operating system, and been promised I would. Of course, this didn't happen. I was put into a team led by one of the (how do I put this?) thick students from my year at Trent.

Our brief was to change every single program in a suite by a couple of lines, because there'd been a mistake, a variable had been wrongly defined, or something. He explained it poorly and managed it badly. When the inevitable inquest came, we programmers who had been following his instructions got the blame, while he sat and smiled. The work got even more boring, and I had nothing in common with my colleagues. Even four days a week was too much. I wanted to be home with Anna. I wanted to be a writer. I didn't want this crap.

I understood then that it wasn't the particular jobs that got me down, it was the whole career.

I set up a computer consultancy and called it "Computer Friendly". I got some work, and I was in charge of my own time. I solved a lot of problems for people. I was undercharging because I had no confidence. When I fixed someone's computer by the easy method of plugging it in, I didn't want to make him feel stupid by telling him that, so I told him I'd used my "special discs". There were people who opened up their boxes while I was working on the software, poked their fingers around in it, and then looked accusingly at me when everything went dead.

I hated the other stuff I had to do – the paperwork, and particularly promoting my business. Advertising was expensive, and you are at the end of a phone to all manner of charlatans producing calendars and booklets you would just have to be in. It was wearying. I wrote some databases, which was creative and therefore more fun. I produced a database system for an ostrich farm, which promptly went bust, but thankfully a woman in accounts had warned me to get paid immediately just before. I received correspondence regarding criminal investigations into the ostrich farm for ages afterwards.

Tasks were varied: I worked on a travel agents' salary software, and helped a woman come to terms with her computer aided embroidery machine. I backed up data. I fixed problems. This was all before the internet caught hold.

The consultancy was supplemented by word processing work. I typed up lots of theses and dissertations, and was amazed at how stupid some of the students could be. I couldn't believe the essay which began "The title of this essay is called ...". I found myself at first correcting spelling, then grammar, finally facts. It pained me to type such shit. And they got good value for money. Another thing I typed was the complete sodding works of Malcolm Muggeridge. Somebody wanted to edit these, and produce a book. Thankfully for us all, it was never published.

I diversified the Computer Friendly portfolio even more once by translating German boiler standards into English; Bob got me the job when he was working at International Combustion. It would have been easier had I had any knowledge of technical German, but this was sadly lacking, and there wasn't much mention of my German language speciality – cake – in the standards. So Bob and I sat together at a table in the university library, surrounded by dictionaries technical and general, engineering books, and mounting panic. Between us we cobbled something together. I'd tell him what I thought the words meant, and he translated it into Engineering. When I'd finished, I had visions of my translation causing life-threatening disasters, and decided it would be wise to add a disclaimer at the end. The stress had been too great; I accidentally missed out a vital word, so that my disclaimer read that I accepted responsibility for any errors or mistranslations.

The document had already been copied and distributed by the time I realised. Bob had to rush around at work, into the offices of people he didn't know, smile and grab their documents from their desks and replace them with a new copy bearing the word "not" in the disclaimer.

As more and more people got the internet, I knew I hadn't been trained to deal with it. I also knew I wasn't enjoying this most of the time. And that my heart sank every time the phone rang with a potential client. I should stop this malarkey!

Sadly, the writing career never happened, because I stupidly forgot to do one thing: write.

Luckily, there was another string to my bow by now. I hadn't left the last programming job before I'd found a means of regular income, albeit tiny. I was a Library Assistant! I'd passed the test: addressing an envelope and putting some books into alphabetical order. I could be me again. After my first shift, I came home beaming, and bearing a big cardboard box of discarded books. I really couldn't wait for my next shift. I was working at Basford Library for fewer than ten hours a week, but I was back where I belonged: with books and people. And this was almost better than bookselling, because I didn't have to ask for money. I just stamped the books, and they were free to go. Yes! I had the fun of rubber stamps too!

Not enough emphasis is given to the role of libraries. They are one of the measures of civilisation. They are houses of culture; a refuge from the cold; a place where the lonely might have their only conversations; where young parents meet others; where children learn the joy of books; sources of information; beacons of humanity; a repository for Mills and Boon's greatest works; community centres; places where there are BOOKS; and somewhere for library assistants to chat, chat, chat with each other until the public have to tell them to "shhhh". I liked the people I worked with, they seemed human! That hadn't happened for years.

As with any job, there were inevitable frustrations, but these came later. Meanwhile, this was a huge, huge relief. And entertaining. When you are at the mercy of whoever walks in off the street, it can be worrying, but also a wonderful source of anecdotes. For example, there was the friendly woman, getting on in years, whose aroma was always alcoholic, and who chatted to us as she returned her library books, often about the wonderful holidays she'd had. She was sun-tanned and cheerful. On two separate occasions she returned a book complete with her bookmark. People often did this. These bookmarks were different though – they were amorous holiday notes from (perhaps) waiters, comprising the purest filth: the sort of purest filth that is complete with graphic detail.

A borrower, on being asked the author of the book he wanted to renew, sounded perplexed. "What do you mean?"

"The author, the person who wrote it." "Oh, could it be 'Smith'?"

Some of the librarians and senior staff shocked me by their ignorance, lack of interest in books, and, of course, dreadful spelling and grammar. One librarian consistently put up illiterate notices. A library manager, being asked to get a book by James Joyce, wrote it down as if he were a female writer: Joyce James. When the borrower corrected her, she angrily replied that she couldn't be expected to know every author. She was the same manager who also endeavoured to clear as many books as possible out of the library because she liked nice, tidy, clear space. I was surprised that people who went to the trouble of choosing library jobs could hate books.

When I started at Basford Library, it was completely uncomputerised. Books had book tickets in them (different colours according to type of book; also cassettes and spoken word), and each borrower received six folded brown tickets. We had to handwrite their name and address on each ticket as the queue built up. When a book was borrowed, the book ticket was inserted into the borrower ticket, and stored alphabetically in lovely purpose-made wooden racks. I thought this system was called "brown issue" because of the colour of the tickets (although children had blue ones), but it was in fact "Browne issue" after the ingenious inventor. I loved alphabetising the tickets at the end of the day. I was rather less fond of going through old tickets and handwriting reminder postcards for overdue books, but rewarded myself by putting them into postcode order before posting.

Later, computers were introduced, with a very basic system at first. The changeover was an enormous task, as it involved every book being put on the system. There were two main advantages as far as I could see. We were able to order requests for borrowers immediately, rather than wait for someone to go physically to another library a few days later and order them; and we didn't have to handwrite borrowers' tickets or overdue postcards any more.

Computers were brought in for the public to use, and we had to show them how. This could be immensely frustrating, but also interesting. If someone was researching an unusual family tree it was more fun to work with them than if they wanted to look up a football club. Lots of people needed help in setting up email accounts. More still wanted help, but didn't know what they wanted to do because they didn't know what they could do. I quite enjoyed working with most of them, and would often get them scrolling through old photos of Nottingham, just so that they could learn to use a mouse and work the scroll bars. I found it ironic that I was once again working with computers, but at a fraction of the salary my previous computer work had brought in. However, the people I worked with were so much nicer, and I felt I was doing some social good. There were exceptions, like the man with cardboard on his nose (who used to make me recall the Mushroom customer with a condom on his finger – just: why?) who wanted to use the internet to make a will without paying, and was the sort of student who grabbed the mouse from your hands and undid everything you'd just set up.

We got to know a lot of the borrowers, and there would always be a bit of a chat. Some of them obviously had a penchant for one or other library assistant, but generally there was polite banter. There would be talk about the weather, the buses, holidays, and any social chat that helped people with their loneliness. I used to wonder about regulars who we realised hadn't been in for a while. Sometimes we'd spot death notices in the local paper.

Mr Wood, a true gentleman who loved reading westerns, gave us sweets and tried to give us money. Mrs Guest, who borrowed Douglas Adams, said she felt an affinity with me, and expected I'd seen angels and ethereal beings too. Miss Morgan was offended at having received a card telling her that books were overdue, but after I grovelled and grovelled and apologised and apologised, she took to me and always came to have a chat. Mr Shephard often travelled to eastern Europe, but later developed cancer. All the years he came, he always carried his books in the same greasy holdall. One very elderly man shuffled very slowly, and loved books on local history. When I showed him some fascinating oral history cassettes, he explained that he didn't have modern equipment to listen to them. Another man would come in at the same time every week, rub his hands together and exclaim to us that it was a bit parky outside; then settle down in a chair with a newspaper, and maybe close his eyes for the rest of the afternoon. (This was the man we once nearly left in the library overnight. We were about to lock up, and Bob, who had come to fetch me, kept interjecting "but ... but ... but" until we listened for long enough to hear that there was someone asleep in the fiction section.)

A handful of regular borrowers obviously became too disabled or unwell to be able to continue visiting the library, and sometimes we'd take them books in our own time. Mrs Glover was always grateful for the Mills and Boon books I brought her, but the fierce, vicious dogs at her house competed with the ungrateful, rude son who lived with her and piled her garden full of dead cars.

> **READING:**
> Local history
> Deitch's *For the Love of Prague*
> Barker's *The Brontes*

Through the library I got to meet Roya, from Iran, and her family. She wanted someone to speak English with, and I was more than happy to become "Auntie" to her baby son, Parsa. It has been a delight to watch Parsa grow up, although I haven't had the time to see much of him since acquiring the grandchildren we thought we would never have. When he was two or three years old, Roya asked him why he was jumping from chair to chair. "It's my destiny", he replied.

Bob and I had been together four years before we moved in together. Once bitten, twice shy! We'd had a lot of fun though. Our first holiday together was just the two of us by Slattery's bus to Ireland, camping. We arrived in Dublin, and slept in a youth hostel in a private room. We caught a bus to Tralee for the

Dingle Peninsula. Half way there the bus stopped and everyone had to wait ten minutes while the bus driver went home to fetch a jumper. We walked on the seashore, camped in scenic camp sites and secretly in sand dunes, tried out many pubs and enjoyed the craic. I was amused by Bob dangling his boots from their laces as he walked beside the sea, and finding that they had filled up with water. But I was easily amused, I also laughed when he sat on the tomatoes in his jacket pocket.

We'd camped on the Dingle Peninsula again, and further up the coast, when we went in Bob's Lada with Anna. We had plenty of grand, soft days. The tent became sodden, and although we knew we were in the middle of amazingly beautiful scenery, the mist prevented us from actually seeing it. We played rebel music cassettes on the car stereo.

> **READING:**
> Norman's *Terrible Beauty* and anything else about Countess Markievicz

We'd been on protests together, written silly things for whatever publication was being produced at the time, and generally tootled around. We'd camped wild in Derbyshire, where Bob used the opportunity to try out his gadgets: the camping toaster veered from incendiary weapon to slightly warm glow, and nothing in between, and the camping saw took ages to hack through a twig that was easily snapped by hand.

Sometimes Anna and I would stay over at Bob's Chilwell house, sometimes he'd come to Woodborough Road. The Chilwell house was constantly in a state of having work done to it, and the more work was done to it, the more like an unfinished building site it became. Bob put his foot through the floor/ceiling, creating a direct line of vision from kitchen to upstairs. And vice versa, but you wouldn't want to look down to the kitchen much. It had carpet on the floor! And samples of everything that had ever been cooked or eaten there for the past thirty years trodden into that carpet. This was garnished with a fine layer of car parts, topped with a clutch.

Eventually we decided to look for a house together. I was programming by now, so able to help get a mortgage. I don't know why the state of Bob's kitchen hadn't frightened me off.

We thought it would be very difficult to sell our rather run-down houses, but it was faster than we'd anticipated. We sold them directly, involving no estate agents. Although I had priced mine to account for the rotten cellar stairs and other problems, I still felt sorry enough for the purchasers to take them a bottle of wine a week after they'd moved in.

It was the summer when Anna was changing from primary to comprehensive school, so this influenced where we looked for houses. Anna and I had visited a few comprehensives, so that she could choose. Of course she had done very well at Walter Halls, reaching a level of arithmetic that her teachers couldn't keep up with, so the head had to help her. The nearest secondary school, where most of her class would be going, was ruled out when I asked what happened if a child was particularly good at maths, would they get support? The head teacher replied that a lot of children thought they were good at things, but they never were. Anna instead chose Frank Wheldon School, in Carlton.

We chose our house, where we still live as I write this, for a number of reasons. Mainly, it had enough bedrooms that all the children could sleep in their own rooms when they visited (Bob has a daughter, Sarah, and a son, Adam). You could go out of the kitchen straight into the garden, something I'd never been able to do at Woodborough Road, due to the hill making the back garden one floor lower. It was clean and didn't need too much doing – stairs to the converted attic being the main thing (we had these fitted by Wayne, Wayne and Brother-in-law) – and it had a garage. And there was a whirlpool bath! Bob had briefly suggested buying something like a derelict church, and converting it. When I later found it took him ten years to build an airing cupboard, I was so relieved that I'd rejected that idea.

Although there was a nearer comprehensive, Anna was able to get to her school on her own from our new home. Sometimes I gave her a lift.

Bob excitedly told me that he had borrowed a van, and would be able to move a first load of stuff in. I was excited too. Maybe we could get some chairs in, and be able to sit down, or other furniture, even maybe make a start with moving books. But Bob used the opportunity to move his most precious stuff – his collection of pieces of wood. They were of various lengths. Thus did our life together start.

We were both used to living alone. We both ordered milk deliveries from different milkmen without talking to each other first.

At first, I took on the cleaning and shopping, and Bob took on cooking. But his (usually good) cooking resulted in the kitchen looking like a field of devastation, the walls were splattered, and dozens of pots were used, so I decided it would be easier if I cooked. In this way were the children deprived of yet more veg bobbing about in tinned tomatoes. (I did say "usually" good.) It was handy living with someone with lots of practical skills; it would have been handier still if procrastination hadn't been one of those skills. But, if I could be patient, Bob would eventually mend/make/fix/build whatever needed mending/making/fixing/building.

Mum came to visit, and liked the house. She admired next doors' garden, which was beautifully maintained. Joyce and John grew vegetables and fruit as well as flowers and shrubs. The runner beans were near the fence. "Look at the garden next door. They might give you some beans," said Mum, in her loud voice. "Shh!" I whispered, embarrassed. "I only said, they might give you some beans", shouted Mum, even more loudly. We got beans.

We had a camping holiday in Scotland, with all three children. We imagined the Loch Ness monster, fought off midges with an unsuccessful vengeance, got wet, and were amazed when Adam chose to put his tent up with the entrance next to the only tree in the entire empty field, so that he then couldn't get into it.

In 1992, Bob, Anna, Adam and I were to fly to St Petersburg. We still look back on that holiday with excitement. We realised that food availability might be a problem in Russia, so we bought a large selection of snacks to see us through the lean times. We forgot to take the Hoola Hoops. Now our diet would be unbalanced!

It was a package holiday arranged by Voyages Jules Verne, and quite an adventure in those days. We stayed in the Hotel Moskva overlooking the River Neva. We could see a bridge lifting and lowering as ships passed through. The hotel was interesting, in that some of it looked grand, and some of it looked like a demolition site. My favourite floor was the one full of rolls of carpet. Each floor had a bufyet (café) on it in the same place, with a limited offering. Adam gradually worked his way down through the stack of bufyets, consuming all that was edible. Russia certainly had a food availability problem.

It was very exciting to explore on our own, and I remember walking up and down Nevsky Prospekt, and seeing a notice which told people which side of the road was safest during the siege. I had taught myself a little Russian (mainly the Cyrillic alphabet), so delighted in trying to translate things, and seeing signs for книги. But one time early on we were stuck. Well and truly stuck. We were looking for the Metro station, and although we were standing outside the Metro station with an upside down map, that didn't seem to help. We were approached and offered help. While some in our party were suspicious, I accepted immediately, and so we made friends with Victor, or Buktopy.

Victor spent nearly all his time off from work with us. He wanted to improve his English. He lived in a prefabricated Stalin-era flat in a block in an estate of very many of these things. We were invited to visit, and got there in an alarmingly ramshackle Lada taxi, which leapt and jumped around the potholes. Victor's flat was small, and decorated with family trees of Czars. He offered us Georgian brandy, which we can recommend. He had a large collection of self-help/health books, and explained that the safest and surest way to stay healthy in the strange capitalism Russia now had, was to look after yourself and prevent problems from starting. Reminding me of East Berlin days, Victor had asked us not to talk while we were outside the flats, in case anyone heard that he had foreign friends, and therefore possibly also stuff that might be worth robbing.

We went on a boat trip, to the Hermitage, to palaces, and had one of those experiences where the hairs on your arms stand on end as we explored the Aurora, and imagined that the revolution was just starting. Sailors sold their hats; we bought watches, balalaikas, samovars, painted wooden spoons, Soviet army belts, and all manner of shit. After trying to haggle at one stall, it was pointed out to me "One dollar is nothing to you. It is very much to us", and I always paid full price after that.

Of course Bob wanted to go to the maritime museum, and it was there, in the cloakroom, that his passport was stolen. During the Soviet era, no-one had been allowed to find out about the Kronstadt uprising, so news about that was only just coming out in Russia seventy five years later.

We visited the Peter and Paul Fortress, passing by an extremely talented child violin busker. There was a lot to see. While I was looking at something on my own, a Russian couple approached me, and asked "где касса?" It may have been my proudest moment. I understood the question and was able to point them towards the ticket office.

What Victor described as "our strange capitalism", which replaced "our strange communism", created massive poverty. There were people, many of them looking ancient, begging or selling small piles of tat everywhere. This was in contrast to the opulence we also saw, and not only in the Hermitage museum. We went in one café for an ice cream; it had armed guards, and the cost of an ice cream was about the same as an average weekly wage. We wanted to invite Victor into our hotel's bar or restaurant, but he didn't want to go in there because of "krimi people". We probably saw many krimi people when we watched a ridiculous "Folklore evening" in the bar. We hadn't heard of the Russian Mafia at that point, and didn't take Victor's concerns as seriously as they deserved to be.

Victor also warned against biting into a mushroom pasty in a museum café. This was a shame, as it was so difficult to get vegetarian food, we thought we'd hit lucky on finding these pasties. But Victor explained that the mushrooms would be from the Chernobyl area, and unsafe to eat. We realised that was a narrow escape; without Victor, we would probably have eaten several.

Towards the end of the holiday, Victor asked us what else we wanted to see. When we appeared uncertain, he suggested Pushkin. Russia worships its national poet Alexander Pushkin, perhaps even more than Shakespeare is admired in England. We thought we would be taken to another statue, or maybe a museum, and agreed. We were led quickly through the streets, and into a railway station. "Interesting", we thought, "Victor's showing us this typical Russian station on the way. It would be great if we could find time for a train ride later." Next thing we knew, he's saying "Quick! Quick!" and pushing the four of us onto a train. Who was more bemused? Bob and I, not having a clue what was going on, or Anna and Adam, wondering why we didn't answer when they asked us where we were going. We hadn't read the following Wikipedia entry: "Pushkin (Russian: Пушкин) is a municipal town in Pushkinsky District of the federal city of St. Petersburg, Russia, located 24 kilometres (15 miles) south from the center of St. Petersburg proper, and its railway station, Tsarskoye Selo, is directly connected by railway to the Vitebsky Rail Terminal of the city. Population: 92,889."

We eventually got out of the train, still to many questions from Anna and Adam, and Victor led us to the amazing Catherine Palace. Eventually the rouble dropped: we were in a *place* called "Pushkin". And when Anna and Adam wanted to know where we were, we could say "here". Victor as always was well prepared for any eventuality, pulling everything and anything that was needed out of his bag, including – don't panic – a towel. We had a wonderful day out in a stunning park and palace, and it only happened because we put blind trust in a stranger and let him lead us who knew where.

A couple or so years later, Victor was able to come to the UK for a visit, and we showed him Cambridge, Nottingham, London, the Black Country Museum, and other places. As we had been in St Petersburg with Russian life, I think Victor was most interested in UK daily lives. He was astounded by the amount of food in the supermarkets.

When we returned to Gedling from St Petersburg, my head was still full of it. I was automatically still spelling out and pronouncing signs in my head, as I had been with the Cyrillic letters. When we went to a local pub for a drink and someone approached me muttering something incomprehensible (I later found out he was trying to sell me a raffle ticket), my mouth replied, "Sorry. I no speak Gedling."

> **READING:**
> Books about St Petersburg, Soviet Union, Russia

There was another foot-in-mouth occasion after Anna had had some friends round for a sleep-over. One girl left in the morning wearing one of her own shoes, and one (two sizes smaller) of Anna's. What a silly thing to do! I asked Anna for the girl's address, and took her shoe there. I rang the bell of what I thought was the right house, held up the miscreant shoe, and announced "I've come to swap shoes." The man at the door stared at me stunned, and possibly just a little bit frightened as well. Of course it was the wrong house.

Sometimes Bob got home from work after me, and after Anna got home from school. One day he opened the door and was startled to find Anna and me cooing over a cage. We just hadn't been able to resist, and had to introduce him to Houdini Hamster. Houdini, like all hamsters, was fat, furry, twitchy-nosed and beady-eyed.

We went to the Rhineland with Adam and Anna, called up our relatives, and found that we'd arrived in time for "Rhein in Flammen", when castles are floodlit and boats are decoratively illuminated, all to the accompaniment of fireworks, music and much, much alcohol. Our relatives ran a hostelry overlooking the Rhine, where much celebration – including a pig being roasted on a spit – took place, but they brought us a vegetarian meal.

This was probably the same trip as our drive to Prague. Yes, I drove in Prague! I'd booked accommodation through an agency, and when that fell through, the agent suggested that we use his house instead. He would be away; only his aging mother would be in the house. This was all fine, and aging mother (with whom we had about three words in common) did us a great favour one day. Anna, around fourteen years old, had told us she wanted to stay behind one day, because she was too tired or had a headache, or some such excuse. We agreed a time and metro station to meet later. Anna had secret plans: once we were out of the way, she wanted to go into the city and explore on her own. Luckily, the aged mother spotted her, and detained her long enough with a dictionary-based argument (pointing to words like "stupid", "idiot", while Anna pointed to other words she hoped would advance her case), that Anna didn't have time to enact her plan. She barely got out of the house in time to meet us at the arranged time!

On a later Rhine visit, Bob wanted to tour a hydroelectric station. We were the only two on the tour. The tour guide told us lots and lots about it – all in German. Bob was the one who was interested. Someone had to interpret. I did the best I could, but there was so much to say, and my German had remained at the level of a five year old's (with a few extra non-cake related words added) so didn't include hydroelectric terms. I think I gave a pretty good interpretation of most of it. However, at one point I had to resort to "This bit goes up and down. Don't ask."

We went to Beverley Folk Festival, and thought it was hilarious when we heard a phone ringing in the next tent. We went to a ceilidh there, to discover to our horror that everyone else was serious about it, and knew what they were doing. I was really pleased to listen to Roy Bailey.

We also visited Chesterfield Folk Festival a couple of times. On one occasion we turned up with the car packed to the roof with camping equipment, food, probably useless camping toaster, and wondered where everyone else was. It turned out we were a week early – my mistake. I made a similar mistake around then, when I took Anna to the theatre a week early, and wondered why everyone else was going to a different play. Chesterfield Folk Festival was the last time I camped. Having set up the tent, laid stuff out, and surveyed our quarters for the next two or three nights, I suddenly realised how miserable this was compared with my comfy bed and ensuite bathroom just down the motorway.

I was very happy to be reunited with some English relatives: I got Aunty Doris's address from Mum, and we drove to Enfield to visit her. Anna was startled to go into the flat of someone she'd never met before and find a photo of herself on the TV. We met some cousins. Irene was the only one I had met before, and that was in Debenham when we were both children. John has remained a friend as well as a cousin, and we see each other once or twice a year. He found some more relatives in Debenham, and we were invited to Joan's ninetieth birthday celebrations, which was an honour. Joan, John and I (and probably half of Suffolk) share the same great grandparents. John shares our politics to a large extent; this makes his friendship easier; it is probably also why he has fallen out with his siblings. We took Mum to see Doris, and all had a restaurant meal together. We met the whole lot of them (including cousin Barbara, who had only just found her family after being adopted as a baby) at Aunty Doris's funeral in the 2010s. She had been incapacitated with Alzheimer's for about ten years, but had lived a long, albeit often hard, life.

I lost some very dear people around those times. Cousin Marion died of skin cancer. She'd spent most of her army childhood posted in hot places. I hadn't known she was even ill, until Mum rang me from Portugal to tell me she was about to die. It was a shock out of the blue. I managed to get in touch with Aunt Edith by telegram, but Marion didn't live a day longer. She too had effectively been an only child, so, although we hadn't seen each other frequently, we were the closest thing to sisters to each other that we could have. And we'd shared some dodgy teenage adventures. Mum didn't make it over from Portugal for the funeral, but Bob, Anna and I went. Someone told me I looked like Marion.

Not so long after Marion's death, I arrived home to find a message on the answerphone from Edith. She had lung cancer. We visited, of course. Edith gave me things – suitcases, towels, rings, earrings, etc. – and talked about Marion's husband, who she couldn't stand and blamed partly for Marion's illness. She stayed in her terraced house as long as she could, and when eventually she had to go to hospital, she walked to the ambulance. I had to arrange her funeral as Mum was in Portugal and Edith hadn't wanted her son-in-law to do it. I did this mainly from my desk at work, which felt bizarre. Mum and Bernd came over to Gosport for the funeral.

We took Marion's son on holiday to Kleinmachnow with us, driving to several interesting places on the way. He'd previously visited Kleinmachnow with Mum and Anna and Edith. The trip was great, of course, but taking him was not a success. He complained the whole time, and rang his father to tell him we were stealing from him. The poor child had had terrible traumas, and he was only about ten years old, but we couldn't cope with his behaviour and deliberately lost touch after that holiday. When we left Gosport after taking him home, Bob tore up his map of the town.

Julia had been a friend for years. She at first didn't know what her illness was. It was AIDS and beautiful, feisty Julia died slowly and painfully. She had been living in London, and when we visited she told us how the people upstairs used to be excessively noisy; then she found out they were the Pogues. I saw her in her Hampstead flat, in hospital in London, and at her mum's once she'd moved back to Nottingham. It was awful.

Awful too was Anne's death, of motor neurone disease. Anne had been a very helpful neighbour at Woodborough Road, as well as a friend. Gradually, she was able to do less and less. Her children were young when she developed the disease. I babysat them quite often, and, with Anna's help, took them out for the day to Sundown Pets Corner, as it was then called. Anne moved to family in Sheffield for her final months.

Carole had been the partner of someone I knew, and we became friends. She too had her children later in life, and was a brilliant mum – I think that was the thing she wanted from life. She had been a fantastic and very reliable babysitter for me before she had her own children. She died during an epileptic fit. Afterwards, her parents asked me to swear that she'd told me that if anything happened to her, they were to have the children. It was very difficult, I didn't know them or the father. Carole hadn't discussed that with me, and I couldn't say she had. I often wonder what happened to those children.

Cath was my boss in the library. She was lovely to work with, knew her job really well, and wouldn't ask you to do anything she wouldn't do herself. And she was good company. When I met her, she was in remission from breast cancer, but it came back and grabbed her. We got the phone call as we were opening the library one Saturday morning, and had to carry on cheerfully. Cath had arranged her own funeral, down to the playing of *Pretty Flamingo* as we all trooped out.

In 1996, when Mum and Ken were back in Woodbridge for the summer, we heard that Ken wasn't feeling well. It was Bernd's 60th birthday that year, and Mum and Ken were due to go to Kleinmachnow to celebrate, but Mum had to go alone. Ken's health didn't improve, but the doctor told him it wasn't cancer. Then, next I heard, it was cancer, lung cancer.

I spent a lot of distressing time in Woodbridge that summer, watching Ken's health decline and trying to help where I could. I bought a video player, to give him some distraction, and we watched *Fawlty Towers* videos over and over. Ken was no longer able to go up the stairs, and could do less and less for himself. He had to go into the hospice in Ipswich, and while he had a day out of the hospice at his son Terry's, he died. I had been with them earlier in the day, but decided to go back to Woodbridge to give them some privacy. It didn't feel like there was much need for me at Terry's. I got the phone call from Mum a couple of hours or so later, while I was sitting at her dining table. It had been about five short weeks from diagnosis to death.

Mum's arm started hurting from the day before Ken died. She thought she'd somehow wrenched it while manoeuvring his wheelchair. But it didn't get better, despite physio and other treatments. I was visiting her in Woodbridge most weekends. She had decided to move to Nottingham, and eventually found a small two-bedroomed flat in Gedling, near the church. The legal stuff with house buying and selling was of course stressful. She was also buying some new furniture, in particular a leather reclining sofa set, but hadn't moved yet. All this, while her arm got more painful.

Mum eventually told me that she'd had her arm x-rayed, and the hospital was so thorough, they'd x-rayed her lungs while they were at it. The next weekend, I decided to have the first Saturday at home for a long time, and not go to Woodbridge until Sunday. We went to the caves under the Broadmarsh Centre in Nottingham, and enjoyed it. Arriving in Woodbridge on Sunday, I could see Mum had been doing paperwork. She was in a strange mood, and told me that paperwork helped her to take her mind off things, and that I should sit down. I was worried, but she just insisted that I sit down. Then she told me that she'd been diagnosed with lung cancer. Her GP had called at the house to tell her. The arm was broken, caused by metastasised lung cancer. This was not many weeks after Ken's death. I could not believe it. I couldn't believe that life could throw such a horrible, horrible coincidence. It wasn't true, it just couldn't be.

I remember walking to the GP's surgery with Mum. The GP gave her something to spit into so that her morning phlegm could be inspected. I just kept saying how I didn't, couldn't, believe it. The GP was kind. We walked back up the hill, looking at the low moon. Mum showed me how she found it easier to walk quickly if she imagined she had a puppet's string from the top of her head, and the string was holding her head up and leading her forward.

Mum was in hospital in Ipswich briefly. On my way over from Nottingham the day I was to bring her home, my car was pranged at the back at a roundabout in Ipswich, so I couldn't open the boot.

It wasn't long till xmas. Mum had a row with the estate agent, who was being slow. She had moved into the little room in our house, which is now my library. Bob and I went to Woodbridge and packed all her belongings up. Some, she'd already given away. Her friends Eric and Julie had packed up all her glasses. There was a pile of stuff she didn't want. If I remember rightly, it was to be left in the garage for a charity to collect. I extracted some books from this pile, to keep for myself. It was really difficult, seeing the place that had been my home from age fifteen, and always been a base to return to, being dismantled, becoming less and less a home. Bob and I went to the pub in the evening.

Life was bloody difficult.

Mum was at ours at xmas, and, as every year, Bob's mum Nina was here too. Mum had second thoughts about the leather settee she'd paid for, and debated going back to the shop to cancel it, saying she wasn't going to live long enough to get the value out of it. We managed to persuade her that, if she would enjoy having it, then she should have it.

I had not long had a mobile phone. (I was quite an early adopter; I needed one because of my "Computer Friendly" business.) Nina liked going to church on xmas eve, so it was arranged that when the service was over, Bob would use my mobile to phone me, and I would go to get them. At the expected time, the phone rang at home. I answered, but all I could hear was Nina saying things like "Are you sure you're doing it right, dear?" and Bob muttering "Bloody phones, why does nothing ever work!" They both sounded a very long way away. I said "Hallo Bob. Bob!" ever louder and louder, but it was apparent he couldn't hear me, so I rightly assumed it was time to go and fetch them anyway. I discovered the technological error

Bob had been making. He had been holding the phone at arm's length. I never did know why. Nor did he.

Mum had registered with a GP surgery near us. I went with her, because we were worried that her next hospital appointment was too far into the future. Bernd had found out about some amazing new treatment being trialled in Germany, and we needed a doctor's report to be able to apply for it. The GP, Dr Thornton-like-the-chocolates, was astonishingly rude and uncaring. He told Mum to stop bullying him, and said "By the way, did you know you have another tumour by your stomach?" and "there's no point in rushing to get treatment, it won't cure you." Once he'd reduced us to tears, we left.

We took Mum on outings, such as Wollaton Park, Southwell, and Newark. In Newark, we wanted to have afternoon tea in a lovely traditional tea shoppe, but ended up in a formica dive with nothing delicious.

The next few weeks were a blur, full of hospital visits, tears, fear, and moving Mum's stuff into her new flat. She decided that she wanted one last holiday, and that she had always wanted to go to Istanbul. With her arm in a sling and plaster, off we flew, staying the night before the flight in a hotel near Heathrow. Mum had just bought me a new VW Polo – my mini was ancient, and she thought minis were unsafe anyway – and we drove to the airport in that; I was unhappy at leaving the brand new shiny car in the airport car park.

I found it painful to share a room with Mum, and witness the difficulty she had sleeping at nights, as she tapped on her plaster cast. I was having difficulty too. She had booked us a very nice hotel, and used the safe in the room to store her supply of Ritter Sport chocolate. She recited the various colours and flavours of Ritter Sport; I was amazed at her expertise. We had a cushion with us all the time, and Mum used this to rest her arm on when she sat down. She told me that, apart from the arm, she felt no cancer symptoms.

It was Mum's 71st birthday soon after we arrived. I gave her a card, but couldn't think of anything she wanted. All my ideas (sleeveless cardigan, Coronation Street tea) had been used up at xmas.

Our hotel was in area of ramshackle but interesting wooden houses. We walked around a lot, looking at sights. Mum had a list of must-sees, so we went to the stunning Blue Mosque, the Topkapi Palace, and Hagia Sofia. Luckily, the Topkapi Palace had public toilets; unluckily, they were the squat style, with a blocked drain, so to use them you had to wade ankle deep in piss. I wasn't impressed and decided to give them a miss.

I found Istanbul a wonderful, fascinating city, and have been back two or three times since, although it was a number of years before I felt able to return. Climbing the wide, winding ramp up Hagia Sofia, I noticed that Mum was needing to pause and rest every now and then – the first indication that she wasn't as fit as she had been.

Being two females alone, we received a lot of unwanted attention, despite one being elderly with a broken arm and the other being middle-aged and overweight. It was quite annoying. The Grand Bazaar looked so interesting, but it was difficult to pause and look at anything. Crossing the road to the Hagia Sofia, someone approached us, and we waved them away angrily. They explained that they only wanted to tell us that there was a car coming, and we should be careful!

We got lured into a carpet shop and plied with tea. We said that we wouldn't buy a carpet because we didn't have enough money, but still weren't able to get away until I looked at my watch and said we were expected at the hotel.

Then there was the taxi driver. February in Istanbul can be cold and wet, so we'd taken a taxi. The driver invited us for a cup of coffee, and did his best to befriend us. It was beginning to look as if he'd be clamped to our sides for the rest of the holiday. We were being friendly in return, of course. He wanted to discuss which colour belly dancing outfit would suit me best. I felt uncomfortable, but when I used the word "bullshit", Mum rebuked me. Then he got out his big album and started turning the pages, showing them to us. Mum said things like "very nice", "oh yes" and "interesting". She wasn't wearing her glasses. I could read the handwriting underneath the photos of smiling women. They were reviews, like reviews of hotels or books, but these reviews were of his sexual prowess. Some were quite detailed.

Mum wanted to go for a boat trip, but all the boats that bobbed up and down at the quayside, trying to encourage tourists on, seemed to require a massive leap across the water to board them. This wasn't a problem for Mum, of course, but it was for me. Eventually we found one I agreed to try. With her arm in its sling, Mum leapt aboard, and I fearfully followed. Then we sat in this damn boat for ages; the boatman was obviously waiting until he had a full load of tourists. We were getting very cold. We managed to get off it again, and ended up going on the ferry to Asia instead. This was the first time I'd been in Asia, even though it was only for a couple of hours. We had some baklava.

Mum had been attending Hayward House, the hospice in Nottingham City Hospital's grounds, for some time before the Istanbul trip, and continued after we returned. She was very impressed by the volunteers, who drove her there and back, just as volunteers had driven Ken to St Elizabeth's Hospice in Ipswich. (This prompted me, about four years later, to volunteer as a driver myself.) A week or two after we returned from Istanbul, I went to her flat to meet her after her Hayward House visit, but she wasn't there, so I hung around for a while. I had brought some things along – light bulbs for her oddly sized wall lamps, some yoghurt that someone had said would make her feel better ... I did some cleaning and tidying, and was beginning to feel rather irritated that she was so late. I don't remember how I got the message, but the message was that she was staying in Hayward House overnight to get her pain sorted, and could I come and bring some overnight things.

She never came back to live in her flat. The overnight stay lasted six weeks, and when she came out, it was to the undertaker's.

She was in a four-person ward, screaming in agony, when I arrived. Staff were doing all they could, and hooked her up with a pump system that supplied constant morphine. It gradually helped.

Mum was glad when she was soon moved into a one person room. I tried to make it more homely by bringing in photos, putting up silly notices, bringing in tulips, and so on. Once or twice she came out for a few hours, but she was very worried about pain, and I remember her eating a bit of avocado at our house, and then asking to be driven back to hospital quickly. It was very good that she was in Hayward House and not in a normal hospital ward. I was working at the library at the time, but spent the rest of my waking hours there. I could see her becoming more and more ill. She needed help having a bath, and I saw how her tumour had grown. She was still Mum, though. If a nurse said something like, "will you take this medicine for me?" Mum replied, "No, but I'll take it for myself." Staff wanted her to lie down, but she kept sitting bolt upright, using only her stomach muscles like I've never been able to do. Sometimes I took her outside in a wheelchair. Once, she asked me why I was looking so sad.

I rang Bernd, and he came quickly. I drove to Heathrow to pick him up. He had brought videos of the family, and of the new house being built for Ralph, my cousin. Mum rallied tremendously. She was alert, full of energy and laughing. It was wonderful to see. They talked about seeing each other again.

That was the last time that Mum was truly Mum. As her medications increased, she was awake and conscious less and less often, and when she did surface, she was often confused. She asked for banana custard, something she had never wanted in her life previously, because it had been offered to her a couple of days before. The kind staff made some for her. I was told I could stay overnight in her room on the reclining chair, so that was where I lived for the last week of Mum's life. I knew how much she had regretted not being with Dad when he died, and I wanted to be there for her. I passed some of the time when she was asleep reading through a massive stack of Hayward House's *People's Friends*. Once or twice, nurses encouraged me to get out into the grounds for ten minutes; someone else would sit with Mum while I did this.

On April 15th 1997, Bob and Anna had come over to Hayward House in the evening to see me, and we chatted in the reception area. When I returned to Mum's room, she was very different. The quality of her breathing, the rattling sound. I rang the emergency bell. The nurses who arrived made it plain that Mum was dying. Bob was called, and he came back to be with me. Keith had been asked to call Anna. A nurse held Mum's hand and felt her pulse the whole time. I held her other hand, and wanted to say something but had a blank mind. I think I told her I loved her. When she hadn't drawn her breath for what seemed like a long time, I involuntarily called out "Mummy", and she breathed again, maybe even opened her eyes, though I'm not sure. Bob later said that it looked like a scene from a Victorian painting.

The end of this story is obvious. We didn't stay long in that room afterwards, but came home, where I sat on the sofa feeling bereft, strange, and orphaned. I felt very, very brittle and that I would never find comfort.

> **READING:**
> Istanbul guide books
> *People's Friend*
> *Woman's Own*

Mum's funeral was at Wilford Hill, where Robin's had been. Mum hadn't been a church goer, but had wanted a C. of E. funeral "just in case" – just in case there actually was a god, he was C. of E., and didn't recognise when someone was hedging their bets. The vicar fucked it up by stating that Terry was her son – a mathematical impossibility considering their ages and the date she met Ken.

Afterwards, our living room was full of people amazed that they were from Suffolk too, or had Suffolk connections. I tried to explain that it wasn't at all amazing because Mum had lived in Suffolk, but everyone seemed to think these were inexplicable coincidences.

I bought a TV with video player, got a small sign with Mum's name fixed to it, and donated it to Hayward House. For many years after, until we undertook masked bookselling (see later), I would give a donation on the anniversary of Mum's death.

There was a lot of paperwork to do; probate seemed complicated, not made easier by grief. Mum had had lots of different accounts. Her flat needed to be emptied and sold. The caravan in Portugal had already been sold at Mum's request.

Then there was the question of the ashes. I don't really attach much meaning to ashes. They must be coffin ash to a large extent, and anyway, Mum doesn't live in ash but in my heart. However, I had promised her that I would scatter them on her favourite beach in the Algarve, and so I obviously had to do this. I also had possession of Ken's ashes, which had been in Mum's flat. These would be scattered at the same time as Mum's, but I had to organise this with Ken's son Terry. Terry wanted me to give them to him, so they went to Ipswich by courier. Not finding anyone at home, the courier left them outside Terry's front door, which didn't please Terry.

I put off going to the Algarve to scatter the ashes until autumn, as I hoped that some of Mum and Ken's friends would be there again, and they might like to be present. Communication with Terry wasn't easy. He blamed me for something, maybe only selling the Algarve caravan (he afterwards said he wanted it), maybe the ashes left outside his front door, maybe something else that I never understood. I had given Terry the money Ken had left to Mum, and a little more besides, which although not legally his, was definitely his morally. In the end we flew separately to the Algarve, each with an urn of ashes in our luggage. We met some of Mum and Ken's friends, but when it came to scattering the ashes, only Terry and his partner and Bob and I were there. We scattered the ashes where the sea would take them, and I wrote Mum's name in the sand.

Mum had always wanted me to go to the Algarve, but this was the first time I was there. While I wasn't impressed by the caravan park, I did like the beaches and scenery, and the white house we rented. I was amused by a restaurant sign that said "Typical Food". That's just typical. I also finally understood what Mum had meant about "Portuguese colours" - she had found them oddly unattractive.

We brought home a couple of bits that had been in the caravan, including broken bits of the Christmas "Pyramide". Bob later bought me a new one from a German xmas market.

A couple or so months after Mum's death, we treated ourselves to a holiday. Bob and I went to Venice. We liked it very much, and didn't find it stinky, as we'd been led to expect. I kept remembering photos of Mum and Dad in Venice, and thinking about how they had seen the places I was seeing.

We also had a holiday with Anna, in Tallinn. I was excited. It was a fascinating place to explore. The old centre of Tallinn is beautiful and interesting. It is wrapped in a more recent, more soviet-style, but none-the-less also interesting outer city.

When Bob wasn't looking, Anna and I leapt onto the tourist "train" that trundled along the tourist trail. It was called "Toomas", and ever since I have delighted in riding in Toomases in different cities. Bob was appalled at our naff tourist behaviour. He, on the other hand, wasn't beyond crticism when he proposed a day on the beach in Pirita for a change. When we got there, he suddenly discovered there was a submarine he could look at. Amazing! Who would have thought it! We'd already been round the Estonian Maritime Museum housed in the medieval tower called Fat Margaret.

We decided that a good way to see some of Estonia was to get on a train going somewhere random, but not too far away. That's how we arrived in Aegviidu. It was fun, with a station toilet that convinced me I was now a world traveller rather than a tourist. We walked in the countryside a little, and didn't get ticks; we only found out that the fields were full of ticks later. We found Aegviidu's library. Even in a remote, non-tourist, sleepy place like Aegviidu, the young woman at the cash desk in the only shop spoke English.

I was still working in, and enjoying, the library. I worked at Meadows Library too for a while, but that was too much, and I felt closest to my colleagues at Basford. I was spending most of a day each fortnight visiting Nina, Bob's elderly mum, and helping him to support her.

But not everything can flow smoothly all of the time. The Council was attempting to display its eco credentials by publishing an environmental magazine of immense superficiality (I say this even though I managed to get an article about Bob's wind turbine company into it). Piles of this magazine would be delivered to libraries, where maybe one or two would be taken, and then the rest would be disposed of – to landfill, as there was no recycling provision. The irony of this overwhelmed me, and I had to take it on. I knew a journalist who was willing to write about this if I would agree to be photographed with piles of these magazines "for human interest". Thus began a lengthy and, to me, entertaining correspondence with the council's head of the library service. "Just checking: it would be ok for me to be photographed, in my own time, sitting on a heap of magazines?" "No, no, that would be a dreadful crime, bringing the library service into disrepute." "If it's disreputable to chuck environmental magazines into landfill, why not provide recycling facilities?" "You don't understand, you lowly library assistant, if we put recycling bins outside Basford Library, the uncouth locals would tip them over and create a mess." And so the correspondence went on. In the (almost) end, he told me to stop writing to him. In the (actual) end, I told him that that was an unsatisfactory response.

Some years later, there was another big fight with library management, when they wanted to put frontline staff into uniforms while management continued wearing what they wanted. The last day I took off my school uniform was the last day someone else was going to tell me what to wear. I could see no point in library assistants being uniformed – we didn't need to be identified in a roaring hurry in some kind of mis-shelved book emergency, and it was quite easy to recognise us because we were the ones standing (chatting) behind the counter, or tidying the bookshelves or cleaning the toys. Badges could identify us anyway.

THE SOCIALIST REPUBLIC OF IZIA

Uniforms of the People's Revolutionary Militia, No 27.

Sergeant, Third Logistics Corps, Mountain Archivists Battalion.

All library workers must serve part-time in Mountain Archivists Battalion. In time of tension, eg filthy American-backed Zhenovian aggression, Mountain Archivists Battalion transports Izia's National Archives and Library to secret locations in mountains and protects precious collection from eg illiterate Zhenovian terrorists and such like. On some days, all library workers are required to be at their libraries in full kit as shown below, to show borrowers that Izia is ready to deal with imperialist book thieves.

FEATHER OF STUTU BIRD

SHAPELESS HAT (D.D.R.?)

WHITE BLOUSE DISCARDED BY NOTTINGHAM CITY COUNCIL AFTER GLORIOUS LIBRARY WORKERS' STRIKE OF 2006-2008

SPAZCHTU Mk III CARBINE

DATE STAMP

BATTLE DRESS BLOUSE, BRITISH WW II SURPLUS

9mm AMMUNITION (30 ROUNDS)

THE BEAUTIFUL DEYATI MOUNTAINS

BOOK BAG

BOOK KNIFE

BOOTS (POLISH)

SKIRT DISCARDED BY NOTTINGHAM CITY COUNCIL (SEE ABOVE)

Bob's take on library assistants' uniforms.

It felt like a plan for someone in management to make their mark, whilst putting us in our place and removing the close informality that was a highlight of friendly relations with borrowers.

So I campaigned. I campaigned officially via "the usual channels", unofficially with leaflets and friends writing letters to the local press, and incredibly unofficially with friends sending spoof emails to libraries, about regulation underwear, and how management would want to be addressed as "sir" or "madam" in future because they were so superior to library assistants. In the end, possibly because of the expense that would have been incurred, uniforms for library assistants were not introduced while I was still on the staff.

Before Anna's 'A' levels, she and I toured some universities she was interested in. We headed north. We stayed nights in student accommodation (mainly: yuck) in York (which was full of buzzy wasp-like things I trapped under drinking glasses), Stirling (whose campus was overrun with cute furry rabbits that no-one mentioned), St Andrews (stunning architecture and too much golf), Aberdeen (the maths department resembled someone's living room), and drove through Edinburgh, which looked nice. I really enjoyed spending the time with Anna, and hope she enjoyed it too.

For Anna's eighteenth birthday the three of us went to Barcelona for the first time. It was February but we were warm, although people who lived there were wrapped in fur coats. We loved it. We explored a lot. Our hotel was in the Gothic Quarter, and we explored Roman remains, St Martin's Tower (where I borrowed an idea from Anna and took my shoes off so it didn't feel so high), and lots of gorgeous Gaudi buildings. We had a favourite restaurant, where we often ate "salad self" (help yourself salad).

In 1998, about a year after Mum died, Anna passed her driving test. She tried to tell Keith, but he wasn't answering his phone. It transpired he'd been walking in Derbyshire and gone missing. The police were alerted. Keith had got lost, and spent the night wandering around in the Peak District. A few days later, he was at his house and had a stroke. I don't know which of these two events caused the other. After the stroke, Keith was in hospital for a long time. He never regained the use of his left arm, but managed to learn to walk with aids, although he lost this when he had a fall a few years later.

Anna was taking her 'A' levels, and planning a gap year abroad. I began regular visits to Keith so that she would feel free to spread her wings. When she had originally proposed a gap year, I thought she might go to Germany or elsewhere in Europe. However, Anna organised it all herself. She'd spend half a year in Alabama, going to college, and half a year teaching English in a Prague school. We went to London (and stayed in an expensive hotel that provided a bucket at the breakfast table, to catch the rain coming in) so she could make the USA arrangements, and we did a day trip to Reading for the Prague arrangements.

As the time for Anna to fly to the USA approached, my stomach knotted up more and more. I was dreading her going, whilst also so very proud of her, and hoping she would have a wonderful and amazing time. I would just miss her so very much. After she'd gone, we went to Hampton Court for the rest of the day. Bob thought it would help to take my mind off how much I was missing Anna, but I kept looking at it and thinking that Anna would enjoy it.

I gradually learned to live with Anna away, although she was at the front of my mind and heart most of the time. We joined a Lambley local history society outing to explore the caves under the Broadmarsh Centre that aren't usually open to the public; a teacher who'd known Anna was there, and I clung to her as a connection with Anna. (There was plenty to see in the fascinating caves.)

We were discouraged from having too much contact with Anna in Alabama, and we definitely couldn't visit, so it was a long half year. Anna returned for a break at home, then was off to Prague. At least that was a bit nearer, and we were able to visit. It was freezing cold winter when we arrived. Anna was living in a room at the top of the school where she was teaching. When we saw the room, it was knee deep in clothing and *stuff*. But Anna was only nineteen, so that's healthy, I suppose. We'd found a room nearby for ourselves. Anna came to see us one morning just as the owners arrived, and there was an almighty argument as they accused us of having Anna stay in the place too, and wouldn't listen to us or accept Anna's offer to show them her room. They tore our paperwork up. But we found we'd taken their key with us afterwards. Their name was Drha. Luckily, we'd booked a hotel for the rest of the visit.

During this Prague visit, I did something I never thought I would ever do. I hung underwear on the backs of chairs and all around a Prague school classroom. Well, Anna had to dry her laundry somewhere.

Although the late 1990s had been painful in a variety of ways, the twentieth century ended quite beautifully for me. I had never been married, or wanted to be. I didn't see why church or state should impinge on my very personal life. But. Despite my inheritance from Mum, I was feeling insecure about the more distant future with my low income. Bob had got divorced. He clearly believed enough in marriage to go to the trouble of formally ending one. He would get good pensions while I would get almost none. He suggested to me that one way I could be more financially secure would be if we married. "Is that a proposal?" I asked, startled. He said something like "not yet, it should be more romantic".

On holiday in Paris, I was delighted to spot that their bins were the same as ours.

So I waited. We went to Paris and wandered around the streets, leant on picturesque bridges, went up the Eiffel Tower (and I wasn't very afraid; was brave enough even to say out loud that old Paris was so well preserved because the French had given up early in the war), drank Cointreau and Calvados in little cafes, but nothing ... Maybe this marriage thing wasn't going to happen after all. Never mind.

We decided to go camping in the Czech Republic. My Czech had got good enough to understand "kde klíč" (Where's the key?), ask for more bread, cheese and beer, and whether there was a room available. I later found out that by dint of a fair bit of looking up, I was also capable of making myself understood when I asked if I could keep some of the beermats. We loaded up all the camping stuff, and drove to Czechland.

The camping stuff was on the car roof. And there it stayed. Hotels were so cheap, there was no point in struggling with tents and the lumpy ground. In Karlovy Vary, we got an entire multi-roomed huge suite with a number of TVs and a giant hot tub that kept fusing, for only a few quid.

> **READING:**
> Books on Czech language
> Czech history

We liked Karlovy Vary for other reasons too: its beautiful spa architecture, its setting in the woods and hills, and the fact that Bob proposed to me there while wearing a Hawaiian shirt. We'd gone for a walk up a wooded hillside to a lookout cabin, and when we got there, both a bit breathless, he said "It's romantic here, isn't it? Will you marry me?" I think I'd answered before he'd finished. What had started as a no-nonsense desire for financial security suddenly became something else, and though this surprised me, I liked it very much. I was very, very happy. When, that evening, Bob turned his salad plate upside down at the (outdoor) restaurant to drain out the water ("Czech salads are always wetter, sweeter and smaller than you expect"), I looked on lovingly. And giggled, of course.

To get married, you didn't just have to propose. I think Bob was a little surprised to find that there were arrangements to be made too. Sarah was in Australia, and Anna was at Edinburgh University, so we decided to wait until December, when both could be with us. Then we had to find somewhere to do the deed. For some reason, this became tricky, although I can't remember that reason. Certainly, there were fewer venues where it was possible to marry than there are these days. It had to be accessible to elderly ladies – Nina and Aunty Doris. We fixed on Gedling House, a mile or so away from our house, and hired a minibus to transport us there and back.

My main memory of our wedding is of manhandling elderly ladies in and out of the minibus.

It was a home-made event. Nina did the flowers, which we'd bought that morning from a local shop. I made the cake. Anna made a tape of music. Adam's girlfriend was studying photography and offered to take photos; that is why the only visual record of our wedding is half a dozen blurred, dim pictures.

In the evening, we all went for a meal at Bestwood Lodge Hotel, using the tablecloth Mum had been saving for my wedding. Otherwise, we were just another table of pre-xmas guests. Nina looked at cousin John very disapprovingly. We had driven there earlier in the day to leave a car in the car park. I'd reversed my Polo rapidly into what I thought was a wide open space, then spotted absolute horror on the faces of Bob and a hotel employee who happened to be there. It wasn't a wide open space at all. There was a bollard on either side. Incredible luck was on my side, as I reversed between the bollards, with about five centimetres between the car and the concrete on either side.

Sarah offered to drive Nina home, so Bob and I were able to stay at the hotel overnight. The following day we were due to go on honeymoon. We caught a plane from Leeds/Bradford airport to a cold, wet, wonderful Venice. It took us some time to realise that the plethora of very low tables around St Mark's and elsewhere was actually a plethora of benches to walk on to keep feet dry out of the floodwater. It was a honeymoon, so we went in a gondola; fearfully expensive and touristy – and lovely.

On honeymoon in cold, wet, romantic Venice, 1999.

I found it difficult to decide what to do about my married name. I wanted it to acknowledge my marriage, but I also wanted to keep the connection with where I came from, and, most importantly, with Anna. The names on offer were ridiculous, especially the "Cann Cook" option. I plumped for the rhyming "Christine Anne Cook Cann", but tended to use only the simpler "Cann" for everyday. This resulted in my payslips for around a year being addressed to "Chris Cook Cann Informally Cann".

Around the 2000s: Solidarity with refugees, cycling and more travels

The new millenium was greeted by Bob, Anna (who was visiting from Edinburgh) and me in Nottingham's Old Market Square. It was packed with revellers, but we were probably the only ones with a nice thermos of mushroom soup, that I'd made earlier from mushrooms going cheap before the holiday.

Anna's third undergraduate year was spent in Bonn, under the Erasmus scheme. She had decided to specialise in linguistics, and, bravely, to start doing this in German. I visited her a couple of times, once on my own, and once with Bob. I was full of admiration for her courage/foolhardiness. As she was settling in, her mentor asked her whether there were any problems. "Yes," replied Anna, "they've given me orange curtains." Anna needed a number of items for her Bonn student flat, and we discovered "Sperrmüll". On a designated day, people would leave items they no longer needed or wanted at the side of the street. You could walk about and help yourself. It was marvellous! We pushed back a heavy reclining chair, managing to get it in and – happily – out of the lift. Now I had somewhere to sleep.

When I returned to Gedling, I emailed the council and suggested they consider instituting Sperrmüll; if there was cash in all the times I've been fobbed off with nonsense, I'd buy you all some Kuchen.

Around the turn of the century, I saw a leaflet from my union, UNISON, in the library staffroom. It was about Nottingham and Notts Refugee Forum, who were asking for support. I had of course always felt that people who had to abandon everything they ever knew to make a dangerous journey in order to seek safety, deserved all the sympathy and support they could get, and it hadn't occurred to me that not everyone would feel the same way.

I made a donation, or whatever the leaflet was requesting, and ticked the box asking for more information. That was the beginning of around fifteen years of NNRF playing a huge part in my life. Because I enjoyed writing databases, I was volunteered to be the membership secretary. I refurbished the database and made an efficient membership system, which I kept updated. I produced forms to recruit more members, and sent emails out regularly to keep members informed and involved.

I was also one of the original volunteers of the anti-destitution group. On Tuesday mornings, we'd give asylum seekers, who were not allowed to work and had no recourse to public funds, a tiny allowance and vouchers for free food. I felt it was very important that they had some cash, so that they could feel part of society and have a little amount of choice in their lives. How else would they catch buses or use phones?

We needed donations to fund this project, and I was one of those who sometimes went out to give talks as part of the fundraising effort. My favourite talk was to the Seventh Day Adventists. I decided to do my best to fit in, so wore a hat. Anyway, I like wearing hats. My talk was after the main part of the service, so I enjoyed listening to a lot of heart-felt gospel singing. I was listened to attentively, and afterwards there was a prayer: "Oh Lord, thank you for sending us Chris." (This is something that Bob also exclaims quite often, albeit in a different tone of voice.)

I helped organise a forty-eight hour sponsored fast, to raise funds for anti-destitution work and highlight the situation asylum seekers found themselves in. I'd mentioned to someone that it would be a good idea if someone organised something like this; then found that I was doing it. We were loaned church premises in the city centre so we could be together if we wanted. Forty-eight hours wasn't such a long time for me – the fasting was easier than the organising, where very large groups of people with many different backgrounds, agendas, languages and interpreting needs would meet and try to move forward. However, it was a positive time. Asylum seekers and refugees were empowering themselves by being part of the planning.

I joined a large group to stand bail for a family who had made their home and friendships in Nottingham, but had been taken away and incarcerated in Harmondsworth detention centre. As well as the parents, there were four primary school age children. We were all overjoyed when they were released, and I visited the family often, and became especially close to the youngest daughter, Marwa. Against their wishes, they were eventually sent to Spain, so a friend and I flew out to meet them as they arrived. Bob and I also visited them once in the small town where they had been settled.

My disgust at immigration detention centres led to my volunteering to stand bail again for someone else, via BID (Bail for Immigration Detainees). Roger, also from Nottingham, joined me in this. Sandra was released on our bail, but seemed less interested in building a friendship with me than the Iraqi family had been, although I called round a few times. She had her own life. Eventually she became terrified that she would be deported, and went missing. Roger and I had to appear in court, and I received a large fine (I should have maintained closer contact with Sandra; the fact that my mother-in-law had become ill and required a lot of my care and time was deemed irrelevant) as a claim on the bail I had stood. Roger very kindly made a contribution, as his fine had been smaller. It had been worth doing as it had freed someone from Harmondsworth, but I couldn't do it again – both, I couldn't afford to lose that amount of money again, and I would probably be regarded as unsuitable because previously someone I had bailed had absconded.

Asylum seekers have to report and sign at whatever random intervals the powers over them choose. When the Nottingham reporting centre closed, people with no income were expected to make their own seventeen mile way to Loughborough instead. In 2007, Bob and I organised a protest/sponsored walk to the Loughborough reporting centre. This didn't achieve its purpose (the situation hasn't changed), but I still felt positive about it, mainly because of the way the arrangements came together. Someone arranged that we could have stops in churches along the way. Others attended with their cars to pick up the walking wounded, ferry people to and from the nearest toilets, and hand out snacks. Others appeared at the end with vehicles, to take everyone home. Whatever needed doing, someone had done it almost before we asked.

The Lord Mayor of Nottingham had agreed to give a speech and send us off from the Council House, but he wanted someone else to write it. When Bob told me he'd written the mayor's speech, I thought it was bound to be funny, but not something we could use. Of course. I was amazed when I read it – it was serious, and said everything that needed saying, with no piss-taking about mayors at all. The Lord Mayor read it aloud, and many people commented on what a good speech he'd given.

I still have a bag of antiseptic cream and blister plasters that I carried on the day of the walk, in case anyone needed them.

May Days in Nottingham. Half my placard had dropped off, so I was left proudly displaying the special offer on the back.

As a member of the NNRF Campaign Group, I became part of a small subgroup which organised Nottingham's May Day marches and ralliesfor about four years. These events, previously organised by the Trades' Council, had lapsed, and we felt it was important to bring them back. We can be proud that we started them going again, had good turnouts, colourful marches with samba bands and dancers, and fun as well as serious rallies, with stalls, music, and speakers. It was a disappointment that the unions didn't participate more, but eventually the Trades' Council reclaimed the event, gaining more union participation and losing most of the fun. We had done it enough by then, and it was seeming more difficult to get council co-operation. We can look back on a good series of photos, including many of us struggling to erect the massive gazebo/stage cover.

I met many amazing people while volunteering for NNRF, both from the host community and refuges/asylum seekers. We occasionally hosted people I met doing anti-destitution work, who would otherwise have been street homeless. The family from Mongolia was with us for a while. There were also: a man from Ivory Coast, a young man from Romania, and a young woman from Eritrea, among others. They made lasting impressions on me.

I was membership secretary and on the anti-destitution group for over ten years each. I was also on the management committee for around five years, until I had no more to give.

About four years after Mum's death, I felt I was able to step inside Hayward House again. I wanted to volunteer as a driver. Mum had so admired the volunteer drivers, and I felt that doing this would bring me closer to her, as well as repaying what Hayward House had done for her, and helping people who were at a time in their lives when they needed support. There were some hoops to jump through, but in a few weeks I was a volunteer. At first I only wanted to fill in when other regular drivers were off, but then I started doing a regular day every week. I'd take patients to day care in the mornings, and back home again in the afternoons. I met many wonderful, brave, funny, interesting, delightful people (and one or two bastards) in the last years, months, or weeks of their lives. It is a privilege.

In 2001, I fulfilled an ambition of many, many years. I cycled end-to-end. I didn't cycle with the prevailing wind the way most people do (and the way I would do it if I were mad enough to do it again), but from John O'Groats to Land's End.

I didn't undertake any special training for the ride, arguing that cycling the first few days would be training for the next. I didn't push myself hard very often, but took it easily in three weeks. I thought that cycling a long way would be just like cycling a short way – but repeatedly. And so it was.

Solo cycle ride from John o'Groats to Land's End, 2001.

I decided to cycle at the end of May and beginning of June because I would get long days then. I also managed to pass through the Scottish Highlands just before the midges got seriously nasty, and the timing fitted in with visiting Anna in Edinburgh. This meant I would be cycling during a general election, and the backdrop to my journey was a succession of changing election posters. I was also cycling during the period of foot and mouth disease, which had not hit the north of Scotland at all, but was rife in many other parts I cycled through, particularly Cumbria, Lancashire and the West Country. In those places I was frequently cycling over disinfectant mats fastened across roads, but as I stayed on roads and lanes I never had to divert from my route because of it.

The route I rode was based very closely on the Cyclists' Touring Club B&B route, which followed minor roads and country lanes as much as possible. I detoured from this to avoid the Forth Road Bridge, when I was lost, when I thought I could see an easier way of doing it and when I got plain fed up with too many hills or too much navigating.

I wanted to use this ride as a fund-raising opportunity. I decided to choose one local and one international charity to collect sponsorship for. The local one was Hayward House Cancer Care. The international one was ActionAid, in particular their AIDS project in Africa.

There were no smartphones then. I chose a road atlas with a mile to two-and-a-half-inches scale, from which I tore out the relevant pages. I spent a very long time on the internet, typing up a list of B&Bs, guest houses and cheap hotels along the route. I also noted tourist offices and bike shops. By the time I had done all this, it felt as if I had done the trip several times already.

The weather on my ride was very good. I was lucky. In the three weeks, I only had about three hours of rain despite hearing dire warnings most evenings on the weather forecast. Sometimes, particularly in Scotland, it was too hot, and I got burned despite using factor 45 sunblock repeatedly. I did experience a lot of headwinds, possibly because I was doing the route backwards.

I was amazed by the amount of support I received. I was being congratulated even before I had set off! Before, during and after the trip I received countless good wishes and practical expressions of support and help, and am now left with a lovely warm afterglow. Maybe people think it was more difficult than it really was ...

Bob drove my bike and me to John O'Groats to start off, met me both weekends with clean clothes and dried figs, and was there when I arrived at Land's End three weeks later.

I cycled alone, but talked to the cows and sheep I passed; I also spotted several scampering bunny rabbits and little chickens. At Melvich I met Ian from Norfolk, who had cycled from Norfolk to Land's End, then up, aiming for John O'Groats the next day, then he would cycle back to Norfolk. (My Granny had warned me about people from Norfolk.) He told me repeatedly about the terrible climbs on the route, and that he hadn't walked up any. I walked up plenty.

I stopped for the first night at Bettyhill, and met a couple of elderly brothers, who, in full lycra, were touring the north coast and islands. They were on something like their 35th or 40th tour together. They were very enthusiastic about packing scientifically, and reduced the weight of their luggage to thirteen somethings. By the time I was half way through my pint, they'd extracted most of my life story from me – and expressed astonished horror at my carrying four pairs of shoes!

Near Nairn I had been concerned about not finding anywhere to sleep, so was delighted to see a B&B sign. I found the farmhouse B&B, and its owner Toby explained that a stick had hit him on the head. He showed me a room I could have for £15. ("It's usually £18, but you can have it for £15 because you're nice." When I looked in the mirror, I realised that what he actually meant was "because you look really funny with all those streaks and blobs of sunscreen all over your face.") The next morning, Toby played the accordion to me as I uncomfortably ate breakfast on my own, wondering when to applaud.

There followed some very steep climbs (I walked) but also some descents, including a spectacular one to Bridge of Brown. This was followed by a 20% climb, but as it started to flatten out a bit, I got on my bike. I hadn't cycled far when – phutt – a puncture in the front wheel. I pushed my bike, knowing I could make Tomintoul before evening. But when a car came by, without really thinking about what I was doing, I flagged it down and asked Bert and his secretary whether either of them were any good at changing inner tubes. Bert got the wheel off easily, and also the tyre, but he could not put the spare inner tube on because it was much bigger than the rim. All parts of my bike, my panniers and me were loaded into the back of the car and I was driven the two or three miles to Tomintoul. Bert found a truck-mending type place there, and left me waiting for the workmen to arrive. They pointed out that the spare inner tube was not only too big, but also had a hole in it already, so they used my puncture repair kit and fixed my original tyre.

I had been urged to visit the bike shop at Ballater for new inner tubes, but thought maybe I could wait until Blairgowrie, which was on my route. However, going past Gairnshiel Lodge, I noticed that my front tyre was flat again. There was nowhere else for miles around, so I knocked on their door. The owners tried really hard to mend my tyre, but couldn't find a hole, although the tyre kept deflating after being pumped up. I was given a lift to Ballater bike shop about five miles away, and received new inner tubes (front and a spare). Bicycle Repairman charged me £3 for each inner tube. When I asked, "What about your labour?" He replied, "Ach, I wasna doin' anythin' anyway."

At Bridge of Cally Hotel, some bloke in the bar said he'd sponsor me 10p a mile. Yes, he was aware that that would be about £100. About four weeks after returning home I received a cheque for £100 and a "well done" card from him!

Near Blairgowrie, I realised that my folder of maps and routes wasn't there! I remembered putting it down when I was loading up my bike. I rang up the previous night's hotel to ask if they could post it to Anna. They did better than that. They drove the folder over to me!

I got mixed up in the Midlothian Triathlon. Loads of beefy blokes in swimming trunks shot past me on racing bikes. This gave me an advantage in that all junctions gave priority to cyclists – including me. One of the athletes, who must have read about my journey on my vest, said, "Great stuff, keep it up" as he zoomed past me.

In Peebles, I stopped to rearrange my maps. Three overweight late-middle-aged men approached, presumably on their way to or from a pub – or between pubs. They guffawed at the unlikelihood of a woman understanding maps, so I told them that I'd done all right so far from John O'Groats. They actually jumped back a step. They asked where I was going, and then insisted I should go a different way from my planned route – "I should know, I'm from Manchester." One of them asked whether I was doing it for charity, and he gave me a £10 note: "This is from the three of us."

I'd stayed the first Saturday at Anna's in Edinburgh, and Bob had met us there. I had booked a room near Chepstow, where Bob was going to meet me for the second weekend. The house was incredible, Georgian and obviously well loved. It was big with very large rooms filled with fascinating antique furniture, lots of lace, patterned carpets, wallpaper. It had not been redecorated for a long time and looked right that way. There were books all over the place, and interesting objects in every corner. It felt a bit like being in an interesting museum. Our landlady, Eileen had been collecting the lovely contents at auctions and in other ways for years (some were inherited and some were gifts). She'd previously lived abroad, including in Singapore and Malaya, and had been a professional opera singer.

Bob and I had a lovely afternoon and evening together. We explored a second-hand bookshop (I was able to buy because Bob could carry my purchases home), had some drinks and ate a meal in a quiet pub. I was intrigued by the random scattering of black and brown combs (nothing else) in a shop window – a barber's attempt at artistry. The next morning, Bob drove my bike and me over the Severn Bridge because I found it too scary to cycle over, then I was on my own again with my bike.

At Wedmore, I tried to pay for my night's accommodation, but the landlord wouldn't take my £25. He said he was inspired by what I was doing and didn't want paying – "we're fairly relaxed about things down here". In Bampton, a couple of elderly ladies, starched white blouses tucked into flowered elasticated-waistband skirts, asked me whether I had far to go. "Land's End." "You are a good girl. We should all love each other more, don't you think?"

In Bude, the hotel bathroom tiles appeared to have been grouted with snot.

Somewhere around Trispen or St Erne, I was happily wheeling my bike up a hilly lane in the sunshine, thinking what a nice time I was having, when – SPLATT! There was a thud on my right arm. It was splattered with horrible brown and white birdshit! As was my bike. I wiped away at my arm with tissues. I picked up my bike to wipe that, and discovered that I'd thrown it into nettles. I used my last remaining Refreshing Wipe on my arm and then my bike – saddle, handlebars, triangular bag, mudguards, rear pannier, map holder needed wiping. It must have been an eagle or an albatross. Maybe a condor. I emptied both water bottles over my arm and bike. Because I was in urgent need of a good wash, I cycled the last few miles into Truro on the A39, and found the Tourist Information Office. My first tourist enquiry was, "Have I got bird shit on my face?"

I came across a Cornish mobile library parked in the middle of nowhere, so took photos and stopped for a chat. The library was staffed by the driver, who'd been in this job for twenty-six years. He was accompanied by his wife, along for the ride. Also in the van was a borrower, emerging with an armful of books. She said how important the mobile library was to the area, which no longer had any public transport.

In Penzance, I met an Australian cyclist, who was just setting off for John O'Groats, accompanied by his wife carrying all the luggage in a car. He told me he'd done it before, years and years ago. He said he wasn't looking forward to it, so I asked him why he was doing it in that case. He looked at a loss. "You have to, don't you." The hotel owner's wife and daughter appeared, to watch me load up the bike and discuss cycling shorts. (The wife had not come across these before, and had been put off cycling by the common sore-bum syndrome, which she'd tried to avert by tying two cushions to her saddle.)

I booked a room in Sennen, and cycled to Land's End once Bob had arrived. He photographed my moment of glory. Bob had brought champagne all the way from Nottingham in a cool bag, and it was still cold. I celebrated, and my bike enjoyed as much champagne as a bike can.

Being back home again was a bit of a shock! I had slipped so easily into the lifestyle of moving on every day, and never having to worry about mail, bills, cleaning, shopping, what to wear, putting the bin out, appointments or work. When I was cycling, all I had to do was cycle, eat or sleep (and sometimes talk or drink). The first morning I woke up at home, I couldn't remember which B&B I was in, or where the bathroom was. I had cycled 1,034 miles in three weeks, raised more than £1,034 in sponsorship, and then raised even more by giving talks about my ride afterwards. Also, I'd had a fabulous time and felt good about the world and myself, if not my puncture-repairing abilities.

READING:
  Anne Mustoe
  Travel books

My solo epic adventure was followed by two cycling holidays with Bob. We spent a week repeating some of my favourite Scottish part of the end-to-end, and saw some wonderful birds. Mrs Breastmilk's B&B was full of cross-stitch. We found a large farm that farmed rubbish – extensively. Sheds, shacks and piles of might-turn-out-to-be-usefuls stretched for miles.

Belgium is flat and cycle-friendly, so we carried our bikes over on the channel ferry, and were delighted to be able to cycle off well before the car drivers could start revving their engines. I loved this holiday – I always love Belgium – but Bob got very tired, especially on the final leg back to the port. The precedence given to cyclists was outstanding, except at the Bicycle Museum, which realised the irony when we found they had nowhere safe to park bicycles. At Ghent, the hotel owner looked at our bikes and declared to us: "You are sporty!" We were too shocked to say anything, so he continued by offering us his discounted room. The reason it was discounted was because entry to it was up a ladder, into a trapdoor cut in the bathroom floor. Our sportiness enabled us to take full advantage of this discount.

Both Bob and I had been spending a lot of time helping to look after Nina, his elderly mum. We'd take it in turns to visit every week, and also took her to the hospital and doctor and arranged care and visits and did all the paperwork and made all the arrangements that someone has to do.

Sometimes it would be my turn to take her to the smelly, cramped hairdressers, or to the Co-op. At other times we were able to make more exciting excursions. We drove up a track into the rhododendron-filled woods near her village. (Bob later told me I shouldn't have done this in case the car broke down in the woods, but Nina adored it.) We explored the grounds of a privately-owned castle (we both loved exploring places with "no entry" signs best) and went to tea shops. At xmas, I would take her shopping in Lincoln, and try to prevent too many unsuitable presents. I think she had a good time on these adventures.

Before Bob and I were married, Nina was at a loss as to how to introduce me to people. "This is Chris, my son's ... er ... er ... she's my friend." One way she dealt with this was by asking me to stay in the car when she went to talk to people – so she didn't have to introduce me at all. It must have been a relief to her when she was finally able to introduce me as her daughter-in-law. I could no longer stay hidden in the car and had to meet them.

To celebrate turning ninety, she invited lots of her friends to her house for a party. When we heard about this, we realised we'd better hurry up and provide a party! It seemed that Nina and her guests enjoyed it; Bob, Adam and Sarah were showing off taekwondo moves to each other in the corridor, and I was handing round plates of defrosted dainties, as the guests sat waiting to be served from the buffet.

In late 2004, I turned up to visit, and could see that something was wrong. Her cup was on the floor and her speech was a bit indistinct. She'd had a small stroke. I called, and the ambulance arrived very quickly, to take her to hospital in Lincoln.

She'd been there before and recovered, though it had taken us a long time to get her out because of the care arrangements and aids (the "package") that took so long to arrange. Then, she'd been given two walking frames, "one for upstairs and one for downstairs". I remember pointing out that she lived in a bungalow, to be told, "Never mind. She's got two." They cluttered the place up, and she refused to use them, though occasionally she would pick one up and carry it around with her.

This time, she was obviously unhappy at being back in hospital, and that she was missing *Casualty* on TV. She was kept on a trolley for a seemingly long time, and without the cup of tea she desperately wanted, because first she had to pass a swallow test.

Nina was in hospital for a few days. She didn't get any better, but instead seemed to gradually fade away. Until she was gone.

It was shortly before her ninety-fourth birthday. She'd led a full life, left behind many anecdotes (a lot of them about her driving), and her funeral was very well attended. Back at her bungalow, we displayed the badges and rosettes and trophies she'd won at the W.I. and elsewhere. She is missed.

Then we had to empty the house, a job that makes me so very sad.

Anna studied at Edinburgh all this time. She changed from maths to linguistics, and obtained a first at MA level, then an MSc, then a PhD. Unfortunately she didn't feel able to continue in linguistics. There was a shortage of jobs and too much nepotism. She became an accountant instead. Before she started work, when she still had a long summer break, the two of us set off with our backpacks to explore Eastern Europe. This was wonderful fun.

We flew to Prague, then caught trains, spending a lot of time in Hungary, as well as some in Poland, Slovakia, etc. In Krakow an angry wasp made a wasp-line for me and stung my arm, prompting a hunt for onions. We stayed in rented rooms in people's houses. We saw the Krakow salt mines and the mysterious labyrinth in Budapest, which included a red wine fountain. We thought this was marvellous, and after we had drunk we filled up our bottles. In the cold light of day, outside the labyrinth, this wonderful fountain wine proved to taste disgusting. In one small Hungarian town, Anna mended their public phone system. In another, we hailed a passing empty Toomas (tourist train), and the driver stopped for us, then proceeded to zoom up and down the hills and around the sharp corners at breakneck speed, while we clung on grimly.

That was good practice. Even grimmer clinging on was required when a train we were on was severely delayed at a station. In the same compartment as us were several British football fans, who had just been to a match. (Zilina were playing Chelsea – we had wondered why so many British men with sunburnt torsos were stumbling about drunkenly. We often manage to meet up with weirder aspects of the UK when we're on holiday – previously that's included the Croydon Youth Orchestra in Karlovy Vary, the Mansfield Caravan Club on the Rhine, and the Basingstoke Male Voice Choir at another part of the Rhine.) Also in the compartment was Jonathan Wilson, the *Financial Times'* football correspondent. Jonathan was on his way to a flight from Krakow, which had been booked from work. He had to make this flight. As the train was ever more delayed, the chances of him catching his flight receded. He decided to get a taxi across Czechland and Poland for many miles, and he invited Anna and me along. I thought I was helping when I told the taxi driver that it was important not to delay. The driver phoned his brother, who helpfully stood at the side of the road holding out his passport. Then all haste was made. And I mean "all" haste. Every bit of it you could make. The speed limit was exceeded by a respectably Czech amount, and corners were taken with Czech enthusiasm. There was no hanging back on the overtaking, oncoming traffic or not. At the border, the driver zoomed past the queue and pushed in at the front. Then there was ever more speed. By the side of the road, I spotted numerous accident blackspot signs. Anna and I held hands in the back of the taxi, hardly breathing, and I dug my nails too deeply into her palm. Eventually we arrived at Krakow airport, in plenty of time for

Jonathan's flight. We were all bathed in sweat, especially Jonathan. Anna told me never again to tell a Czech driver that we were in a hurry. We had all survived.

> **READING:**
> *The Timewaster Letters*
> Other funny things

Bob and I later made several exciting rail holidays, including to Anna's friend's wedding in Nafplion, Greece, to Istanbul, and interrailing randomly but including Croatia. I loved these holidays, and made sure never again to tell a Czech driver we were in a hurry. A taxi driver in Croatia was interesting, in that he didn't believe in looking at the road, but rather at us on the back seat. He was delighted when the time on his watch said "22.22", and turned around for some time, proudly showing it to us, and repeating "22.22". We must thank the magic of time which soon became "22.23" that he eventually turned to look forwards again. Later we needed a taxi again, as we were staying in a cheap out-of-town hotel whose claim to fame was that it sold something called "Eurocrem Bloc" in its vending machine, but when we saw this man touting for business beside his taxi we hid.

I have had so many "holidays of a lifetime", and our 2003 trip to Cuba, my present from Bob for my fiftieth birthday, was up there with them. I had wanted to go to Cuba for a long, long time; I also wanted to go while Fidel was still president, and realised we couldn't wait forever. We found a tour organised by Australian Oxfam, which toured lots of sites of huge interest, so we could learn about life in Cuba rather than go sun-bathing. First we had to get there. Our flight from Heathrow to Paris was uneventful, despite the January snow. At Charles de Gaulle airport we were delayed for over two full days, with no information and very little support. We couldn't go and enjoy Paris because we had no idea when our flight would be. The first night, we had to find a hotel ourselves as we were refused help. Eventually I was too angry and decided to rally the comrades. To gain a little height to speak to them, I climbed up on the check-in luggage belt, unwittingly displaying my weight to anyone interested. The French check-in staff continued to file their nails and shrug. (I don't like stereotypes, but this happened.) At long last, and after an altercation with Italians, we got a flight. Luckily, we'd arranged to fly out a day earlier than the start of the tour, so it was still in Havana when we finally landed and got a taxi to the hotel late at night. (For years afterwards, my email signature included "Don't fly Air France".)

Waking the next morning was tremendously exciting. We looked out of our bedroom window, and indeed Havana was below, with a row of cocotaxis lined up along the side of the street. We found we were two of three English people in a minibus of Australians who liked to take the piss, particularly of my antipathy to insects in my bathroom.

The tour took us all over the mid and eastern parts of Cuba, and we learned so much that I'm still not sure whether I've assimilated it all. We spent some time in Havana, and visited markets, the Museum of the Revolution and saw behind the scenes at the theatre. We visited a hospital, a school, an eco-resort, a GP surgery, organic gardens, a music college, Che's mausoleum, and more. We heard talks about collective farming and tourism from people high up in their organisations. We went to a remote village which benefited from solar power to run its surgery and school room, and learned about the basic rations for everyone. We went to a cultural exchange food and dance evening, where everyone except Brits and Australians danced. And they danced so well. While the rest of the group ate lunch, we usually explored on our own, and so saw many libraries, beautiful buildings where books were highly prized and not thrown out after a few years. It was all very impressive. Everywhere we were made very welcome.

The only place we didn't enjoy was the tourist resort, where we were to stay a couple of nights. Our damp room smelled bad, and the piles of plenty on the buffet tables looked obscene after the carefully husbanded food that was available to Cubans.

Qualified lawyers and doctors worked as waiters and porters because they could earn more that way. Cubans who didn't work there weren't allowed in, but we were free to come and go, so we went, and explored the adjoining town instead. We'd already had time on a beautiful sandy quiet palm-treed Caribbean beach by a nature resort, and didn't need this. We never did get answers as to how the resorts coped with infrastructure needs, where the sewage went ...

Anna and Sara had been together since about the turn of the millennium. Sara's father was working for UNHCR in Albania, and we were all invited to Tirana for new year 2005/6. Albania was another place I'd always wanted to visit, and it proved to be as fascinating as I'd expected. It still seemed to be in recovery from Enver Hoxha. The road between the airport and the capital city was a narrow, pot-hole-filled dirt track. Tirana's pavements were lined by huge piles of litter and happy rats. The pyramid which was to have been Hoxha's mausoleum was a shabby shopping mall. The pathetic zoo was disgusting in the tiny cages housing moth-eaten animals who longed to run and roam. And yet. The mayor, Edi Rama, had made the place look cheerful by painting the high rises in a variety of bright colours and patterns. There were bookshops. Albanians put infrastructure second to a love of fireworks – as it was new year, fireworks were being let off on pavements all over. The raki was phenomenal, but when Bob selected a bottle at random in a shop with a huge display, the shopkeeper advised him that it wasn't for him.

Out of Tirana, we noticed that the main economic activity seemed to be car washing, and still wonder how that worked. A man directed traffic, not because he was in the police or traffic department, but because he wanted to. Our phrase books had emphasised learning "Are there mines here?" and "Don't shoot", but we felt safe enough.

We took several trips out, up and down mountainsides and to traditional markets. In the countryside, the scenery was really, really stunning. I can only describe it by saying it's the first place where the beauty of the scenery made me cry.

We had been invited to a flat overlooking the main square, so we could see the official firework displays as well as the random street corner incendiary events, on New Year's Eve. Diplomats and other international professionals were there. It was a more formal occasion than I am comfortable with, and included ballroom dancing, which I had no clue about. I think I was considered rude by turning down offers to dance, while poor Bob had to stamp on a woman's toes a lot of times before he was given his freedom. The fireworks, however, were as spectacular as expected.

> **READING:**
> Albanian history
> Richard Holmes's *Shelley: The Pursuit*
> Dervla Murphy

Anna and Sara had a big civil partnership wedding in Edinburgh in 2006, and our Kleinmachnow relatives came over for it, to join the dozens of others in the Royal College of Physicians. I was asked to walk down the aisle with Anna, and also to give a speech. It was a happy occasion, as was the lower key surprise Blackhall back garden wedding ten years later, during a second birthday party, to convert the civil partnership into marriage. Like so often, and very, very sadly, the happiness was not to last.

Our main holiday in 2006 was a fortnight in Hungary, in Budapest, Szentendre and Eger. Szentendre is a very pretty little place, with narrow streets, little cafes, lots of museums and galleries, and Roman remains. One day we took a bus to the Skanzen (folk museum of village life), where I had been before with Anna.

On the train to Eger, we won an argument with the no-red-hatted ticket collector, who was insisting on us paying a fine because we hadn't understood the intricacies of ticket purchase. We kept her arguing until we arrived and she had to run off to do something else.

We enjoyed the spa at Eger; also the Archbishop's Library, and the astronomical museum. At the Valley of Beautiful Women, where there are dozens of wine cellars, we sampled the produce and were serenaded by stereotypical Hungarian folk musicians. You can wander around, tasting wines for a few pence, and buying what takes your fancy for very little more. An oldish man staggering up the hill away from the valley at the end of the evening must have enjoyed himself a little too much: we watched with horror as he swayed from side to side, then suddenly vanished over the handrail down into the valley below. Bob ran to help him with un-Bob-like speed. A very spiky, prickly bush had saved the man from falling down the hill, and his legs were protruding from the low wall. With the aid of two young men I enlisted by calling: "Help!", Bob managed to pull the drunk out of the bushes. Rescued, the man sat there grinning at everyone, and shaking hands. Also in Hungary, we visited three different marzipan museums, and saw life-size marzipan models of Kantor the police dog and Hunyadi Emese the speed skating champion.

A marzipan museum in Hungary. One of those figures is made entirely from marzipan – but which one?

In 2007 it was our twentieth anniversary of being together. We were unable to book Barcelona, so celebrated in Girona instead, which was lovely. Bob finally gave me an engagement ring, although we had been married about eight years. I treasure it.

Yet another holiday of a lifetime occurred in 2009, when we went to China. This was an organised tour, as we would not have felt confident in a country where we couldn't understand – or be able to look up – any notices. Another utterly amazing time was had. Highlights for me were of course the Forbidden City in Beijing, exploring Beijing's Hutongs, walking along the Great Wall, Hangzhou, and seeing the Terracotta Warriors. And we spent a day with pandas in the panda sanctuary; they were so delightful, especially the babies and toddlers in the panda nursery. Bamboo everywhere!

Holiday in China.

As the tour group travelled along in a bus between sights, the tour leader, Leonard, announced that we would make a stop for a "car museum". "Oh bugger, boring," thought I; "Oh wow, exciting," thought Bob. We drove up the driveway to a large, prepossessing mansion, and were led in to the museum. But there were no cars to be seen. Zilch. It was carless in that so-called car museum. The multi-billionaire owner greeted us, and gave a speech, during which it gradually became apparent that this was no "car museum", but rather a "cow museum" – not a thing we'd imagined existed. As his speech ended, a shelf filled with priceless-looking statues of bulls rose into the air, to reveal a huge painting of Chairman Mao beaming at us in front of idyllic hills. Bob and I managed not to laugh. This multi-multi-billionaire and party member, who must have amassed his wealth in the few short years since private business had been allowed, had a vast collection of ancient priceless objects, mostly based on the theme of bulls – bull statues, bull-decorated vases, bull-decorated bulls, porcelain worth more than all the bulls in the world. If an item was rare, exotic, ancient and valuable enough and not a bull, it was also allowed. There were some very beautiful objects. Frightened-looking immaculately turned-out young women served us tea. This private museum probably held more treasures than many state-owned museums. For years afterwards we wondered why we had been taken there. At enforced detours to jade, brocade and silk factories, we were obviously encouraged to buy. This could not be in question at the "cow museum". We can only surmise that Mr Big got some kind of grant or tax break by calling his private collection a tourist attraction.

The China holiday included a fabulous cruise through the Three Gorges, with scenery to make you gasp. We also got to go up a tributary on a smaller boat, to see even more wonderful scenery. This was in the area where naked men climbed along precarious paths, towing boats – in the olden days; none did it while we were there!

After the organised mainland tour, we had a few days in Hong Kong on our own which I enjoyed, much more than I'd expected. We seemed to be on the Star Ferry lots of the time. I discovered – and, bless me, told Bob – that there was still a proper junk extant in the harbour, and it was possible to take trips. As we boarded the Duk Ling, I settled myself with the other tourists, to enjoy a relaxing trip in the harbour. Bob, meanwhile, was leaping from side to side, climbing over stuff, tape measure out, recording every possible length, photographing joints in the woodwork, and generally appearing as mad as only Bob can.

The holiday included one train ride (the train was impressive) and several internal flights. We had been collecting Chinglish, and I think I found the best example in the Ladies' at an airport.

I tried to find western-style toilets where I could, and here there was one with this sign:

We had been part of a campaign protesting at Nottingham-based small arms dealers Heckler & Koch. Usually this meant standing on a boring Nottingham pavement holding banners for a couple of hours, but in 2009 we and a couple of other campaigners took the train to south Germany, and join the protests at the factory there. We received a very warm welcome and were accommodated in people's houses. I gave an off the cuff speech in German, and have no idea what I said or how I did it, but people applauded. Sadly, this was another of those campaigns that achieved little, and it fizzled out, at least in Nottingham. To the best of my knowledge, Heckler and Koch are still peddling death weapons from Lenton Lane.

Protesting against Heckler und Koch in Freiburg, Germany.

Towards the end of the decade, long-time friends Claire and Mike set up the Sparrows' Nest Library and Archive, and asked us whether we would be on the collective. We agreed, because it was such an excellent idea. They bought a house in St. Anns, Nottingham, for the project. I sorted out a large chunk of my memorabilia for the Nest. I created an Access database to log all the books and other items, and I used to sit in the library for a few hours once a week, in case of visitors. Very few visitors came during my shifts, and after two or three years I wanted my time back. However, although we no longer do much for the Nest, we are still on the collective, and I gather that there are now more visitors. It is a brilliant, unique place, with many special treasures.

In the early years, I organised a talk there. Ray Gosling, author, broadcaster and activist, had been very involved in St. Anns, and I thought it would be interesting to hear him talk. However, he arrived worse for wear. The room was packed, but Ray was mainly intent on taking mobile calls from his lover. After he died, ExLibris (see later) was gifted much of his personal library, which had many exceptional books.

Partially overlapping the Sparrows' Nest is Nottingham People's Histreh – a group exploring local history from below. We have very good friends in this group, where quite often eating and drinking together supersede historical investigations. Philipp does most of the research work, and we make hummus. We spent a marvellous day at the National Archives at Kew, researching courts martial proceedings against Sherwood Foresters during WW1.

> **READING:**
> Gosling's *Personal Copy*

With Anna living in Edinburgh, we had got into the fun habit of staying with her for a week or so most Augusts, and enjoying the Edinburgh Fringe. We saw some very, very funny shows, some shows that made you go "OOOH!", and some that were complete rubbish. The ones that stick in my mind mainly are the site-specific ones, including ones set in: a Ladies' toilet (during which a lady in need of a pee came in, not realising it was a venue); a migrant workers' caravan; an upstairs office (a job recruitment piece); and the one with a coffin on a bus. Also *Jesus: the Guantanamo Years* was unforgettable.

In 2006 we finished our week at the Fringe with a flourish: we'd watched a lot of people being silly on the streets, and thought, "we can do that too!" So Anna, Bob and I donned Ampelmann hats and tee-shirts, painted faces green and red, and crossed the road repeatedly at the pedestrian lights. (An Ampelmann is the former DDR's traffic light figure, much more appealing than the standard western version.) We soon accumulated fans. The Japanese were particularly enthralled by us, and took lots of photos. One man joined in behind us, briefly. Another was overheard saying, "I'm not sure about this." Nor were we.

In 2009, Bob and I were in Malta. Sara's dad Hossein was working there, and he'd invited Sara and Anna and us over for a holiday. One wonderful part of that holiday was meeting up with the Galea family again. They had been Herentals neighbours fifty years previously. Anna got badly stung by jellyfish, but struggled back to the flat, covered in balsamic vinegar; Vida tried to hide Anna's accident from me by offering me more watermelon.

While in Malta, Keith's brother John phoned Anna. He was worried because he couldn't get through to Keith. We found out that Keith had been taken into hospital. Returning from Malta, Anna came to us in Nottingham, so that she could see Keith every day. After a week or so he seemed to be improving, and was looking forward to going home. Anna had things to do in Edinburgh, all would be well, and I would visit Keith some days. I think it was Sunday evening when, during my visit, he asked me to buy Tictac sweets to help his indigestion. I did this. He seemed the same as ever, just looking forward very much to going home the next day. The next morning, the hospital rang, asking for Anna. I explained that she was back in Scotland. Could they speak to me? No, but could I help them to contact

Anna, they had been trying to do so since six o'clock, the phone number they had wasn't being answered. I said, "This sounds very worrying", and they didn't reply. Several phone calls to and from Scotland tracked Anna down at the dentist. When she rang me back, she told me Keith had died.

We had planned to drive up to Edinburgh that day with my friend Margaret for our annual Fringe visit. Anna told us all to come anyway. Nothing could be done in Nottingham until after a post-mortem, so we should all enjoy as much of the Fringe as we could.

That was a very strange Fringe visit, the laughter floating thinly above waves of grief, uncertainty and darkness. I was extremely worried about Anna, and wanted so much to protect her without really knowing how to, but outwardly at least she was doing very well.

Eventually Anna received the phone call that the post-mortem was over and Keith's arteries had been furred up (his "indigestion" for which he'd requested Tictac sweets had been a heart attack?); funeral arrangements could proceed. We left the Fringe and returned to Nottingham, where Anna made arrangements. She organised a moving and appropriate funeral, at which some of Keith's most precious music was played. I was very proud of her honest and loving eulogy. A lot of people had turned up. Margaret was very kind and let us hold the post-funeral get-together at her house, ours being unsuitable as Keith's mum wouldn't have got up the stairs to the bathroom.

Then Sara and I helped Anna to empty Keith's flat. This was a difficult task. Not only was there so much stuff, in no order at all, other than it was piled on top of other stuff, which was piled on top of other stuff, but it was also heart-breaking to come across items from the years when he had hope and the future in front of him. There were large numbers of *Together* poetry magazine, and *Laughing Water*, his self-published poetry book.

Around the 2010s: A masked Omi sells books, I am still very little

In 2011, I heard terrible news. Hayward House daycare, for which I had been a volunteer driver for a number of years, was to close. I was not the only one upset. So were other volunteers, and of course all the patients. I was determined that this could not go ahead.

I campaigned fiercely, together with other HH volunteers and many patients who, despite coming towards end of life, felt strongly enough to give interviews, set up petitions, help with fundraising and give all they could. This was a local issue; we might have some influence. Letters were written. Placards were brandished. The petition took off wildly; so many Nottingham citizens had had a loved one in Hayward House and felt very strongly that daycare there should be saved. We went to meetings. We organised meetings. The "opposition" played their cards close to their chests. When I went to Radio Nottingham to be interviewed, I had no idea what the hospital managers had said. On television they claimed that daycare was unfeasible and unnecessary.

The upshot, though, is that we won! Hospital management denied they'd ever considered stopping hospital daycare, and we rejoiced, mightily relieved and a little surprised.

We tried to extract lessons from this success, but I think it was a unique situation. We were campaigning around a very well loved place, with the emotional aspect of dying patients themselves being part of the campaign. It was local and small enough for local people to have an influence. Management had the face-saving exit possibility of saying we'd completely misunderstood, they'd never meant to do this cruel thing at all. And, probably above all, it was a standalone, discrete campaign – not "Abolish capitalism" or even "Defend the NHS". We were very clear on the one thing we wanted to achieve.

The incredible hamfistedness of hospital management gave one more shuddering gasp before this episode was wholly over. They wrote to current patients to reassure them that their daycare would continue, but did it in such unintelligible, bureaucratic language, under a heading "Daycare at Hayward House", that many patients glanced at it and were convinced it was telling them that daycare at Hayward House was over. I contacted the "public relations" person responsible for this piece of managementese, and she understood my point, and asked me to write another letter to send to patients! Patients thus soon received my letter from the hospital, which was in English, and headed "Your daycare at Hayward House is safe".

2010 was another year with a "holiday of a lifetime". Sarah and her husband Matt were living in Cairo, where Matt was working for BP. They invited us over. This was exciting. We travelled to Istanbul by train, an adventure in itself, then flew to Cairo from there.

Istanbul, whose Maritime Museum is very strange. 2012.

We had a wonderful time, working hard at sightseeing. Of course we saw the Giza pyramids (Bob went inside; I was scared of climbing the unrailed stones to get to the entrance.) We went inside another unused pyramid, with rank millennia-old air and a weird, mysterious, atmosphere. We spent a long time in the Egyptian Museum, and in various shopping areas, bazaars, and markets. And many, many toilets. If it hadn't been for Sarah's magic pills, we would have seen only toilets. Matt and Sarah drove us out to the desert; it was our first ever visit to a desert, and utterly amazing. It went on and on, dotted with the most unusual, surreal rock formations; one of the strangest places I've been.

Outside Bibliotheca Alexandrina – I am still very little.

We cruised the Nile for a week, exploring temples and tombs. We saw the temple of Hatshepsut. The cruise tour guide told us that there was one special excursion which wasn't included in the price: would anyone like to visit Tutankhamun's tomb? We would probably never be in Egypt again. This was unmissable! But Bob wasn't keen? I asked him why he didn't want to do this. "I'm not interested in riding a camel," he explained, displaying his desperate need for hearing aids. We explored the Valley of the Kings, and did pay extra to see Tutankhamun's tomb.

It was very, very hot. We found that difficult, as we also found the sight of armed police everywhere difficult. Some of them were "tourist police", apparently there to protect us. During the Nile cruise, I woke from a snooze on the deck for Bob to tell me that while I'd been dozing, machine guns had been set up overlooking the back of the boat. I thought he was making it up, but no, we were now overlooked by machine guns.

Emerging from most tourist sites was via compulsory souvenir stalls, and there was a knack to keeping your head down and rushing past them without getting apprehended by probably desperate and ingenious salesmen. Shoe shiners were also keen on the tourist EGP (Egyptian pound). When Bob refused the advances of one, he was told his shoes were rubbish. (They were; they were still covered in desert dust.) Most souvenir dealers spoke some English, often very good, and often learned from

1950s films or the British army presence in those days. They used expressions (e.g. "Have a shufty") that were long obsolete back home, but helped them to sell their plastic pyramids.

It was another fabulous holiday, which I added to my store of precious memories.

We went on our first cruise in 2008. Onkel Bernd had showed us many, many videos of cruises he and Hannelore had been on, and recommended cruising to us. We felt that if we did go on a cruise, we'd have to be able to avoid the snake puppets. I wanted to do something special for Bob's sixtieth birthday, and hit upon a cruise that went to lots of places that had maritime museums. What could be shippier than that? In secret, I booked us onto a Thomson (i.e. cheaper end of the market) cruise to the Baltic, where Bob would be able to explore shippiness in Stockholm, Helsinki, Tallinn, Warnemünde ... places of much shippiness. Bob at first thought I'd given him a holiday in Newcastle, but it was only where we embarked. We were lucky that we did manage to embark, as despite desperate and strenuous efforts on my (secret) part, the agents would not divulge whereabouts in Newcastle we should go, basically telling me that we should go to the embarkation dock in order to find out where the embarkation dock was. Bob got an extra treat as a result of this: we mistakenly climbed up to the harbourmaster's office, thinking it might be the cruise terminal, so we got a quick peep at that. The harbourmaster's staff told us where we should be.

We saw ships. And we saw boats. And we saw ships and boats. Bob was bloody ecstatic. I enjoyed everything about this cruise but may have been a little less enthusiastic about the many ships. I had done right to take Bob on a cruise of maritime museums. In Tallinn, Fat Margaret, the maritime museum (which we had already visited some years previously) was closed for setting up a new exhibition. Museum staff told us to come back tomorrow. We explained that we couldn't, we were only there for one day. Bob's disappointed face melted their hearts, and they let us in despite it being shut. We had a maritime museum to ourselves! I have (unfortunately) been to maritime museums all over the world, but to be alone in one (museum staff were mostly at the other end of the tower) was exciting, I must admit.

We found we both liked cruising and didn't have to watch puppets or any of the other awful entertainment – it was quite easy to go somewhere else. There was too much food about, and we watched, astonished, as grown people returned to help themselves to more and more helpings of jelly. It seemed to be the most popular buffet item!

Since then, we've been on various other cruises, mainly back to the Baltic or round the Mediterranean. A Baltic cruise on the sailing ship *Star Flyer* made me angry because the ship was freezing cold, being exposed to the outside wind nearly everywhere except in the freezingly air-conditioned cabin or the small library. The library was usually crowded, and dominated by an American woman called Bobby and her voice. I dismantled the cabin air-conditioning. In Heligoland I looked for a jacket or coat, and amazed shop keepers by asking for a warm one. "Eine *warme* Jacke?" they repeated in surprise, obviously unaware that we were in a howling gale with temperatures approaching too icy for words.

The *Star Flyer* was able to visit some delightful, quiet ports, which were too small for large cruise ships, so although the ship was horrendous, the places we visited were lovely. Flaske Peters Samling in Aeroskobing can never be forgotten: a museum of hundreds of ships in bottles made by Peter, plus a small, creepy, medical display.

We discovered the luxury of cruising with Cunard, with their beautiful art deco ships, including ballroom, swing bands, extensive gorgeous two-level wood-panelled library, lovely dining rooms, string quartets, bookshop, and huge theatre. Cunard doesn't do bowls of jelly.

I disgraced myself on one Cunard cruise. We'd been attending an event in one part of the ship, and then rushed to the buffet area where an "Evening of Chocolate" was ending. Unfortunately, we were too late. The chocolate evening had actually ended, and staff were clearing – and throwing – away all sorts of chocolate delights. "This can't happen, it's so wasteful, and it's chocolate," I panicked as I stuck my hands into bowls of it, licking up what I could, my face covered in chocolate like Sister Assumpta's. What did I think I was doing?

READING:
>
> Bernard Newman's travel books
> Alan Bennett
> Mass Observation diaries
> Dickens
> Vonnegut
> Oliver Sacks
> Valentine Yarnspinner
> Chris Richardson's *City of Light*

Possibly even more embarrassing was the occasion when I showed Bob my swimsuit, prior to going to the pool. "I think this old one's had it," I said to him. "Maybe it's time to throw it away." Bob, however, thought there was lots of life in it still, so I believed him. Coming out of the pool, I discovered that the entire bum portion had rotted away, and I was hanging out for everyone to see! Quick! A towel! (This reminds me of looking down in the pool at the local gym, and realising I'd put my swimsuit on back to front. Although my back was modestly covered, my chest was on complete display.)

In 2012 I turned sixty, and had a big party. One present was a trip to Tedfest (by and for fans of TV series *Father Ted*) on Craggy Island the following February. We drove across Ireland, then caught a tiny plane in which you were seated according to your weight. Anna had made the arrangements, and booked a self-catering cottage. My Ted character was naturally Chris the Sheep, which was convenient, as the many woolly layers helped to keep me warm. I had an excellent cameo part in the remaking of "The Passion of St Tibulus"; joined in with some bishops to do an unrehearsed acrobatics display (and got placed!); and got nowhere in the King of the Sheep competition. Much alcohol was consumed, and nuns, priests and bishops were round every corner.

Another holiday of a lifetime was our trip to South America. I'd always wanted to explore there, but where to go? Which area to select? A cruise seemed the perfect opportunity to sample many different places without constant packing and unpacking. The holiday we booked included land-based excursions before and after the cruise. We flew to Lima. We were taken to see lots of places, including cuddly llamas and alpacas and places we could buy alpaca wool. I bought.

There were lots of Inca sites, and we were taken to Cusco and by special train through the cloud forest to Machu Picchu (somewhere I'd always wanted to see). I hadn't been prepared for the scenery there to be as wonderful as it was. It was another place beautiful enough to make me weep. The ruins were extensive and fascinating, and I tried to understand how they could have done all that without inventing the wheel. When the heavy rains started, it was time to go back down to the town in the valley. Public buses drove us back. As our bus filled with wet, rained-upon passengers breathing heavily, its windows steamed up more and more. The bus was nearly full, so Bob sat at the back and I sat at the front. From my vantage point, I could see that the windscreen was entirely misted up. It was so opaque, it may as well have had a brick wall in front of it. Surprisingly, and also frighteningly, this didn't bother our bus driver, who descended the steep and twisting mountain road at a speed that would have worried me had he been able to see. Possibly he was blind, so not concerned? This was another drive where I was surprised to have survived.

We embarked on our ship, and continued south along the west coast. In Santiago, my thoughts were wholly with Allende and his overthrow by Thatcher's mate Pinochet. I loved being in Punta Arenas and Ushuaia; I have always been fascinated by really remote places, and these were really, really remote.

I wanted to see penguins, but without going on a cruise tour with hundreds of others. We asked at a tourist info in Punta

Arenas, and were directed to a taxi company. The taxi driver agreed to take us to the penguins at Otway Bay, so we climbed into his disintegrating taxi with its reassuring sign ("Jesus is my co-pilot") and drove into the wilderness. It was a long way. We were stopped once, and required to pay either a fee or a bribe, who could tell. On we trundled, the road getting ever bumpier, and more and more bits falling off the taxi. Eventually, we got to the penguin car park, and did our utmost to instruct the driver to wait there for us, although we had little language in common. Then we walked into remoteness. I pointed out that, even if we didn't see any penguins, this was an amazing place to be. And we didn't see any penguins. At first. Then: "Oh look, a penguin." And: "Oh look, another penguin." Then, soon: "There's penguins everywhere! Penguins! Penguins! Penguins!" It was wonderful. What was also wonderful was that our taxi was still in the car park when we returned to it, and it got us back safely so that we had plenty of time to get back on the ship. In fact, Bob had time to visit another maritime museum while I sat in a café frantically and unsuccessfully trying to connect to the internet.

I loved all the ports, but particularly Montevideo. Uruguay was a lovely place, on a human scale, with a Place of Sexual Diversity. I should love a holiday in Uruguay. It felt very safe, unlike Buenos Aires, where we spent a couple of days, and which was also interesting. Bookshops were everywhere, and we took many photos. In Buenos Aires we went to El Ateneo bookshop, one of the world's most beautiful bookshops in an old theatre. We loved being there; although their English language selection was tiny and pitiful, the shop was gorgeous.

After the cruise, the final trip was to the Iguazu Falls, which somehow we'd never heard of. "We're going to a waterfall, that might be nice," we thought, ignorantly. How could we not have heard of the Iguazu Falls? I know I've said places are stunning before, but the Iguazu Falls are on a whole different level. They go on and on for miles, round bends and on further, throwing their spray high into the air. We walked a long way, always finding new falls, getting more and more amazed, and wet. Cute coatis appeared frequently, after people's biscuits and sandwiches. We were in the lucky group, whose flights didn't get messed up, so we were able to view the Falls from both the Argentinian and Brazilian sides, as we had two days to see them. We went on a boat trip, ducking behind falls, getting soaked to the skin, and feeling exhilarated as Bob's dollars got saturated because he'd forgotten to put his wallet into the waterproof wrap.

On the flight back, we were offered something white, soggy and wrapped in cling film, in the middle of the night. I asked Bob what it was. "Refreshing flannel," he replied, being wholly responsible for my attempt to wipe my face with a ham sandwich.

In 2006, I was working at the library, and Bob and I were volunteering at a charity bookshop. I was distressed by the quantity of books thrown away by both these establishments, and other libraries too. Librarians would descend and start "weeding" – pulling out books over a certain age, sometimes only a very few years. Irrespective of whether or not this was the last copy of a seminal work on a subject, we then had to "discard" it: remove it from the system, after which it might go to a sale, or, more likely, a bin. The charity had a minimum price. Anything not expected to sell for this price would be chucked out. Books which had been on the shelves for longer than six weeks, and not special enough to be reduced or sent to a different shop, were "culled". They too met a sad fate.

One day Bob and I were discussing this after enjoying a drink or two, when one of us (I still insist it was Bob) had a brainwave. We could rescue these books, sell them cheaply on stalls, and give the proceeds to good causes. Yes, and we could wear masks when we did it. Thus we became Masked Booksellers, followers of the legendary Josiah Saithwaite. ExLibris started off very small, with some books from the charity shop and the library. They fitted comfortably on the shelves under the stairs to Anna's room. We priced them very cheaply, as we wanted quick throughput and to make bargains available to readers. Despite the low prices, our first stall at Nottingham Green Festival took

£116 for NNRF's anti-destitution work. In 2006, we ran five stalls, and raised £254 altogether. It seemed like we had had a good idea.

We continued collecting books, and running stalls at events. The shelves under the stairs overflowed, and gradually Anna's room filled up with boxes of books. ExLibris was becoming a larger and larger part of our lives. Constantly loading and unloading the car to take books to stalls was a bit of a pain, so I hit on a brilliant idea. In September 2007, we had the first sale at our house. We put up shelves across the front of the house and in the front part of the garage. A gazebo and a table were on the drive. Astonishingly, we made £189 during the day! We shared this between Nottingham and Notts Refugee Forum and Hayward House.

A tradition was born. By 2019, what started as a one day sale at our house has become eight days of selling over two long weekends; the month of the sale moved from September to April as it was stealing our summer by taking longer and longer to organise; publicity includes posters in shops, pubs, cafes and centres for miles around, and thousands of leaflets pushed through doors; we are on many local news media and over the internet like a rash; sales have been opened by masked mayors of Gedling and masked well-known writers; a café feeds book buyers; a poetry event runs itself in the back garden; and sometimes people point at us and tell us we're "those guys". Dozens of friends and enthusiasts help us with all aspects of the booksale. They are indispensable as the sale has become a monster we could never manage alone. We continue to run stalls, but the "easy" option, avoiding loading and unloading the ExLibrismobile, and replacing it with months of shelf-building, book-carrying, publicity, interviews, leaflet pushing, pricing, shelving (I LOVE that bit) and panic, has become our focus. We've had a shed (Saithwaite House) built and insulated specially to store books, but still we run out of storage space. Books just turn up. We've had to do something I never thought I would have to do: put a notice in front of the house asking people not to leave books outside.

Between 2006 and 2019, ExLibris, the Masked Booksellers have sold enough books to be able to donate nearly £24,000 to (mainly local) good causes. We've rescued probably hundreds of thousands of books from landfill. We've made a lot of booklovers happy. We've found a way to make a difference. And we can do it while wearing masks.

We obviously can't do this forever, but we see no exit strategy. How to get rid of the books? Sell them. How to entice people to the sale to buy them? Have some new stock available. Oh dear, we're not getting rid of books.

> **READING:**
> Books about Berlin
> *Stasiland*
> Andrew Drummond's *A Handbook of Volapük*

Sarah, Bob's daughter, married Matt in 2008. The wedding took place in a hotel in the beautiful Yorkshire countryside, and we watched Sarah and Matt perform a wonderful first dance before everything got very, very loud – as young people's celebrations should be. There were now Norrises in our family.

I've been wondering how to write about grandchildren, as I haven't yet invented the words that express my joy in, and love for, them. But then I realised that I managed to write something about Anna; despite it being inadequate, it was something.

I'd sadly accepted that we'd never get grandchildren. Anna had told me she wasn't interested in having children. Adam was nowhere near the right place to become a dad, and Sarah was getting older and babyless. But it turned out like buses – three nearly at once, and Leon a little later. (I don't know where Leon fits into the bus analogy.)

Anyway, Sarah and Matt were living in Houston, Texas, when we heard she was pregnant. Our first grandchild, Jack, was born in summer 2012. It was so exciting! And terrifying, because he was premature, very tiny, and had a lot of dangerous problems. And across the Atlantic. Sarah seemed to take this in her stride, as she does most things, and gradually Jack grew and grew, and soon he will be taller than me. He has a head full of ginger hair and off-beat ideas, and is a really kind, thoughtful little boy.

Their second US citizen child, Alfie, came not even two years later. Alfie has a head full of very, very fair sticky-up hair, bright ideas, and mischief.

We were happy when Sarah and Matt moved back to the UK, and we could see our grandsons frequently. As a toddler, Jack was fascinated by our washing machine, and always wanted to climb our stairs.

Anna and Sara had several fraught attempts to become pregnant, and eventually succeeded, with Anna giving birth to Lily with the long eyelashes in 2014, a few months after Alfie was born. I was allowed to be the first person to see her, after Anna and Sara.

Lily's early weeks were very frightening. She wasn't thriving because milk was going into her lungs rather than her stomach, so her oxygen levels were also a worry. She had an operation to mend her epiglottis, but ended up in intensive care for some time when she caught an infection after this. These were stomach-churning, horrible weeks. We all spent our time in Edinburgh's Sick Kids hospital, which luckily was within twenty minutes' walk of the flat. Lily was eventually able to go home, but only after parents and grandparents had been given a lesson on infant resuscitation. However, she remained tube-fed, with a tube permanently inserted into her stomach via a nostril, because her swallow tests were still not safe. Anna spent all her spare time researching this, and managed to learn enough that Lily could be weaned off the tube and onto thickened bottle milk. Just before Lily's first xmas, when I had been trying to find out how Lily's tube could be replaced if it came out while she was visiting us, Lily pulled it out herself, and she was well without it. That was a wonderful xmas present! Lily has a head full of Rapunzel dreams, unicorns and schemes.

Anna became pregnant the second time much more easily, and Leon with the huge smile was born without any problems like this, although Anna herself was in more pain. Leon did need a hospital night under lights to fix his jaundice, and has also spent a couple of other brief spells in the Sick Kids for coughs and infections, but there was nothing terrifying as there had been with Lily. Leon has a head of the curliest hair, escape plans, and dreams of food.

I see the children quite often, and they fill me with love, fun, and wonder. Each one is different, and each one is perfect.

Jack and Alfie stay alone with us for up to a week every August, and we enjoy finding lots and lots of fun things for them to do; even before the end of the day, they and we are falling asleep. They are friends as well as brothers. They love climbing and horse riding and making things from our huge stashes of craft materials. And they love TV in bed and tomato ketchup.

Anna and Sara split up when Leon was a few months old. I travel to Edinburgh to see Anna and the children every four to six weeks usually, sometimes alone on the train, sometimes with Bob in the car. Occasionally, they are able to visit us in Nottingham. We have been lucky enough to see them every xmas. Lily has become a brilliant climber/gymnast, and she has always been a great dancer – even when she was a baby in intensive care, she was doing a lying-down dance to the music. She loves clothes: the pinker and more princessy, the more she loves them. She can concentrate on colouring-in and copying. Leon admires and loves Lily, and likes it best when he can do "big child" things with her. He likes to cuddle soft toys, and to say "No". If you turn around for more than the blink of an eye, he has run away.

For Bob's seventieth birthday, I booked us a holiday in Cornwall. What I didn't tell him was that Sarah, Matt, Jack, Alfie, Anna, Lily, Leon, Adam, and Dominique (Adam's lovely partner) were coming too. Sarah and Matt overtook us on the motorway and beeped, and I waved. "Who was that?" asked Bob. "Never you mind" was not a reply guaranteed to allay suspicions, but it was the best I could come up with. It was still a surprise for him when we finally arrived, and everyone emerged from the hedge they'd been hiding behind to greet him. They'd had to hide behind that hedge for some time, as I kept going to the wrong cottage.

Celebrating Bob's birthday at Broadway, Nottingham 2019. Photo by Mike.

Having all four children together for a week was a total joy to me. Beaches, Eden Centre, more beaches, toys and ice creams ...

This grandparenting lark takes up a lot of time. Luckily, I had anticipated that, and, as things weren't going well with library management anyway, I decided to retire, just a little early, shortly before Lily was born. It must have been contagious, as my colleagues Lynda and Margaret decided to retire at the same time. We gave a leaving party, not for other library staff, but for the public who'd used the library and been served by us over the years. It was humbling to see how many turned up, to read the cards they gave us, and to see how many presents we were given. A professional chef made a cake. We couldn't have been doing it all wrong. Our immediate boss was there, to appear sad that we were leaving and to ensure we handed our keys back. (When I had been stretchered urgently out of the library by paramedics a year or two previously, with a suspected heart attack that was in fact gallstones, she had shown no interest in my predicament.)

I have retired. The last time I leave Basford Library. 2014.

It's only recently that my life-long embarrassing difficulty with recognising people's faces has acquired a name. I have prosopagnosia! It's a real thing, a neurological abnormality, and not just laziness or carelessness. This difficulty has probably shaped my life in ways I don't even recognise. But face blindness has also caused embarrassing moments I remember only too well, and not only with the Holbrook boys.

I couldn't recognise my cousin's teenage son when we went to meet him off a plane, prior to him spending a fortnight with us, learning English. I have hidden from people, because I didn't know whether I was supposed to know them or not. Recently, at Hayward House, I was telling another volunteer that I have face blindness, when she helpfully said, "But you know who this is, don't you?" Of course I didn't recognise the nurse who'd been running the place for years, as she was out of uniform. Working in bookselling and libraries, where meeting people – who often become regulars – is a major part of a day, is maybe not the easiest path I could have chosen. But just because I can't recognise people doesn't mean I don't like them. I have developed coping strategies. In the library, I tried to treat everyone as if they were my favourite customers; this is why my colleagues thought I was "gracious"; in truth, I just didn't recognise the trouble-makers. Had I done so, I'd have kicked them. Another trick was to use leading questions. The leading question "Where are you working these days?" tripped me up when the reply was "I'm programming. You sat next to me this afternoon." I can't complain. Prosopagnosia has given me anecdotes, and if it has helped shaped my life, then I'm happy with that shape. It helps a lot now that I can name the condition, and warn people that I meet that I probably won't recognise them next time. In my ideal world, we'd all wear MASSIVE name badges.

Prosopagnosia of course is just one of many factors that has shaped my life, made me who I am.

Retirement is wonderful! I can do what I want to do, and I want to do so much. It is true, though, that it is hard work, and makes you busier than ever. This is probably because of the grandchildren, and because of ExLibris.

When Anna was expecting Lily, I resurrected my lifelong hobby of crochet, and started to produce an epic layette. I learned to knit as well – something I had not tried to do since my dismal Brownie failure – and then acquired a sewing machine! Sewing had always been something I'd avoided, and I'd used much glue and many staples instead. Now it was suddenly fun! I started making our greetings cards, I went on a mosaic course, I discovered the joy of making stuff. And I inundated the children and grandchildren with some shite and some stuff I was proud of.

> **READING:**
>   Books about knitting
>   Richard Dawkins
>   Henry Normal
>   *A Woman in Berlin*
>   David Sedaris
>   Children's books, to children

There is still some travelling in retirement. I had always wanted to go to Norway, and we cruised there once in the winter to see the Northern Lights, and once in the summer, to see the fjords. Cruising must be the most affordable way to see Norway; prices were a shock. Norway is very beautiful, and appealed to my love of remoteness. It was very civilised despite being remote. We did see the Northern Lights, although not on the tour to the special place where we were most likely to see them. We saw them from the ship. I couldn't fathom the lights: they seemed not to move or change while you looked at them, but turn away for a second and look back, and they were quite different. I was so glad to have seen them. You can do ballroom dancing on cruises, too.

I still feel close connections with what I consider my two opposite sides – Suffolk and Berlin. We visit both as often as we can; it probably averages at once a year for each.

We enjoyed an Aldeburgh holiday in a cottage with Sara's parents Vida and Hossein. In the middle of one night, I was trying to find my way back to our bedroom guided only by the flickering street light outside the window. I thought I was walking along the landing as I stepped out. In fact, I stepped out into fresh air above the stairs, found nothing beneath me, and tumbled all the way down, bouncing heavily on each stair ... I grabbed out, and pulled a huge abstract canvas of forgettable content off the wall. It bounced down with me. My glasses and dressing gown flew off. In trying to creep quietly so as not to wake anyone, I had probably been loud enough to wake much of Aldeburgh.

We also had an amazing holiday with Adam and Dominique in the Martello Tower (owned by the Landmark Trust) in Aldeburgh. Exploring Orfordness was thrilling; we spent so long there that the National Trust ferry people worried that we'd got lost.

On one trip with Bob, I decided to show him Royal Hospital School, Holbrook, scene of many a teenage dancing nightmare. The frontage was still as prepossessing as I remembered it, and we were very surprised to find the driveway unbarred. Happy explorers, we continued driving into the school grounds, until we came upon a huge parade ground, where pupils (girls as well as boys by now) were being marched up and down in what looked like the antithesis of fun. A prefect caught sight of us. My last visit ever to Holbrook ended with us reversing rapidly back along the drive, with a sweaty, angry prefect in full pursuit.

We had been going to Berlin/Kleinmachnow nearly every year. Onkel Bernd died in 2018; now Hannelore has moved from Kleinmachnow to Teltow and the Jentzsch family house since 1936 will probably be demolished soon. We went to Bernd's funeral, and also had a week in Berlin in summer 2019. This meant we could go to Hannelore's birthday celebrations, now held at Ralph's house, and see her new flat. We also enjoyed time pootling around Berlin. Many previous visits have included me dragging Bob round historic Chris sites. During this trip, we spent a fascinating day touring the, now closed, Tempelhof Airport. I go to the Commonwealth War Cemetery on the

Heerstrasse nearly every time I'm in Berlin; it always feels as if it's still 1962 when I'm at Dad's grave. We also visited the Tränenpalast, where I was suddenly immersed in the past – and prompted to write about it.

The back garden in Kleinmachnow, with Bernd and Hannelore. 2009.

Now it is 2019. All of us in this country are in difficult, uncertain times. Often I can't face listening to the news. We are too close to fascism. So we continue to march and write and march again. Maybe we can make no difference, but at least I can say I tried.

Can an atheist be blessed? Because if so, then I have been blessed with a childhood where I was loved; a happy, loving, entertaining and witty marriage; the best daughter in the world; four amazing grandchildren who make my heart sing; precious friends; memories of wonderful times and people; reasonable health so far; and a language which provides semi-colons.

Are there any lessons I've learned? Any wise information to pass on? Only the obvious, I think. Be kind. Solidarity! Enid Blyton isn't true. Appreciate your friends and family. Don't waste your one life in a job you hate. Careful with that superglue. Tobacco kills. Don't stare at gorillas. You are what you eat. Never have your armpits waxed. Question everything. Don't let the bastards grind you down. We are many, they are few. Resist! Revolt! Rebel! Don't delay getting your ear wax removed.

Actually, just the first and last of the above list will do. And I've never understood why some people put used tea bags into the sink before transferring them to the bin.

And that candle, that was bought for Onkel Bernd's twenty-fifth birthday, but never lit because the Berlin Wall stopped celebrations? I found that candle many years later among Mum's things. For his seventy-fifth birthday, I decided to surprise him with it, so I dug it out. The "25" appeared to have rubbed off it in the intervening fifty years, but he was overjoyed to receive it. He showed it to everyone, and even wrote a thoughtful article about it, that was published in the local press.

Please don't tell anyone, but some months later I was having another root around stuff, and came across an old candle with a "25" on it.

Rise, like lions after slumber
In unvanquishable number!
Shake your chains to earth like dew
Which in sleep had fallen on you:
Ye are many—they are few!

Percy Bysshe Shelley

A bit more about the family

Dad Don was one of eight. He was a twin with Doris. His dad James, who died before I was born, was one of 16, all of whom survived childhood, but then WW1 took some. The Cooks had large families and laboured on the Suffolk land going back generations. Dad was able to change his life in the army.

Granny Blanche, Dad's Mum, was one of five. As a teenager, she was "in service" at a big house, as was her sister Maggie. Her first husband was killed in WW1. Left a widow with children, she married James. Some of her children were from each husband; possibly some from neither.

Aunty Doris moved to London. She had a hard life and seven children, one of whom was only discovered as Doris was incapacitated with Alzheimer's.

Mum Inge was one of three. Her older sister Edith shared the same father, but Edith's mother was Olga Höflich. Olga died, probably during a miscarriage, when Edith was a toddler. Opi Albert then married Olga's youngest sister, Omi Gerda, who was only 18. Omi's family fled from Posen (now Poznan) after WW1, and Omi never went to school again because she was too shy. Omi and Olga had three other siblings: Elfriede, Grete and Paul. Paul was a mathematician who lost touch with his siblings after pointing a gun at them in a dispute about housing.

Opi came from the Oberlahnstein on the Rhine, but WW1 moved him away, so he met the Höflich family. He came from a long line of wood cutters, foresters, etc.

Aunt Edith married during WW2, and had a child. Her husband Wilhelm was called to the Russian front, and did not return. He was pronounced dead, and Edith married Sgt Charley, who was in the army with Dad. Then Wilhelm returned from Soviet captivity. The child was taken by his mother.

Mum's brother, Bernd Albert, was ten years younger than her. He had two children, five grandchildren, and the number of great grandchildren grows almost weekly.

William Cook 1762-1838	William Cook 1805-1884; m Sarah 1833; at least 4 siblings; agricultural labourer	James Cook 1844(Saxtead)-1922(Debenham); min 6 siblings; agricultural labourer
Susannah Capon 1761-1821		
	Sarah Pizzey 1803-1884	m 1868
John Hammond 1781-1870	Thomas Hannond 1818-1904; m Mary Ann 1844; 13 siblings	Sarah Hammond 1846(Bedingfield)-1928(S'market); 11 siblings
Hannah Cracknell 1785-1853		
Thomas Cracknell 1797-1880	Mary Ann Foreman 1823-1881; 10 siblings; 1st husband Stephen Cracknell	
Elizabeth Rodwell 1789-?		
David Milson Brunning 1819-1876	Mileson John Brunning 1851(Witnesham)-1919(Essex); min 2 siblings	Charles Henry Brunning 1872-1926; 12 siblings; agricultural labourer; horseman; inn keeper
Eliza Osbourne 1815-1894		
William Leach 1818-1886	Rebeckah Leach 1852(Framsden)-1935(Essex); min 6 siblings	
Amy Osborn 1811-1894		m 1890
George Frederick Scott 1814-1876	George Scott 1842(Earl Stonham)-1911; 16 siblings	Laura Scott 1868(Earl Stonham)-1933(Blything); 5 siblings
Sarah Bryant/Begant? 1813-1896		
Robert Finbow 1822-1899	Eliza Finbow 1844(Mendlesham)-?; 11 siblings	
Mary Ann Syrett 1826-1906		
Christian F Jentzsch	Friedrich A Jentzsch 1815-1891	Karl Friedrich August Jentzsch 1855(Stangerode)- 1920(Oberlahnstein)
Christiane F Fritsche 1792-?		
Karl Wilhem Abesser 1774-1869	Wilhelmine Abesser 1824-?	
Karolina F Reinhardt 1803-?		m 1883
Jakob Blum 1767-1803	Ludwig Ernst Blum 1803-1874	Mathilde Blum 1857(Runkel)-1944(Oberlahnstein)
Anna Elizabet Schenk 1772-?		
Andreas Metz 1801-?	Marianne Metz 1826-1881	
Margarete Muth		
Anton Höflich 1791-1852	Anton Höflich 1831-1871	Josef S Höflich 1858(Labschuetz)-1939(Berlin); remarried after Ida died
Klara Boehm ?-1858		
Anton Peschke 1802-1866	Marie A Peschke 1833-?	
Theressia Blaschke 1806-1866		m1890
Adalbert Goschin	Valentin Goschin 1827-1916	Ida Justine Goschin 1864(Tirschtiegel)-1924(Berlin)
Hedwig	Mathilde Klische 1835-1878	

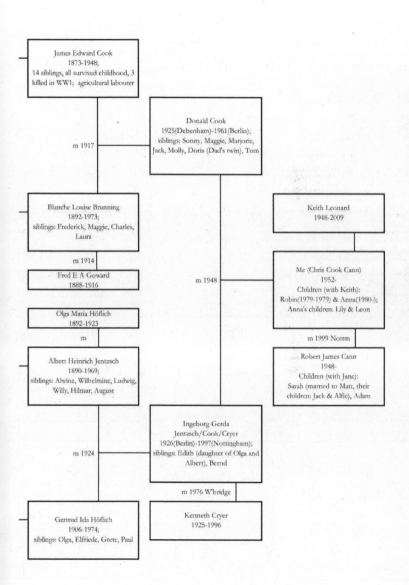

James Edward Cook
1873-1948;
14 siblings, all survived childhood, 3
killed in WW1; agricultural labourer

m 1917

Donald Cook
1925(Debenham)-1961(Berlin);
siblings: Sonny, Maggie, Marjorie,
Jack, Molly, Doris (Dad's twin), Tom

Blanche Louise Brunning
1892-1973;
siblings: Frederick, Maggie, Charles,
Laura

m 1914

Fred E A Goward
1888-1916

Olga Maria Höflich
1892-1923

m

Albert Heinrich Jentzsch
1890-1969;
siblings: Alwine, Wilhelmine, Ludwig,
Willy, Hilmar, August

m 1924

Gertrud Ida Höflich
1906-1974;
siblings: Olga, Elfriede, Grete, Paul

Keith Leonard
1948-2009

m 1948

Me (Chris Cook Cann)
1952-
Children (with Keith):
Robin(1979-1979) & Anna(1980-);
Anna's children: Lily & Leon

m 1999 Nottm

Robert James Cann
1948-
Children (with Jane):
Sarah (married to Matt, their
children: Jack & Alfie), Adam

Ingeborg Gerda
Jentzsch/Cook/Cryer
1926(Berlin)-1997(Nottingham);
siblings: Edith (daughter of Olga and
Albert), Bernd

m 1976 W'bridge

Kenneth Cryer
1925-1996

Who's who in this story of a life

(Non-human in italics.)

ADAM. Bob's son. Partner to Dominique.

ALFIE. Our grandson. Son of Sarah and Matt.

ANNA JANE. My daughter.

ANNE. Friend and Woodborough Road Neighbour. Mother of Tim and Amy.

AUNT EDITH. Mum's older three quarters sister. Mother of Cousin Marion. Wife of Uncle Charley.

AUNT MAGGIE. Granny's sister, Dad's aunt. Lived near Ipswich.

AUNTY DORIS. Dad's twin sister.

BARNABY. Guinea pig at Woodborough Road.

BEN AND LIBERTAD. Anarchists living in East Bergholt.

BERND; see ONKEL BERND.

BERT. Gamekeeper who rescued me when my bike had a puncture.

BETTY. MISS LANGSHAW. Headmistress at Mills Grammar School.

BILLY. A budgie. (See Peter.)

BOB. My husband and love. And proof reader.

BODO. The boy who lived next door to us in Hanover.

BUTCH. Fulbeck protestor, proud of his wig collection.

CAROL. Nottingham friend 1970s, 1980s.

CAT. Nottingham friend in the 1980s.

CATH. Basford Library manager when I first arrived there.

CLAIRE. Friend in 1980s and again 2000s onwards. Co-founder of Sparrows' Nest Library and Archive. (See Mike.)

COLIN. Boyfriend around 1985, 1986.

COUSIN IRENE. My cousin. Daughter of Aunty Doris, sister of Cousin John.

COUSIN JOHN. My cousin and friend. Son of Aunty Doris, sister of Irene.

COUSIN JUDY. Daughter of Aunt Marjorie, Dad's sister. Brought up by Granny. Married a U.S. serviceman.

COUSIN MARION. My cousin. Edith and Charley's daughter.

COUSIN RALPH. My cousin. Son of Bernd and Hannelore, father of Dominic, Benny, Tobias and Robert.

COUSIN STEPHANIE. My cousin. Daughter of Bernd and Hannelore, mother of Elias.

DAD; DONALD COOK. 1925-1961. My dad.

DAVE. A friend from Arkwright Street days, he worked over the road at Fine Fare minimarket.

DOMINIQUE. Adam's partner.

DON; see DAD.

DORIS; see AUNTY DORIS.

DR BLISS. He befuddled us with economics at Essex University.

DR FROBENIUS; LORE FROBENIUS; FROB. German and psychology teacher at Mills Grammar School; became a personal friend.

EDITH; see AUNT EDITH.

ERIC AND JULIE. Friends of Mum's in Woodbridge.

FRANCES. Friend at Cransford Hall and Mills Grammar School, she became a day girl a year before me.

FROB; see DR FROBENIUS.

GABI. Daughter (my age) of parents' friends.

GALEA FAMILY. Next door neighbours in Herentals. From Malta.

GEORGE; a Mushroom customer who invited Keith and me to Cork.

GRACE. Neighbour of George, a Mushroom customer who invited Keith and me to Cork.

GRANNY; BLANCHE BRUNNING/GOWARD/COOK. My grandmother. Dad's mother.

GRETE; see TANTE GRETE.

HANNELORE; see TANTE HANNELORE.

HELEN. A day girl at Mills Grammar School, two years older than me. I stayed with her family at half term.

HOSSEIN. Sara's father. One-time father-in-law to Anna.

HOUDINI. Hamster in Gedling.

HUNYADI EMESE. The speed skating champion made out of marzipan.

IAN from Norfolk. Mad cyclist, met on End-to-End ride.

INGE; see MUM.

IRENE; see COUSIN IRENE.

JACK. Our grandson. Son of Sarah and Matt.

JAMIE. Cellmate in Risley, and friend for a short while afterwards.

JANE. Berlin school friend.

JOAN. Second cousin in Debenham. James and Sarah were mutual great grandparents.

JOHN; see COUSIN JOHN.

JOHN; Keith's brother, Anna's uncle.

JONATHAN WILSON. Football correspondent and man who gave Anna and me a lift in a terrifying taxi.

JOSEPH KIAME. Lebanese man I met on a French train, who wanted me to visit him in Lebanon.

JOSIE. Woman I befriended via Mencap, and went to pottery classes with.

JOYCE AND JOHN. Vernon Avenue, Gedling, neighbours.

JUDITH. Friend at Cransford Hall.

JULIA. Friend in 1970s, 1980s.

JUNE CAMPBELL-CRAMER; see LADY JUNE.

KEITH ALLEN. Friend at Charlottenburg School, Berlin.

KEITH LEONARD. My partner from 1970 until 1982. Father of Robin and Anna.

KEN CRYER. Mum's second husband. Father of Karen and Terry.

KEV. Lodger and babysitter at Woodborough Road.

LADY JUNE; JUNE CAMPBELL-CRAMER. Poet and artist. Lived in Maida Vale. Keith and I stayed in her flat when in London, early 1970s. First place we turned on.

LEON. Our grandson. Son of Anna and Sara.

LIANA. Berlin school friend.

LILY. Our granddaughter. Daughter of Anna and Sara.

LINDA CHURCHYARD. Girl in my class in Berlin – her mother was Brown Owl.

LINDA MÜLLER. Daughter of Tante Luise. My age.

LUISE MÜLLER; see TANTE LUISE.

LYNDA. Colleague at Basford Library, and friend.

MARGARET. Berlin school friend.

MARGARET. Colleague at Basford Library, and friend.

MARILYN. Friend at Cransford Hall and now. Brilliant proof reader.

MARION; see COUSIN MARION.

MARTIN WITH THE EMPTY SHOE. Party goer from Shoeburyness.

MARTINE. French pupil.

MARY. Colleague at Copystatic Systems.

MATT. Husband of Sarah. Father of Jack and Alfie. Son-in-law.

MIKE. Friend in 2000s onwards. Co-founder of Sparrows' Nest Library and Archive. (See Claire.)

MISS LANGSHAW; see BETTY.

MISS MICHELLE. French teacher at Mills Grammar School.

MISS MORGAN. A borrower at Basford Library.

MISS PERRIN. English teacher at Mills Grammar School, left to become a missionary.

MISS TETT. Biology teacher at Mills Grammar School.

MISS THIMBLETHORPE. Old woman who lived along the road from us in Ipswich.

MISS WILSON. Maths teacher at Mills Grammar School. Resident at Cransford Hall.

MITZY. Assistant matron at Cransford Hall.

MOCK HARPO. Hamster at Woodborough Road.

MR BASHFORD. Teacher in Berlin.

MR JONES. English teacher at Mills Grammar School.

MR ROGERS. Lab technician at Mills Grammar School.

MR SHEPHARD. A borrower at Basford Library.

MR SMITH. Music teacher at Mills Grammar School.

MR THICKETT. Vicar at Peasenhall.

MR VASEY. The Nottingham surgeon who delivered Anna.

MR WOOD. A borrower at Basford Library.

MR WRIGHT. Caretaker at Cransford Hall.

MRS FERGUSON. Domestic Science teacher at Mills Grammar School.

MRS GLOVER. A borrower at Basford Library.

MRS GUEST. A borrower at Basford Library.

MRS RAE. Berlin Charlottenburg School head teacher.

MRS WELCH. Ivy Hulme Welch. Matron at Cransford Hall.

MUM; INGEBORG GERDA JENTZSCH/COOK/CRYER. 1926-1997. My mum.

NINA CANN. Bob's mum.

NINA. Anna's friend in Woodborough Road days.

NULLY; see ONKEL NULLY.

OLGA HÖFLICH. Omi's older sister. Opi's first wife. Aunt Edith's mother. Died 1923.

OMI; GERDA; GERTRUD HÖFLICH/JENTZSCH. My lovely grandmother, Inge's mother, Opi's second wife.

ONKEL BERND; BERND ALBERT JENTZSCH. My uncle. Inge's younger brother. Husband of Hannelore.

ONKEL LUDWIG. Rhineland relative, brother of Opi.

ONKEL NULLY; ERNST WEDEL. Mum's aunt's second husband. We lived with them in Berlin. Married to Tante Grete.

OPI; ALBERT HEINRICH JENTZSCH. My grandfather, Inge's father, Omi's husband.

PATRICIA. Rich girl I shared a room with at Les Sables d'Olonne.

PEGGY. Uncle Len's dog, Debenham.

PERCY. Hamster in Arkwright Street.

PETER. A budgie. (See Billy.)

PHILIPP. Friend 2000s onwards; Sparrows' Nester and People's Histerian.

PIP. A close friend since the mid-1970s. Wife first of Andy, then of Paul.

POPPY. Friend at Mills Grammar School and now.

PRINCE. My pretend horse.

PRODNOSE. Black, white and dirty mongrel who adopted us in Arkwright Street.

RALPH; see COUSIN RALPH.

RAY GOSLING. Writer and broadcaster, who gave a talk at the Sparrows' Nest.

REG. Mum's partner early 1970s. He had a boat.

RENATE. Mum's friend from her Kleinmachnow teenage years, married to a German PoW and living in Stratford on Avon.

REV TODD. Clergyman who presided at Robin's funeral and who blessed Anna.

ROBIN EDWARD LEONARD COOK. My son.

ROGER. A kind friend who joined me in bailing Sandra from immigration detention, then helped me to pay my fine.

RONALD HALFPENNY. Nominal "boyfriend" in Herentals.

ROYA. Iranian friend met at Basford Library. Mother of Parsa.

SANDRA. Jamaican woman who needed to be rescued from immigration detention.

SARA. Anna's wife until 2018. Co-mother of Lily and Leon.

SARAH. Bob's daughter. Wife to Matt. Mother to Jack and Alfie.

SEPPEL. Short-haired dachshund belonging to Tante Grete and Onkel Nully, with a fondness for chocolate.

SLOWY. Tortoise in Berlin.

STAMP FRIEND. Man who recruited Mum into spying for West German intelligence.

STEPHANIE; see COUSIN STEPHANIE.

STEVE FROM WOODBRIDGE. A colleague of Keith's at Nottscutts Nurseries.

STEVE. Woodborough Road lodger.

SUE. Also known as Fanny. Lived in Woodbridge. Friend at Mills Grammar School and later.

TANTE GRETE; Margarete Wedel. Mum's aunt, older sister to Omi. We lived with them in Berlin. Married to Onkel Nully.

TANTE HANNELORE. Onkel Bernd's childhood sweetheart and his wife.

TANTE LUISE. Mum's cousin (on the Rhineland side), living in Berlin. Married to band leader Werner Müller.

TEGWYN. Latin teacher at Mills Grammar School. Resident at Cransford Hall.

TERRY. Ken's (Mum's husband's) son.

THIBAUT FAMILY. Stars of French audio-visual teaching slides at Mills Grammar School.

TOM; see UNCLE TOM.

ULLY. Mum's friend from her earliest years, married to an Englishman.

UNCLE LEN. LEN GILLINGS. Dad's friend in Debenham.

UNCLE TOM. Dad's younger brother.

VICTOR. Our Russian friend in St Petersburg.

VIDA. Sara's mother. One-time mother-in-law to Anna.

WOOKY. Betty's dog. Betty eventually ran it over.

ZAMPY. Hamster in Berlin.